INFORMATION, ORGANIZATION AND INFORMATION SYSTEMS DESIGN

Information, Organization and Information Systems Design

An Integrated Approach to Information Problems

by

Bart Prakken

Nijmegen Business School,
Nijmegen University, The Netherlands

KLUWER ACADEMIC PUBLISHERS
BOSTON / DORDRECHT / LONDON

A C.I.P. Catalogue record for this book is available from the Library of Congress.

ISBN 0-7923-7784-2

Published by Kluwer Academic Publishers,
P.O. Box 17, 3300 AA Dordrecht, The Netherlands.

Sold and distributed in North, Central and South America
by Kluwer Academic Publishers,
101 Philip Drive, Norwell, MA 02061, U.S.A.

In all other countries, sold and distributed
by Kluwer Academic Publishers,
P.O. Box 322, 3300 AH Dordrecht, The Netherlands.

Printed on acid-free paper

Printed in the Netherlands.

PREFACE

When dealing with information problems, we are confronted with organizational aspects in three ways.

Firstly, information problems can often be solved more efficiently and effectively by organizational redesign, especially one which is based on the sociotechnical approach, than by the use of ICT applications.

Secondly, if organizations still prefer ICT solutions, they have to be aware that they are freezing the existing information/communication structure, including its shortcomings, for a number of years, since it is a part of the overall structure. Before we design new information systems it is therefore of the utmost importance to examine the organization's information and communication structure carefully, and to improve them where necessary.

Thirdly, new information systems often change the way people work together. As a result, those systems are not neutral from the organizational point of view but have an impact which is sometimes far-reaching.

Because of these reasons it may be disastrous to neglect the organizational aspects of information systems, and failure to take them into account is one of the main explanations for the shortfall of ICT applications which is reported by so many students. As a matter of fact, it is not the technology but rather its organizational embedment which is crucial for reaping the fruits of any technology in general and of ICT in particular.

This book focuses on the organizational aspects of ICT, particularly with respect to the first point mentioned above. In addition to this, other relevant topics will be discussed, such as the design (process) of information systems, their project management, and a sophisticated economic evaluation procedure which ensures that well-considered decisions are taken. In fact, the book offers a comprehensive framework for coping with the major factors that are responsible for the shortfall of information systems which is identified in the first chapter.

The book also contains a description of the most important information systems for controlling organizations. The final chapter is devoted to an evaluation procedure for projects in the field of ICT. This evaluation procedure goes beyond popular techniques like business scorecards, because the latter have a number of shortcomings that are related to the changing character of such projects. Unfortunately, business score cards, although intended for measuring both quantitative and qualitative effects, are unable to treat all of the latter adequately.

Of course, the realization of this book was only possible thanks to the support of my dear and loving family (Els, Nynke and Sybrand) and of my colleague Prof. Grahame Lock, who was so kind to read the text very closely and critically. I also want to thank Filip VanDijk and Dr. Hanne Meihuizen for a final check of some chapters.

Nijmegen, spring 2000

CONTENTS

I	**Why do information systems fail**	1
1.	Introduction	1
2.	Failure factors of information projects	3
3.	Possible solutions to neutralize failure factors	7
4.	Plan of the book	11
II	**Concepts**	13
1.	Introduction	13
2.	Systems	13
3.	Control, policy and decision making	22
4.	Some more concepts	34
III	**The identity of management information systems**	51
1.	Introduction	51
2.	The identity of management information systems as a scientific discipline	52
3.	A (more) fundamental approach to information problems	55
4.	Measures to reduce internal flows of information	56
5.	Measures to reduce external flows of information	64
IV	**The sociotechnical approach of organizations**	67
1.	Introduction	67
2.	The sociotechnical structure of organizations: design principles	68
3.	Paving the way to the sociotechnical organization: the implementation	72
4.	The sociotechnical organization; its exploitation	75
5.	The sociotechnical structure; a universal principle?	78
6.	The principle of dialogical control	83
V	**Information policy**	85
1.	Introduction	85
2.	The levels of information policy	88
3.	Nolan's stage model	91
4.	Task and position of the information centre	95
5.	Outsourcing of ICT	99
VI	**Project management**	105
1.	Introduction	105
2.	Organizing information projects	106
3.	The organization structure of information projects	108
4.	Systems Development Methodology	111

VII Design and management methods 115
1. Introduction 115
2. Information projects and project risks 120
3. General design methods 124
4. Information management and flexibility 133
5. Specific design methods 136

VIII Power and the control of conflicts due to information systems and ICT 139
1. Introduction 139
2. Changes in the power structure of organizations due to new information systems based on ICT 142
3. The control of conflicts 144

IX Information systems for the control of organizations; categorization and application 149
1. Introduction 149
2. Executive information systems and strategic information systems 153
3. Data base systems and document information systems 156
4. Idea processing systems 158
5. Group information systems 161
6. Decision support systems 166
7. Knowledge-based systems and artificial intelligence 170
8. Structured decision systems and electronic data interchange 173
9. Transaction processing systems 176
10. Business process redesign 180
11. Telework 190
12. The relationship between information systems and the decision making *process* 194

X The (economic) evaluation of investments in information systems and in ICT 197
1. Introduction 197
2. Traditional capital budgeting techniques 199
3. Quantitative and qualitative factors and the evaluation of information projects 201
4. A procedure to handle the risks of information projects 206
5. The evaluation of information projects 207
6. A decision procedure for ICT projects 213
7. The mutual comparison between projects and the final decision once again 221

References 223

Index 227

I WHY DO INFORMATION SYSTEMS FAIL

1. Introduction

In the last twenty-five years a great deal of money has been spent on investments in Information and communication technology (ICT); especially in the services branch (in this book we explicitly speak of information *and* communication technology, instead of information technology only, because the communication component of information systems becomes more and more important; actually, information and communication are two sides of the same coin). For instance, in the United States of America this branch is responsible for 80% of total investments in ICT. And in the Netherlands (the author's native country) ICT showed a growth rate of 8.4% in 1995.

However, the positive value created by investments in ICT has been under attack for some time. This is because of the moderate growth of labour productivity during the last twenty years. Since the sixties, labour productivity in the services sector has even slowed down to zero (Roach, 1991). As Solow says: 'Computers are found everywhere in society except in the productivity statistics'.

Apparently, in spite of the – information/communication – technologies that are applied in the services branch we are unable to reduce the number of people necessary to generate a given level of output. This phenomenon is called the 'productivity paradox' or 'information paradox'; although some authors claim that, especially in Europe, the situation is changing for the better (Cabelo, 1996; Thorp, 1998).

In addition to the limited impact ICT has had until now, some people think that the productivity paradox is also caused by the difficulties involved in measuring productivity in the services branch (Bjyrnjolfsson, 1993).

Moreover, it is legitimate to question the validity of *partial* relations, such as the relation between technology and productivity, on a *macro* economic level. For instance, in some branches in the United States, such as warehousing, labour productivity rose in the last ten years, whereas in others, such as health care, labour productivity was falling in the same period.

In spite of this last modification of the relevance of the productivity paradox, it is quite clear that ICT, in connection with a complex of other factors, on the whole has not had the positive effects society hoped for or expected.

When we zoom in on the success – or failure – of individual information projects this conclusion should not surprise us. After all, with some regularity articles are written with labels such as 'Information projects keep failing' (Pruijm, 1995).

Several students have reported lately on the success and failure of information projects. For instance, a field research project in The Netherlands showed the following results (Riesewijk and Warmerdam, 1988):
- 51% succeeded,
- 44% were problematic,
- 5% failed.

For sure, these data are not very hopeful.

Research outcomes in the United States regarding the application of software at some ministries were even disastrous (De Snoo, 1990):
- 47% was implemented but never used,
- 28% was never implemented,
- 20.6% was used for some time,
- 3% was useful after adaptation,
- 1.4% was useful from the beginning.

From another point of view, i.e. the costs of information projects, we can also come to the conclusion that 'something' is really wrong. For example, research by the *Automation Guide* showed the following cost categorization:
- 67% maintenance costs,
- 15% testing costs,
- 8% costs of analysis and design,
- 8% costs of identifying of user needs.

These results mean that more than two-thirds of project costs are generated *after* implementation, and are often not foreseen before the project is started.

Further specification of maintenance costs identified:
- 43% costs of adapting to – changed – user needs,
- 21% costs of correcting mistakes,
- 6% costs of adapting to new hardware,
- 6% costs of adapting documentation,
- 4% costs of improving efficiency,
- 3% other costs.

The only conclusion that can be drawn from these data is that the identification of – future – information needs is a great problem when traditional design methods are used.

Naumann and Jenkins came to similar, though slightly more favourable, numerical conclusions (Naumann and Jenkins, 1987):
- 40% development costs,
- 15% costs because of delayed use,
- 45% exploitation costs.

Obviously, this research also identified the disappointment of the users, which resulted in (additional) exploitation costs, as a major reason for the failure of information projects.

Finally, Jenkins, Naumann and Wetherbe reported that the costs of information projects in the cases they studied were 66% higher than planned, that the lead time was 22% longer and that the project specifications of 65% were insufficient (Jenkins, Naumann and Wetherbe, 1984).

The research mentioned so far dates from approximately five to fifteen years ago. More recent data reveals only very modest improvements. For instance, yearly research of the Standish Group International, based on the Fortune 500 list, showed the following results (Project Leadership Conference, Paris, 1998):
- 26% of the projects would be delivered without delay and without exceeding budget limits,
- almost 50% of the projects took more time and money,
- 28% of the projects would never be implemented.

Compared with data from the past there is some improvement on account of:
- better project management,
- increased use of standard components and
- smaller projects.

It is especially the third factor which is important for the requirements with reagrd to time and money. 50% of projects cheaper than $ 750,000 do not exceed budget limits and will be delivered in time. For projects between $ 1,500,000 and $ 3,000,000 this percentage is 25. If projects cost more than $ 10,000,000, the number that is successful in realizing planned time and money is zero.

So, there is still sufficient room for further improvement.

The research outcomes mentioned so far make us very curious about the reasons for these modest results. However, it is mostly a waste of effort to look in the same publications for explanations why so many information projects fail because researchers often present their data without telling us for what reasons their results were so very disappointing, or they only give specific explanations – such as lack of user involvement during the design process of information systems – meanwhile ignoring other factors which are perhaps even more important.

In this book we will therefore try to close this gap between theory and empirical results by developing a more complex theoretical framework for explaining the limited success of information systems.

In the next section we start our analysis with a thorough identification of the factors we hold responsible for the failure of information systems. In section 3 we discuss possible solutions. Finally, in section 4 we take a look at the different subjects that will be discussed in the chapters after that.

2. Failure factors of information projects

When we are talking about the failure of information projects we must wonder which failure factors, also called 'critical success factors', are responsible. In our opinion the

following factors, partly mentioned by other authors, can be identified (Akkerman and De Weerd, 1995):
- project management,
- gaps between users and automation experts,
- acceptance,
- maintenance,
- implementation,
- budgeting,
- inadequate formulation of information problems,
- lack of a policy framework for information systems,
- limited scope of ICT applications,
- difficulties with the economic evaluation of information projects,
- insufficient attention paid to the power structure of organizations,
- mismatch between information systems and organizations.

Project management
Information systems are normally rather complex and have far-reaching consequences for the organization. Therefore these sort of projects must be planned and managed carefully. In addition, project management should have an open eye for processes of organizational change which are caused by information projects.

Gaps
Because of their differences in education, background, culture, etc., there is a *communication* gap between users and automation experts; as a result they do not understand each other. Moreover, the latter group aims to build information systems with which they gain respect from peers and/or about which they can write contributions in scientific periodicals. Users on the other hand only need systems that give them a little additional help with solving daily information problems. These two starting points, resulting in an *aspiration* gap, can hardly be reconciled.

Because of these two gaps traditional design methods – so-called 'turn key' approaches – are unsatisfactory.

Acceptance
Future users of information systems are forced by designers to give their opinion about new systems on the basis of rather global specifications which give a very limited picture of the final system. Only when the complete system is ready and tested does the user get the opportunity to give a final evaluation. However, it is usually too late then to refuse the system or to adapt it to the users' wishes, unless large additional amounts of money are spent.

Maintenance
In the preceding pages we have referred to the phenomenon that a substantial part of the costs of the development and exploitation of information systems is caused by adaptation *after* implementation. Apart from the problem of specifications mentioned under 'acceptance', this adaptation is often necessary for several reasons. In the first

place, the methods which are employed to investigate the users' needs often fail. Secondly, it is well-known that users, once they have worked with new information systems for some time, become aware of additional needs which could not be identified at the start of the design process. Thirdly, environmental turbulence is responsible for frequent changes in the initial needs after they were first identified.

Implementation

Implementation means that information systems become operational in such a way that the aim of functionality is completely realized. Unfortunately, this is often not the case. Systems still contain several bugs for instance; bugs that do not become manifest until these systems are used in daily practice.

Another complaint relates to the user (un)friendliness of information systems. Often bulky handbooks have to be read before the user is well-instructed to operate the system satisfactorily.

Budgeting

The design of information systems is characterized by budgeting problems with respect to maintenance problems; i.e. the planning of information systems is very difficult as to time and money. Unfortunately, it is a phenomenon which is almost universally accepted that information systems get out of hand on these two dimensions.

Inadequate formulation of information problems

There is a strong tendency in our world to translate information problems almost automatically into ICT solutions. Because of this preference other solutions, which might be more fundamental and even better, are excluded in advance. The risk of using ICT solutions is that information problems are then formulated in terms of rather superficial problem specifications instead of in terms of more fundamental causes; a tendency by the way which is not just unique to information problems (Mitroff and Featheringham, 1974). As a result, users come to the conclusion after some time that the chosen solution does not eliminate their problem. In other words: information problems are laid down on the 'Procrustes'-bed of ICT solutions.

As a matter of fact we consider this failure factor – the wrong formulation of information problems – one of the key factors for the success – or failure – of information systems.

Lack of policy framework

In many organizations solving information problems is a bottom-up process in which top management hardly participates, on account of the absence of an overall vision. This approach may lead to a configuration of information systems in which on the one hand particular systems overlap too much, and on the other they are insufficiently compatible. It is clear that such an interpretation of the notion 'emerging strategy' means a lot of wasted money. Moreover, a climate for collective learning is absent in this way.

Limited scope of ICT applications

In the beginning, nearly all revolutionary technological developments are used to *replace* existing technologies. This means that new technologies are deployed in a rather defensive attitude and are aimed at realizing cost reduction benefits (*efficiency* targets). When applied in this way, the productivity contribution of (new) technologies is rather modest. It is only after several – sometimes a great number of – years that more innovative applications are generated which contribute to the *effectiveness* of organizations.

This course of events is also illustrative for the use of ICT. In many cases, this technology is used to replace people by machines (automation) which do the same things more cheaply, i.e. more efficiently. If the promise of ICT for the future is to come true, we will have to search for radically new applications in products and in (production) control structures as well.

Dutch research on the possible use of ICT in 1994 showed that:

- 33% of the respondents were interested in using ICT to replace existing techniques,
- 18% of the respondents were trying to improve the design of business processes and *only*
- 16% of the respondents mentioned strategic considerations for using ICT.

Economic evaluation of investments in ICT

Investments in ICT have some characteristics that make their economic evaluation difficult. In the first place, investments in ICT may have side-effects, either positive or negative, on other departments. Secondly, the positive effects of using ICT are often only realized after several years. And the longer this period, the more difficult it is to predict such effects. That is why information projects are rather risky. Thirdly, in many cases ICT will be evaluated on the basis of different criteria which are sometimes fuzzy and/or qualitative, which makes it difficult to measure those effects (Mirani and Lederer, 1998). Moreover, all these criteria should be translated into a common standard if you want to compare several investment proposals to reach an unambiguous priority order and a well-considered decision. Finally, if investments in ICT are innovative, this is an additional reason why the prediction of the outcome of these investments is so very difficult. So, in the field of information systems and ICT we have to deal with risky interrelated investments and a mixture of qualitative and quantitative effects.

For these reasons, organizations tend to allocate investment funds for ICT at face value without a thorough analysis, using the slogan 'what is good for our competitors is also good for us'.

A technique which stimulates this sort of behaviour is the so-called 'value analysis' (Keen, 1986). Although we do not reject this method out of hand, other – more sophisticated – evaluation methods should be tried before using value analysis.

Information systems and the power structure of organizations

There is a rather well-known saying in this context: 'information is power'. And this is especially true for the present knowledge society where information – defined as the increase of knowledge – has a very central position, and where the value of people for the organization depends on their information lead (Markus, 1984).

If new information systems are introduced into organizations, the existing information structure will usually change and so will the power structure. To the extent that participants are negatively affected by these changes we cannot expect them do be fully cooperative; they will probably try to undermine the new system instead, with all sorts of consequences for its functioning.

Mismatch between information systems and organizations

When information systems are discussed, in many cases only a single aspect of organizational problems is taken into account. Although information problems may act as a trigger to make decisions and to take action, we have to keep in mind that if we focus on only one aspect of a certain problem, i.c. the information aspect, the balance between that aspect and other aspects will be disturbed.

3. Possible solutions to neutralize failure factors

There are several methods and techniques for reducing the negative effects of the failure factors we discussed in the above section. Some of these are effective for a single failure factor only while others have a broader scope. In this section we will pay attention to the following approaches (Alter, 1999):

- the real meaning of management information systems as an academic discipline,
- design methods,
- information policy,
- methods for the economic evaluation of investments in ICT,
- political processes within organizations,
- project management,
- organizational embedment of information systems.
- integrated approach

Real meaning of management information problems

As we have already pointed out briefly in the preceding section, people and organizations often tend to choose the wrong solutions for information problems; i.e. ICT applications.

In order to reach fundamental solutions to information problems, we first have to make a distinction between two main directions that offer potential solutions (Galbraith, 1973):

- reducing information needs, for instance by organizational measures, or
- meeting these needs by using ICT.

Because there is a wide range of solutions available for information problems, of which ICT is only one specific possibility, management information systems as an academic discipline should concentrate on the *information* phenomenon as such, instead of almost automatically coupling information needs with ICT solutions.

If it is our intention to solve information problems fundamentally – 'dissolving' them according to Ackoff – we must not accept the information needs of organizational participants as given. On the contrary, we must wonder where information needs come from (Ackoff, 1978).

And if, after a thorough investigation in a specific situation, ICT solutions are still preferred, we have to take several precautions.

Design methods

A number of failure factors – i.e. communication problems, implementation problems, acceptance problems and maintenance problems – entirely or partly originate from using the wrong design methods. This especially concerns the so-called 'turn key' methods. These methods are applied as follows.

The design process starts with identifying the information needs of the – future – users of information systems. After this phase, the designers go back to their office and the complete information system is built. It is only in the implementation phase that the users are confronted with the final results. Such an approach is valid under the following conditions, which are not very realistic:

- users are sufficiently aware of their own information needs,
- users are able to make these needs clear to the designers of information systems,
- new information systems do not change information needs.

With regard to this first condition, it is rather problematic to interview humans about their information needs on account of phenomena like 'anchoring', 'concreteness' and 'recency' (Davis and Olson, 1984). That is why the *formulation* of information problems should be part of the design process and why it is comparable to shooting at a moving target (Checkland and Scholes, 1990).

With regard to the second condition there is a communication gap between users and designers of information systems, as we mentioned before. Therefore, users are not only rather unaware of their needs but they also have a problem communicating them.

Finally, the third condition does not apply either because users, confronted with the functionality of new information systems, tend to formulate additional needs that are not foreseen at the start of the project and therefore cannot be fulfilled in the context of traditional design methods.

We have to take care however, that we do not meet every need the user formulates, because many needs are not fundamental to the functionality of the new information system. On the contrary, such needs belong to the 'nice-to-have' category. During the design process Pareto's Law should be kept in mind: with 20% of costs and time 80% of the system's – total potential – functionality can be realized.

Of course we cannot expect adequate design methods to solve all the problems we identified in section 2. However, by applying iterative design methods that give a dominant position to the – future – users of information systems, such as prototyping and Rapid Application Development, radical improvements will be realized, especially with regard to the elicitation of user needs, the communication of user needs to designers, and changes in these needs during the design process which result from the confrontation between users and information systems (Martin, 1991).

Information policy

If decision making in organizations, for instance about the purchase of hardware and software, is not embedded in an overall vision, specific decisions will only lead to local solutions without added value for other parts of the organization, or with even a detrimental effect on them. In respect of ICT island automation is the result.

Consequently we have to look for such a vision. This vision can be found in information policy; this provides a framework which is most relevant for achieving a coherent configuration of information systems and ICT applications within the organization (Earl, 1995).

At the same time we should pay attention to the incorporation of information policy into the organization's strategy to give it a solid position in realizing competitive advantages (Porter and Millar, 1985).

At this level of decision making top management has a specific responsibility (Hamel and Prahalad, 1993).

Economic evaluation of investments in information systems and ICT

For investments in general, and for investments in information systems in particular, there are many evaluation methods available. Methods for risky interrelated projects have been developed as well (Hillier, 1969). Notwithstanding this, the evaluation of investments in information projects is still a real problem.

This problematic situation is not just caused by the limited applicability of many evaluation methods but is particularly due to the absence of relevant data for making reliable calculations related to sensitivity analysis. In general, data can be defined here as the quantitative translation of *facts* in the *past*. But what we need is more *future*-oriented – partly qualitative – data based on sophisticated *expectations*. A method which, in spite of its shortcomings, can be very helpful for generating future-oriented data is Delphi (Linstone and Turoff, 1975).

Methods that combine quantitative and qualitative criteria are needed as well, for evaluating investments in information systems. Techniques that can be applied for this purpose belong to the category 'multi-criteria analysis' (DeVries, 1992). In the field of 'information economics', too, methods have been developed for coping with incomparable criteria such as the 'balanced scorecard' procedure (Parker et al, 1988; Kaplan and Norton, 1992).

Understanding the role and added value of information systems

The disappointments about the results of information systems and ICT are partly caused by – too – high user expectations. Many people see computers as some sort of modern magician but they do not know what computers are really able to. If we give users a clear impression of the (im)possibilities of information systems, their expectations will become more realistic. This means that information systems will be used for purposes where sufficient added value is expected. As a result, users will become less disappointed.

A method that can help to bridge the gap between user expectations and functionality of information systems is the so-called 'project management approach'.

Political processes in organizations

Political processes cannot only be found in the political arena, outside organizations, but also within, think back to our discussion about the relationship between information structure and power structure. As we know, new information systems will change the existing information structure, and this directly affects the power structure. Participants who perceive a reduction of their influence, their power, are not prepared to facilitate the introduction of a new information system. It is more likely that they will try to frustrate its introduction or, if they do not succeed, its functioning afterwards.

The success or failure of information projects is therefore rather heavily dependent on the available techniques that can be used to cope with internal political consequences and conflicts during the design process of information systems; techniques that are well-known from literature (Pfeffer, 1981).

Innovative applications of ICT

As we have seen before, new technologies need a period of time, a so-called incubation period, before their opportunities can be fully exploited. So we have to accept some minimal ripening time, which sometimes may amount to thirty years. In this incubation period, new technologies are generally used to *replace* existing technology. Automation, replacing men by computers, is such an application of ICT.

If we stay rather passive, however, this incubation period can even take much longer. In order to fight the productivity paradox from this angle it is therefore necessary to use ICT in more creative ways and to look for radical innovations, in products and also in production processes (Turban, McLean and Wetherbe, 1996). Only in this way will it be possible to fully realize the potential added value of ICT.

Project management

In the preceding section it was concluded that information projects get out of hand on the dimensions 'time' and 'money'. This is caused by the complex and risky character of these projects and the far-reaching effects on large parts of the organization and on individual participants. In order to cope with such problems, specific techniques should be used for project management, especially techniques that have an open eye for the changing (power) structure of the people involved and the possible threats – real or imaginary – to their individual position.

This means that the composition of the project team is a major point of attention. It is not only technicians and users who have to be members but the team also needs experts on organizational change and political processes within organizations who can facilitate the introduction of new information systems.

Evidently, if information project teams are to achieve successful results, they must be composed on an interdisciplinary basis.

Organizational embedment of information systems

When we solve information problems by using information systems and ICT we often only pay attention to the information (technological) aspects of these problems. This will create an imbalance between the information aspect and other aspects, particularly the organizational aspect. Actually, the use of ICT will usually change the nature of the work of organizational participants. Some people get better and more challenging jobs for instance, whereas others become no more than extensions to the newly introduced technology. So, the quality of labour is changed, either positively or negatively. A well-known information systems design method which can be helpful in coping with labour quality problems that are caused by ICT is the so-called ETHICS method (Mumford, 1983).

Recently, the danger of using aspect-like approaches has risen again due to the development and application of I-CASE (Integrated Computer Assisted Software Engineering) tools with its rather strong technological emphasis.

Integrated approach
Looking back at the several topics which were briefly discussed in this section, we may conclude that information problems have many dimensions. In order to solve those problems we therefore need an approach that takes into account all possible aspects without neglecting one or more of them beforehand. Especially if ICT is part of the solution, the problem field is rather complex. In fact, we are not changing one piece of the puzzle but, because of interdependence between most pieces, the whole puzzle as such. That is why an *integrated* approach is necessary for coping with information problems, which means that when designing information systems we have to analyze, develop and change technology, organization and labour circumstances interdependently, particularly based on technological, social and economic design criteria. The use of such an integrated approach implies that all relevant aspects of the problem field are taken into consideration, without neglecting or emphasizing any aspect in particular. We must carefully look for an acceptable balance between the relevant aspects, i.e. all the aspects discussed in this section, which means that an integrated approach will be applied more or less automatically.

This does not mean however that all aspects have the same importance in every project. Sometimes certain aspects may not be relevant. However, such a conclusion is only feasible after a careful investigation of all the aspects.

After this explanation of 'an integrated approach to information problems' and our emphasis on such a method, it should not surprise us that this is also the subtitle of the book.

4. Plan of the book

With respect to the measures to neutralize the failure factors that accompany the design of information systems which were discussed in the previous section, we come to the conclusion that these same topics are relevant for a description of the relationship between information and the control of organizations. Therefore in the next chapters we will pay attention to these different topics in greater detail.

After a discussion of more general subjects in chapter II – such as the concepts we use, the control cycle, the decision making process, the information flows within the organization, the (social) systems theory, the impact of mental models, etc. – we will pay attention to the identification of management information systems as an academic discipline (chapter III). Chapter IV is devoted to the sociotechnical approach to organizations; an approach that is of the utmost importance in solving information problems in a – more – fundamental way; not as a method for structuring the process of designing information systems but for restructuring the organization. In chapter V the topics 'information policy' and 'information management' come up for discussion. This chapter will also deal with the task of the computer department. Chapter VI is about the management of information projects. In chapter VII we discuss methods for the design and exploitation of information projects. This chapter also pays attention to the topic of information analysis. Chapter VIII will discuss the phenomenon of power and the legitimization of policy (measures) within organizations.

It is almost self-evident that in a book like this there is much room for all sorts of information systems (chapter IX). With regard to this topic we will pay special attention to information systems that support organizations in realizing competitive advantages. As we will see, ICT applications play a dominant role here. Ignoring this potential can also be a reason for the limited success of information projects.

Apart from the fact that this book focuses on information systems there is a second reason for discussing such a topic. It is because a better understanding of information systems contributes to a greater correspondence between the possible added value of using those systems and the expectations the (future) users have of them. This chapter also gives some thought to the subject of business process redesign; a methodology which may help us look for innovative applications of information systems, and of ICT. This is the only type of applications which can be expected to make a substantial contribution to getting rid of the productivity paradox.

Finally, chapter X deals with a sophisticated method to take adequate capital budgeting decisions in the field of information systems, i.e. ICT.

We finish the present chapter by observing that the topic of ICT as such will not be discussed separately in this book, and the reader may wonder why. First of all we argue, especially in chapter III, that in many cases other, and even better, solutions for information problems are available than technological ones. This latter category of solutions is only one option out of several. Secondly, ICT changes very quickly, according to Moore's Law. Therefore an explicit discussion of this topic would make a negative contribution to the obsolescence of this book.

For the rest, ICT is indirectly discussed by talking about its possible applications (especially in chapter IX) and the identification of several design methods (chapter VII). Moreover, we also pay attention to innovative applications (chapter IX) and the economic evaluation of this technology (chapter X), as we mentioned before.

II CONCEPTS

1. Introduction

In this Chapter we will discuss a number of things that are important for understanding the chapters that follow.

Because the concepts 'information' and 'information system', together with 'organization', are the backbone of the book, section 2 focuses on systems in general and information systems in particular.

Section 3 is devoted to a discussion about the purpose we have in mind in generating information: the control of organizations. This section will also explain the control cycle, the levels of policy making and the process of decision making.

Section 4 concludes the chapter by identifying the information flows of organizations and by the definition of some concepts that are important for reading and understanding this book.

2. Systems

In the systems approach two premisses are relevant (Bertlanffy, 1956; 1968):
- the world around us is considered a composition of wholes; this is also called a 'holistic' concept,
- there exists a fundamental difference between a system and its environment.

We define a 'system' as:

a collection of elements (i.e. parts or components) among which there are relations

Relations between elements are effectuated by exchanging:
- goods or services,
- information and
- energy.

Everything that is outside the system is labelled *environment*. This environment can be split up into:
- relevant environment and
- irrelevant environment.

The 'relevant' environment is that part of the universe with which the system actually maintains some sort of relations; as opposed to the rest of the environment which is irrelevant to the system.

The frontier between relevant and irrelevant environment is not always clear. Moreover, this frontier may change over time. We will clarify this with an example. Suppose there is a company that produces wooden toys for the local European market. In spite of this regional limitation it does not mean that products never will be sold outside the European continent. One day the decision might be made to penetrate the American market.

This example illustrates that the whole world is in fact more or less relevant in spite of the present restrictions on the sales area.

Next to this possibility of changing frontiers, another part of the environment which is *ir*relevant at this moment relates to alternative raw materials for wood for instance. In the future, the company may decide to use plastics in addition to, or instead of wood.

The distinction between relevant and irrelevant environment is especially important in the context of the strategic policy of organizations; a topic that will be discussed in Chapter IX, when we deal with the identification of various information systems.

Apart from a division into elements, systems can also be split up into a different category of components called subsystems. With respect to subsystems we make a distinction between *facet systems* and *aspect systems*.

By facet systems we mean concrete parts that can be touched physically, such as the keyboard of a computer system. A business unit of an organization is a facet system, containing people, equipment, etc. of the organization to which it belongs.

In the case of aspect systems it is important from which point of view we are looking at systems. In other words: which specific relations are we interested in. For instance, if we pay attention to the social relations within an organization, then we are interested in the social aspect of organizations. In other words, we focus on the social aspect system. In the same way an economic aspect system can be identified, just like a psychological aspect system, etc.

Evidently, various relations are possible between the elements of a system. When we are dealing with aspect systems, only a limited number of those relations are relevant, depending on the focus of the observer or student.

Unlike facet systems, aspects are not concrete but abstract; they are not physically observable.

Both categories of subsystems are important for the information policy of organizations. If we study organizations from the point of view of information handling, then the information aspect is dominant and we limit our interest to the information aspect of a system.

If, on the contrary, we speak about information systems meaning some specific parts of the organization such as a specific combination of hardware and software, then this is a facet system. Normally, in daily language the term 'information system' is used in this way.

To make things easy, in the remainder of this book we will adhere to this second interpretation too. Only when explicitly stated will information systems be conceived as some specific sort of aspect systems. Otherwise, the concept 'information system' refers to a specific combination of hardware and software, as is the usual interpretation in daily practice.

In order to function a system needs raw materials called inputs. Those raw materials are processed – transformed – from inputs into outputs. This transformation process which is aimed at the production of goods and/or services is called the *primary* process of the system. Thus, primary processes can be defined as the processes that give the system, or subsystem, its right to exist, because inputs are bought and outputs are sold on external markets, i.e. external from the point of view of the (sub)system.

To assess the results of this process an output norm has to be specified, a quantitative as well as a qualitative norm.

To realize this output norm the system must be controlled (see also the next section). The controlling body is charged with this control task.

The relationship between the controlling body and the system that has to be controlled is two-sided. On the one hand the controlling body receives information from the system and on the other hand the controlling body imposes corrective actions on the system. This mutual relationship is illustrated in fig. II.1, where the symbols used have the following meaning:

CB = controlling body,
T = transformation process of the system,
I = output,
O = input.

The straight lines represent the flow of goods, the dashed line represents the information flow and the dotted line represents the corrective action.

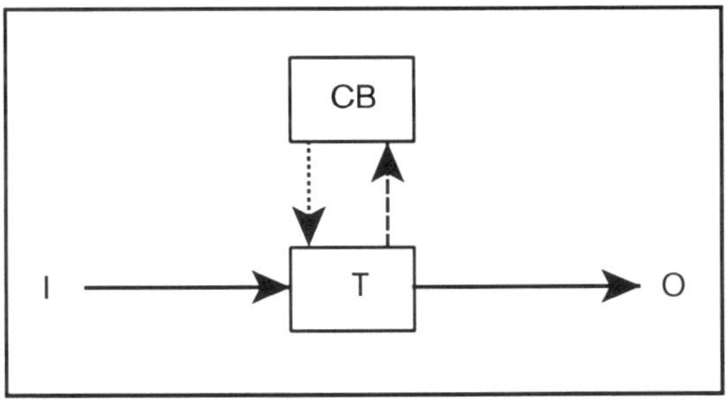

Figuur II.1

This figure depicts two kinds of processes: the transformation process and the controlling process.

As a third category we distinguish *facilitating* processes, also called supporting processes. Those processes give the transformation process the necessary support.

If we look at the definition of primary processes and facilitating processes in greater detail we come to the conclusion that the qualification 'primary process' is not an absolute one. For instance, the organization's bookkeeping department is facilitative as far as the units are concerned for which it registers all sort of transactions. But seen through its own eyes this department is also characterized by a transformation process with input and output that gives this specific department its right to exist. Therefore, bookkeeping can be seen as a primary process for this particular department. And this transformation process must be supported as well. But there is still a fundamental difference. Usually there is only one specific transformation process (the organization) which has relationships with entities *outside* the system as a whole. All the other transformation processes have contacts that are restricted to *inside* clients.

To avoid possible confusion about this terminology the term 'primary process' is exclusively used for the transformation process which has relationships with outside markets. We do admit that facilitating processes themselves must also be supported *and* controlled.

However, for some organizations there is a complicating factor because they allow particular departments to produce for external clients too. For instance, it is increasingly becoming standard procedure that the organization's information centre has external clients as well as internal ones. So our definition could lead to some confusion because the process of this department can also be seen as a primary process. In order to solve this problem we must look at the core business of the organization: the business that is seen as dominant in generating resources.

Information systems are an example of facilitating processes, or facilitating subsystems in which we are particularly interested. Bearing in mind the definition of a system, for the moment information systems can be described as

> *a combination of transformation processes that can be identified as collecting, storing, processing and retrieving data*

As will be demonstrated in section 4 of this chapter, we will modify this definition to some extent because of the specific interpretation of the terms 'data' and 'information'.

Besides, please note that information systems do not automatically imply the application of ICT. In addition to computers we have other technical means at our disposal to generate and handle information in an efficient and an effective way.

When we speak of information systems and information structure we focus on that part of the information handling of the organization that is officially recorded. Such a structure gives a measure of solidity to the organization, just like the rest of its organization structure, which consists of a combination of rules and procedures that have to be observed by its participants. In this way, the organization will not degenerate into chaos and anarchy; a development that may be very threatening.

In this sense, the structure of organizations is comparable with the skeleton of vertebrates. These creatures also need some solidity to survive in a hostile environment.

However, if vertebrates have too much structure, because of arthritis for instance, their mobility will be hampered, with consequences that are probably fatal.

The same arguments apply to the structure of organizations. Too much structure, as in the case of a bureaucratic organization, diminishes the mobility – flexibility –

in an unacceptable way. And flexibility is especially important in turbulent (hostile) environments. Therefore, organization structures (containing information structures), with a well-considered balance between rigidity (structure) and flexibility, are necessary preconditions for creating opportunities for long term survival (see also Chapter III).

As we pointed out before, systems are composed of elements that have mutual relations. This does not mean that every single element has relations with all the others. For instance, the staff department 'Corporate planning' does not have direct relations with the various business units since it is a subsystem of the system 'concern'. It is directly related to the board only.

Moreover, if there is a relationship between some elements, this does not mean that they actually have contact with each other. Therefore, we distinguish *potential* and *actual* relationships. A potential relationship can be defined as the possibility to come to an exchange of goods/services, information or energy. An actual relationship means that such an exchange really takes place.

Now, if we observe a system at a certain moment we can generally conclude that only a part of its potential relationships are activated. So we are confronted with a specific configuration of actual relationships. This configuration is called the system state. And this state may change at each following moment when we observe the system again.

The larger the number of possible system states, dependent on the number of elements and the potential relations, the greater the system's complexity (Beer, 1990). Complexity interpreted in this way is called objective complexity (Willke, 1993).

Various kinds of systems, as they are identified in the real world, can be distinguished on the basis of their amount of complexity. For instance, an organization is much more intricate than a skeleton. To explain this difference in greater detail we will pay attention to the system hierarchy of Kenneth Boulding. This student of systems theory distinguished the following system levels according to their amount of complexity (Boulding, 1956):

1. static systems: frame level,
2. simple dynamic systems: clockwork level,
3. homeostatic systems: thermostat level,
4. open systems: cell level,
5. genetic-social systems: plant level,
6. animal systems: animal level,
7. human systems: human level,
8. social systems: social level,
9. transcendental systems: transcendental level.

From the fourth system level upwards they are also called 'organic' systems.

Because the real world in which organic systems have to function is very complex, and because only a part – a limited set of aspects and facets – of the real world is relevant, this has consequences for the ability of these systems to observe what is going on, internally as well as externally; an ability that is very narrowly oriented.

On account of this limitation, organic systems recognize structures and patterns in the real world that are in fact imposed by themselves. Events in the real world are interpreted using this very pattern. According to Weick, we call this phenomenon *enactment* (Weick, 1979). This means that organic systems create a sort of image of the real world, an image that is used to deal with this supposed world.

In fact, organic systems only refer to themselves, that is to their specific image of the real world. In other words, they produce themselves. Therefore organic systems are autopoeietic (Maturana and Varela, 1992). The noun 'autopoiese' literally means self-production.

Therefore, organic systems are not confronted with some sort of objective knowable world outside themselves but with a world constructed by themselves. The templates resulting from such constructive acts are called 'mental models'.

The function of these mental models is twofold. On the one hand they protect organic systems against a continuous bombardment of – mostly superfluous – information. On the other hand they limit the ability of these systems to observe; sometimes unacceptably so, which means that the system's long-term viability is at stake. In this way the mental model sometimes functions as a mental prison.

We will return to this topic when we discuss information systems that can be used to shape the strategic policy of organizations. The way in which organic systems deal with the world around them is of crucial importance for this policy (Chapter VIII).

Social systems, at the eighth system level, are distinguished from other organic systems by the fact that they are systems whose elements consist of human beings (systems of the seventh level), and in which the *relations* between these human beings (the social aspect system) are very important.

This does not mean, however, that all systems consisting of human beings can be seen as social systems. For instance, the system of traffic participants can hardly be called a system because of the superficial contacts between the elements; let alone that we can consider this a system in the social sense. What is lacking is a lasting relationship between the actors in some sort of structural setting which facilitates social interaction.

Because living systems are continually in motion (physically and mentally) they are governed by other – much more complex – laws than non-living (mechanistic) systems.

We will illustrate this notion by using the results of an experiment with rats performed by the American psychologist Karl Lashley (Morgan, 1986).

In one of his experiments, Lashley kept removing small parts of the brains of his laboratory animals (rats) which had learned to find their way in a labyrinth looking for food. In the course of this experiment, it turned out to be possible to remove about 90% of the rats' brains without significantly deteriorating their ability to orient themselves in the labyrinth in which they had to find their way. This phenomenon is caused by a characteristic of the brain which is shared by other living systems, or parts of these systems. It is the capacity that other parts take over, although sometimes rather inadequately, the functions of the missing parts. It is out of the question that what Lashley showed in his experiment with a living system can be done with mechanical systems. It is impossible to eliminate parts of those systems without seriously affecting the function of the system as a whole. For instance, it is completely unimaginable that some parts of an engine could be removed and that their function would then be taken over by others. This is because all parts of a mechanical system are highly specialized, whereas the learning capacity of such a system is zero. This means that dissimilar parts cannot be taught to behave differently to fill the gaps caused by parts that have been removed.

Analogous to the animals in Lashley's experiment, organizations have the capacity to make elements take over the function(s) of other elements that have failed, on the basis of the principle of 'functional redundancy' (this means that parts are multifunctional).

This fundamental difference between both categories of systems justifies a theoretical framework for living – organic – systems that is completely different from one based on mechanistic principles.

Learning is closely related to the functioning of systems. We will start our discussion of this topic with an anecdote. Earlier generations of boys were brought up playing with *metal* models of automobiles called 'Dinky Toys'. The manufacturer of these toys, however, got the short end of the stick due to severe competition, especially from *plastic* toys with the trade mark 'Fisherprice'. This raises the question: how could such a thing happen?

A plausible explanation for this disaster may be the following. Some decades ago, plastics came into use as a raw material for many different products, toys for instance. Manufacturers such as 'Lego' and 'Fisherprice' got the message and replaced their raw materials (wood, metal, etc.) by plastics. However, the manufacturer of 'Dinky toys' obviously had the self-image that his toys had to be made of metal, ignoring new developments in the field of possible alternative raw materials.

Because this firm was unable to correct its self-image in time, it probably failed in the struggle with competitors who were well aware of the opportunities offered by new raw materials.

As indicated above, people and organizations have self-conceptions which originate from mental models. In other words, organizations only have knowledge about a world constructed by themselves, which results in a specific mental model.

Within the – limits of the – mental model that is in operation, data from the environment will be selected, interpreted and reacted to. This phenomenon is called first order or single loop learning. This sort of learning does not mean that organizations actually select information, but rather that they *produce* information within their current frame of reference.

In this context we are explicitly speaking about the *production* of information by the systems involved instead of by the environment, because it is the system itself, and no one else, which decides on the basis of its frame of reference which signals will be picked up and how they will be interpreted, that is, what meaning will be assigned to them.

As will be demonstrated in the next chapter, self-conceptions are crucial to the way in which information problems are solved most of the time. This approach involves a category of solutions which is largely to blame for the poor success of information systems and ICT projects.

As long as the organization's self-image leads to a net exchange relationship with the environment (cash inflows minus cash outflows) which is at least zero, there is no need to correct this self-image, because the organization's viability is not at stake.

However, the environment in which many organizations have to function is continually variable; or even worse, it is turbulent. As a consequence, there is a real danger that the environment develops requirements that are incompatible with the organization's self-image. The symptom of this dichotomy is a declining net cash flow.

If the organization does not change its self-image, this may have dramatic consequences, and perhaps result in complete disaster. The adaptation of self-images is called second order – or double loop – learning.

Second order learning processes are particularly important for the strategic policy of organizations. That is because this policy involves choosing – new – combinations of products/markets/technologies, something which requires changes in the mental model that is in operation.

With regard to second order learning a number of fundamental problems arise:
- what is the impulse for second order learning,
- how does second order learning take place,
- what is the role of information systems in second order learning?

In most cases the impulse for second order learning is the threat of going bankrupt. Organizations are normally focused on short-term activities, and they neglect their opportunities to survive in the long(er) run. James March and Herbert Simon once formulated this behaviour under the label 'Gresham's Law of Planning' (March and Simon, 1958) as:

'Daily routine drives out planning'

As long as things are going well, organizations prefer daily routine activities. Only if the viability of the organization is at stake are they prepared to take long-term activities (planning) into consideration. However, it may be too late for that.

It is therefore necessary that second order learning becomes a regular part of the policy of organizations, instead of responding ad hoc to calamities which threaten the organization's survival.

As to second order learning on the individual level we face a methodological problem similar to that of a person who tries to pull himself out of the swamp by his own hairs. This is because our self-image determines what we observe and what we fail to see. And this information confirms our self-image instead of challenging it, as is necessary for second order learning. The signals that might change our ideas are not noticed. And this also applies to organizations.

This raises the question in what way, in spite of such kinds of limitations, second order learning might be effected at the individual human level. The answer is that second order learning takes place by people influencing and correcting each other.

The same mechanisms are present in the second order learning process of organizations. For instance, organizations are able to correct their self-image by turnover of personnel on a regular basis. According to Hamel and Prahalad this is called 'creating genetic diversity' (Hamel and Prahalad, 1993). By using this instrument, behaviour patterns that are taken for granted by the present members of the organization will be challenged and possibly changed by newcomers.

In addition to the creation of genetic diversity, organizations can use the mirror of external consultants in the field of organization diagnosis (Kubr, 1986). These are able to give advice on a specific problem, such as the purchase of a new computer, they also have instruments for judging the 'health' of the organization. Training programs, courses, seminars, workshops, etc. can also be used to correct the self-image of organizations.

Finally, in addition to the possibilities we just mentioned, organizations have information systems at their disposal for second order learning; so-called 'idea processing systems'. This subject will be discussed in greater detail in Chapter IX.

An important part of the learning process of organic systems concerns the formulation of problems; i.e. the way in which problems are interpreted. Let us first define a problem as:

> *a perceived discrepancy between a situation as it is and as it should be, now or in the future*

Only if problems are completely structured (meaning that they can be solved in a finite number of steps that can be specified unambiguously) does their formulation not involve any doubt. But in many cases it is not clear in advance how problems should be specified. On the contrary, the problem formulation is part of the problem solving process (Checkland and Scholes, 1990).

By 'playing' with the problem and looking at it from several angles its formulation will be changed during several rounds, in which the picture will become increasingly clear. So initially problems are often rather vague.

It is even possible that this vagueness, for instance with regard to strategic problems, is no more than a feeling of unease; a feeling that the end of the decision making process must result in a concrete solution or a concrete action plan.

A good understanding of how social systems function is of vital importance for designing information systems in organizations.

In the first place, the fact that mental models are involved implies that only a limited number of all the signals from the world around us will be observed. And this mental model will also cause the system to interpret these signals (get information from it) in a specific way.

Secondly, social systems involve a collection of actors with their own individual motives, goals and interests which sometimes conflict with those of others. In such a setting information is not used as a neutral – technical – variable but as an instrument for influencing the behaviour of other participants in the desired direction; not to say for manipulating them.

Thirdly, the significance of knowledge and information in our modern society, and therefore within organizations, is still growing. One of the results of this tendency is that the added value of personnel for organizations is increasingly based on their knowledge and information lead over others. As a result, their willingness to share this knowledge and information with other people will diminish; after all, knowledge (information) means power (Hendriks, 1999).

In the fourth place, the power of people in organizations is not exclusively based on knowledge and information which is purely factual but also on additional knowledge and information which is, as such, not relevant for their position (see also Chapter VII).

As conclusion to this section we can say that information in organizations plays an important role that goes beyond its purely technological content. In fact, information is not an objective phenomenon but it is rather the product of the mind of organizational actors who use it as an instrument to facilitate the realization of their own specific goals; goals that can be detrimental to the organization.

3. Control, policy and decision making

Information and information systems play an important role in the process of the *control* of organizations, the process of *policy* making and the process of *decision* making in mutual dependence. This interdependence can be clarified as follows. In order to control organizations we need some sort of policy which indicates the direction of our actions, the path we have to follow, if this control is to be effectuated. And actions are based on decisions which are the outcomes of the decision making process.

The preceding section introduced the concept of a controlling body which has to ensure that the system concerned realizes its targets. When we look at the control process performed by can identify a so-called 'control cycle'. This cycle is split up into three stages:

- planning,
- execution and
- checkup.

Planning means the design, the preparation of the intended activities so that these activities may be carried out as a cohesive whole.

What is needed after planning is action: *execution*. Finally, planning and execution have to be confronted with each other. This stage is called *checkup*.

In the case of – unacceptable – discrepancies between these two we will have to interfere. We may have to interfere either in the planning, or in the execution, or in both. In other words, the term 'control' refers to a process in which the different phases of the control cycle are gone through time and again.

This process is illustrated in fig. II.2.

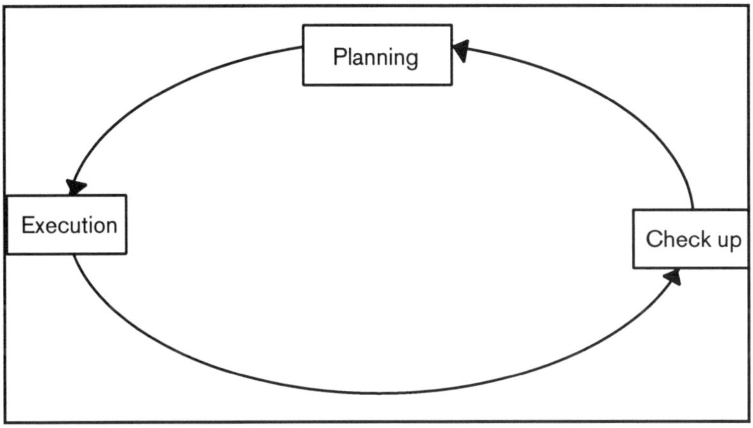

Figure II.2 The control cycle

In practising the control cycle, two fundamentally different approaches can be distinguished: the blueprint approach and the process approach. The *blueprint* approach means that a plan is drawn up which consists of a number of instructions – such as steps to be taken, procedures to be applied, etc. – which have to be followed carefully.

The *process* approach is also based on a – sophisticated – plan. However, for its execution there are many degrees of freedom, depending on the specific combination of circumstances that cannot be predicted in any single detail. In this situation the plan is essentially an enumeration of important elements that have to be taken into account. And if the execution deviates from the plan, we are forced to ascertain where this happens, why it happens, and what consequences there are to be faced. Thus, the process approach involves a flexible application of plans with sufficient imagination and creativity.

Needless to say, neither of both approaches is superior; the choice between these two depends in particular on the structure of the problem at hand (see also section 4).

If the controlling body interferes in the execution it is essential to know which steps can be taken and in what magnitude.

We will illustrate this with a simple example. Suppose that a given system transforms input I into output O. If there is a serious chance that the output target (a certain number of units O) will not be met, the controlling body, on the basis of – sufficient – observations from the past, is able to adapt the input volume in such a way that the output will become acceptable.

This example reveals that the controlling body gets information by measuring the output in the course of the transformation process, while the corrective intervention relates to the input (see the diagram below).

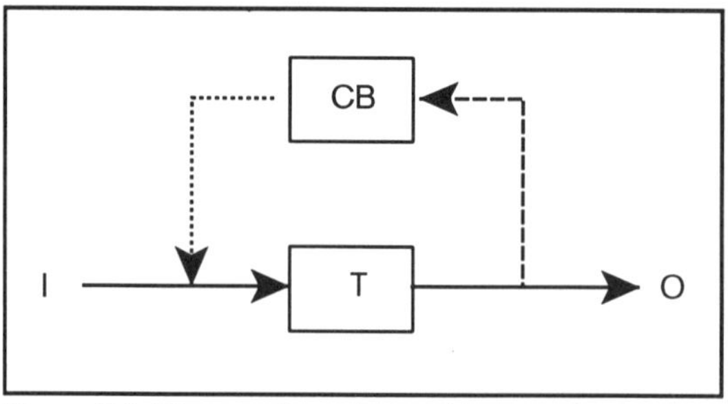

Figuur II.3 The transformation and intervention process

It is essential in this control loop that the controlling body uses two variables outside the system to control it: input and output. This is called 'boundary control'. What is going on inside the system is not observed by the controlling body. We call this a 'black box' approach.

As such this is a simple and transparent control paradigm. But its strength is also its weakness.

Many systems in general, and social systems in particular, contain a transformation process that is composed of many smaller processes. And within each of these processes a lot of disturbances are possible. A cumulation of disturbances may result in a relationship between input and output that is very unreliable, in such a way that systems in which the controlling body uses the black box control paradigm are insufficiently controllable or even uncontrollable.

For this reason, the controlling body may wish to open the black box. This means that for a specific part, or collection of parts, of the system the relationship between input and output will be specified in greater detail. This is done in order to fine-tune the control of the system. If we open the black box, we apply the so-called 'sequential approach', based on the *sequential control paradigm*. As a matter of fact, this paradigm defines the main transformation process of systems as a sequence of smaller transformation processes which work together to meet the system's goals. In other words, by the application of the sequential control paradigm systems will be decomposed. Of course, this decomposition does not go on infinitely. If we are interested in organizations for instance, human beings are the smallest possible parts – the elements – which can be identified; these are elements that are not opened. But these human beings can still be seen as complete systems from the point of view of medical scientists. The number of parts, and partial transformation processes, which will be distinguished in decomposing organizations depends on the measure of control that should be exercised, and the severity of the disturbances in each part.

In summary, we may conclude that the main difference between both control paradigms (black box and sequential) can be formulated as follows. The black box control paradigm considers *complete* systems as a black box, whereas the sequential control paradigm decomposes complete systems in smaller parts, but these parts are black boxes too in the end because they remain closed. It is a matter of degree.

There is a specific category of information systems for which the control paradigm is rather essential: decision support systems. We will discuss these systems in Chapter IX.

For the information policy of organizations their policy in general is rather important. Therefore we start with a definition of *policy*:

the ways in which and the means with which an organization attempts to meet its goals

With regard to the policy of organizations a number of *levels* can be distinguished:
- strategic policy,
- tactical policy and
- operational policy.

Strategic policy is concerned with the positioning of the organization in its environment, embodied in the *products* it makes, the *technologies* that are used, and the *markets* in which these products are sold. In other words, strategic policy means the reflection on combinations of products, markets and technologies in a mutual dependence.

In the field of strategic policy it is usual to make a further distinction between (Hamel and Prahalad, 1993):
- corporate level and
- (strategic) business unit level.

When talking about strategic policy at business unit level, we are interested in the positioning of the goods (and services) produced by those units, and the markets they attend to. Strategic policy at concern level relates to core competencies in which the organization excels and which are materialized in the products at the business unit level. Strategic policy at corporate level means answering the question in what sequence the core competencies will be embodied in the products of the several business units. Sony, for instance, using its core competence 'miniaturisation', started with the production of the walkman, and afterwards this competence was also embodied in wrist television.

Furthermore, there is a second distinction which is important for strategic policy: offensive or proactive and defensive or reactive strategic policy. *Offensive* strategy involves the creation of new opportunities for the organization, while *defensive* strategy concerns the elimination of threats at the strategic level. As we will see later when we discuss the process of decision making, opportunities and threats are phenomena which cannot be determined objectively but result from our perception of developments in the environment.

By *tactical* policy we mean the design of transformation processes for putting the chosen strategy into practice. This design activity concerns both *technical* facilities (which type of machines have to be bought for example) and the *structure* of these processes, i.e. answering the question how processes are embedded in the organization and which rules and procedures have to be followed in carrying out these processes.

Finally, *operational* policy is about the activities that must be executed in order to realize the strategy of the organization. For instance, production and sales planning belong to this policy level.

The control at these three levels is called strategic control, tactical control and operational control respectively.

In addition to these three kinds of control we distinguish a fourth one, so-called *execution* control. Unlike strategic, tactical and operational control, all of which are related to the *preparation* of activities on the work floor, the *execution* of activities means that production, etc. really takes place. The execution as such must be controlled as well, either by a supervisor or by the worker himself.

The notion of the four levels of control is relevant because of the opportunities to support the activities on these levels by the use of information systems, in combination with ICT.

At each of these three policy levels the three stages of the control cycle – planning, execution and checkup – take place. At the strategic level, this cycle starts with the intention to (re)formulate the organization's strategy (planning stage). Then this intention will be executed, for instance by using the instrument of a strategic conference where the organization's present and future product/market/technology combinations are discussed. And finally, at the end of the year, it is checked whether such a conference has really taken place.

At the tactical level, for example, planning may relate to an initiative to invest in new equipment. Execution means ordering and installing this equipment. Checkup is the confrontation between what was intended and how it is later realized.

As to operational planning, we can think about production planning for some future period, the production of goods during this period, and the checkup after production is finished.

Furthermore, it is necessary that the control cycles at the three policy levels are *connected*. This can be achieved by using a goal hierarchy. Operational targets must be derived from tactical goals; and these should derive from the organization's strategic objectives and mission. Thus, in the planning stage, 'higher' goals are incorporated at each level as constraints, which results in the necessary coordination between the three levels. And afterwards, in the checkup stage, it will be evaluated whether these goals have been realized at each level.

Budgeting is closely connected to operational control, for the following reasons.

Before planning can be executed, an organization must take an intermediate step. It is necessary that the financial constraints for the execution are indicated, and the department must be authorized to recruit sufficient employees and means of production for the execution.

Now, budgeting is the translation of working hours and production means into financial terms, as well as the authorization to spend the money that has to be paid to employees and to suppliers to get the job done.

The control of organizations requires many decisions, day after day. Before we can reach a decision a number of activities have to be executed. This is called the decision making *process*. As a matter of fact, in terms of the well-known model of a system, this process is a transformation process, with problems as input and decisions as output.

A thorough knowledge of the decision making process is of the utmost importance because of the role of information systems as support or as a replacement for the decision maker.

Before discussing the phases of the process of decision making we will pay attention what triggers this process: problems.

We are confronted with a *problem* if there is some tension between how things should be and how they really are or will develop. If such a tension occurs in the present, for instance if our sales do not meet our expectations, we call this a *manifest* tension. However, it is also possible that there is no tension today, but that tension may arise in the future. As we know, every product is subject to some sort of life-cycle, which means that after a number of years products become obsolete. If we do not take the necessary measures in time, the organization's viability might be at stake in the long run. Because the development of new products takes time, we have to anticipate the obsolescence of products in the future. This tension is not manifest today but will certainly materialize in the long(er) run. Therefore, we call this *latent* tension.

Now we are able to redefine a problem as:

manifest or latent tensions between what should be and what is

Returning to the process of decision making we can identify four phases (Simon, 1959):
- intelligence,
- design,
- choice and
- implementation.

Two of these phases – intelligence and design – can be split up as follows:
intelligence:
- observation of problems, i.e. catching signals,
- identification of problems/signals,
- interpretation of problems/signals,
- formulation of problems,
- recognition of problems.

design:
- generation of alternatives,
- evaluation of alternatives.

In the rest of this section we will discuss the phases of the process of decision making in more detail.

Every new day we experience a bombardment of signals arising from the world around us; signals which we ignore or to which we might react. Sometimes we actively look for signals, for instance if we have an immediate (manifest) problem. But sometimes we are also rather passive. This may happen if we are screening the organization's environment looking for new opportunities (latent problem).

In spite of the fact that observing the environment is mostly an internal affair, as we demonstrated above, Aguilar makes the following distinction (Aguilar, 1967):

- undirected viewing,
- conditioned viewing,
- informal search and
- formal search.

'Viewing' is a rather passive activity, while 'search' is a rather active one. 'Undirected viewing' means that we are exposed to signals without focusing on any signal in particular. 'Conditioned viewing' differs from undirected viewing because the field of interest is now limited. 'Informal search' is characterized by the same focus as conditioned viewing, but in the former case signals are looked for actively. Finally, 'formal search' means a structured research process focused on narrowly defined signals.

It could be suggested that with 'undirected viewing' our observations of the world around us are completely unprejudiced, whereas the other three types are more or less interest or problem-driven. However, human beings are unable to observe the environment with an open mind, because of the presence of physical and mental filters which signals from outside have to pass.

The physical filters are related to our physical capacity to observe, to our senses. When we are asleep our senses are partially disconnected.

And even when we are awake, the number of signals we are aware of is very limited compared with all the signals that we are exposed to. For instance, compared with the hearing capacity of dogs, our capacity of hearing is much smaller.

'Time' is also a restricting factor which acts as a physical filter too. Normally, we do not have enough time to read all the periodicals available or to join all the conferences and meetings that could be relevant.

In addition to physical filters we can identify mental filters. We are only able to catch signals that can be recognized somehow, because of our mental model. Therefore, when we practise undirected viewing, signals must at least pass this mental filter. Moreover, if we are looking for signals in some specific field, either on the basis of our interest in creating new opportunities, or on the basis of a specific problem that we have to solve in order to eliminate a threat (conditioned viewing, informal search or formal search), signals are subjected to an extra filter.

Aguilar's four observation categories are primarily a part of the first order learning processes (see the preceding section), but they can also serve as a trigger for second order learning processes.

These distinctions in the observation of the environment are important for the structure of problems as well (see also the next section) and the opportunities of information systems to support these activities.

If signals relate to operational problems it is often fairly soon clear in which direction the process of decision making for solving the problem will develop. In the case of offensive strategic control, however, it is usually rather difficult to handle signals adequately. This difference has to do with the *structure* of problems; a topic that will be discussed later on.

Summarizing the ideas about filtering data, we may conclude that which signals we pick up is determined to a great extent by the filters these signals have to pass. Two kinds of filters are important, physical filters and mental filters. The physical filters result from our limited capacity to observe the world, whereas the mental filters are based on our mental model, and eventually on our specific interest in our environment; an interest that is always problem-driven.

The difficulty just mentioned, that of adequately handling signals – especially strategic signals –, is the reason why we distinguish a phase called 'identification'. In this phase the decision maker selects signals at first sight. It is this first impression which determines whether signals should be ignored or should be processed further. Signals that are not recognized as important for action do not trigger the process of decision making. In this phase, too, a mental filter is used to select between important and unimportant signals.

This selection process is, with respect to strategic problems, of crucial importance for the long-term viability of the organization. If this process results in the wrong choices the survival of the organization will be at stake.

After this first impression in the phase of identification, it is necessary to identify what the signals that are perceived mean – or could mean in the future – for the organization. In fact, signals are 'translated' in this phase with a view to their possible contribution to the solution of present and/or future problems, as perceived by the decision maker. Therefore interpretation is not an objective activity but implies that the decision maker's perception of signals plays a dominant role, resulting in a specific – narrowed – meaning, which is attached to signals.

After the signals have been interpreted their meaning will be narrowed down further by asking ourselves how we should perceive the problem at hand; how we have to formulate it.

Although we speak here of 'having to' it is actually preferable to speak of 'wanting to'. Even if we are confronted with a problem which is simple at first sight, it may often be formulated and solved from quite different angles if we invest some time and energy.

If, for instance, we formulate the problem 'buying a new car' to transport us from home to work, the problem can be solved by choosing between a number of brands and types.

If we consider this car-buying problem at a higher level of abstraction, by formulating it as a transportation problem, other means of transport come to mind, such as train, bus, etc. And this problem can be defined at an even higher level as a problem of bilocation; the problem of two different geographical locations where we have to undertake some activities. So we could look for opportunities to eliminate this distance, the distance between home and work. If we formulate the problem in this way solutions such as looking for another job or moving house will also become relevant.

By zooming out on problems we become aware of other categories of solutions that are sometimes very original and revolutionary, more efficient and effective (Ackoff, 1978).

In addition to generating new categories of solutions, there is a second reason for applying this zooming-out procedure. People, and organizations as well, tend to formulate problems in terms of well-known solutions that have proved successful in the past. In other words, we are looking at problems using solutions as 'spectacles'. This approach is very dangerous, because problems may be reshaped in such a way that we solve a supposed problem, meanwhile leaving the original problem unsolved (Mitroff and Featheringham, 1974).

In fact, problems are laid down on the Procrustean bed of preferred solutions (Prakken, 1992).

As we will see in the next Chapter when we discuss the identity of Management Information Science, an important reason for the failure of information systems is the wrong formulation of information problems. We almost automatically formulate them in terms of ICT solutions.

Apparently, the formulation of problems depends on the way people and organizations perceive problems. Therefore it may be misleading, when we are looking at the well-known SWOT (Strengths/Weaknesses/Opportunities/Threats) analysis, to speak of 'opportunities' and 'threats', which suggests that we are confronted here with objective developments in the environment that we have to accept.

Opportunities and threats are not phenomena that happen to us accidentally, but they are the labels we use for developments around us. That is why it is possible that some organizations identify a certain phenomenon as an opportunity, while others perceive it as a threat. Evidently, it would be advisable not to talk any more in terms of 'opportunities' and 'threats' which happen to us, but to replace these terms by *external perception*. By using this term we express our belief that organizations have the capacity to determine what developments contain potential opportunities or potential threats. In fact, in the environment of organizations only neutral developments occur. And depending on our perception the label 'opportunity' or 'threat' will be used.

We will illustrate this with an example from Japan. Many years ago, the Japanese authorities forced the Japanese industry to pay attention to conservation. Initially, Japanese manufactures reacted very defensively, complaining that this policy would lead to competitive disadvantages which would threaten Japanese industrial power. The Japanese government, however, held to its decision and after some time a new sector was born which developed and exploited conservation technologies.

After some time other countries, forced by economic developments and environmental pollution problems, followed the Japanese example. Unfortunately for them, those countries did not have a grown up conservation technology sector yet. So they had to buy their equipment from Japan, thus stimulating a very flourishing Japanese industry in this field, which exports products worth billions of dollars. What originally was perceived as a threat turned into an opportunity after some years.

In the same way that was demonstrated for opportunities and threats we must look at the strengths and weaknesses of organizations. These do not refer to objective qualifications either but result from our perceptions of these organizations. Once these qualifications are settled, a process of self-fulfilling prophecies will be reinforced. If a characteristic is perceived as strong the resources of the organization will be used to make it even stronger. And the opposite will happen to weaknesses. It is advisable then to speak about *internal perceptions*, in the same way we already did for external perceptions.

As a consequence, the name SWOT analysis is no longer adequate and should be replaced by 'IPEP' analysis, which suggests that the organization itself is exclusively responsible for the frontier between opportunities and threats or between strengths and weaknesses, instead of some independent external force that has to be accepted unconditionally.

Finally, in discussing this formulation phase of the decision making process, we notice that the formulation of problems is not always definite. Sometimes it may occur, especially when we are confronted with unstructured problems (see below), that the problem formulation will change because we have generated alternatives in the design phase. In fact, the decision making process is not linear but circular, as will be demonstrated presently at the end of this section.

On the other hand, if problems are completely structured (see below as well) from the start of the decision making process, the problem that has to be solved is perfectly clear; this means that the formulation phase can be omitted. Moreover, in this situation, the decision making process is completely linear because there is no need to return to earlier phases.

As a matter of fact, here we encounter the difference between process approach and blueprint approach that was discussed above.

In addition to the filters and the narrowing of signals we already saw in the preceding phases, the meaning of signals and problems is further narrowed down here, since this is crucial to the final solution of problems.

Often the influence of problems and their solutions is restricted to a specific part of the organization, instead of affecting the organization as a whole. As a rule we do not have enough funds to solve all the problems that exist at a given moment, and choices have to be made.

Therefore, the organizational department that has a problem must convince the organization's management to raise the necessary funds. This means that the management *recognizes* the problem. This is also called authorization (Mintzberg, 1976). Needless to say, such a procedure will only be followed if the department is not authorized to make its own decision because its budget is exhausted or if some predetermined level of expenditures will be exceeded.

Evidently, in respect of our enumeration of phases of the decision making process, we locate 'recognition' at the end of the intelligence phase.

Of course it is possible, depending on the prevailing procedures, to locate the recognition phase elsewhere.

Finally, if recognition is not limited to one phase only, the recognition in the intelligence phase is provisional, and it will afterwards be turned into a definite recognition (or rejection).

In the design phase, we engage in two kinds of activities in order to bring nearer the solution to the problem formulated in the preceding phase. We generate alternatives and evaluate alternatives with a view to their usefulness. With regard to this phase we want to stress that 'doing nothing' or 'doing nothing for the time being' should also be considered possible alternatives.

As we have pointed out before, problems are usually formulated in terms of solutions. Therefore, generating alternatives means looking for a number of those possible solutions to eliminate the problem, temporary or for good.

Generating alternatives is, in addition to identification/interpretation/formulation, a fourth way of narrowing down the problem, because the final choice is limited to the alternatives we want to explore further.

In addition to generating alternatives it is naturally also important to evaluate the alternatives. We look at their contribution to eliminate our problem and at the costs they will bring about.

Because the conditions that are relevant for the outcomes of alternatives are rather uncertain, especially in long(er) term decision making, an important part of the evaluation process consists of evaluating these alternatives under different sets of possible conditions. Such an approach is called sensitivity analysis; a technique that normally is a part of a specific category of information systems: decision support systems. These systems will be discussed in Chapter IX.

If the alternatives which can be used to solve the problem are evaluated it seems a rather logical conclusion that the selection of the best alternative, in terms of the difference between costs and benefits, is only a formality. And this assumption is right if costs and benefits can be unambiguously quantified with a common standard, money for instance.

If this is possible, the alternatives will be evaluated on the basis of their net contribution, and the alternative with the highest net contribution will be preferred.

However, in some situations alternatives are evaluated on the basis of heterogenous criteria, wchich means that it is not possible to express them in a common standard without applying additional transformation techniques. If we have one alternative which has the highest scores on every criterium, it is not necessary to come to a single yardstick. This transformation is only relevant if the score ranks on each criterion are different.

If a transformation technique is not applied in this situation, a number of – arbitrary – ranking orders of alternatives will result, based on different criteria. This may happen for instance if we evaluate information projects which were evaluated with heterogenous yardsticks, as will be demonstrated in Chapter X.

In that case a multi-criteria evaluation is necessary and if there is no single alternative which meets all the criteria, we will have to express the criteria in each other or in a common standard, which facilitates a clear ranking order.

A technique that is very helpful in solving this sort of problem is the so-called 'multi-criteria analysis' (DeVries, 1992). In our opinion, the application of such a procedure is part of the choice phase; a phase that will be concluded with a definite decision to solve the problem in one way or another.

After an alternative has been selected as solution to the existing problem, the process of decision making is in fact complete.

Nevertheless, we will pay attention to the implementation phase, which is also important for the success of this process. In organizations it is often usual not to involve everyone whose work will be affected by the decision in the process of reaching that decision. Therefore, it is necessary to convince those employees that the decision is in their best interests too, in order to prevent them from thwarting that very decision.

Gaining consensus is the main activity in this phase of the decision making process.

A fifth phase is sometimes distinguished: the auditing phase. Actually, it is not only important to go through a sophisticated planning – decision making – process, but afterwards, if the decision is implemented, we must also monitor its results carefully, so that we will be able to interfere if necessary. This is especially important for projects in the field of ICT, because, as we have seen in Chapter I, sometimes seventy percent of the total costs of these projects will be generated after implementation. Of course, a major reason for this is the poor decision making process which has gone before. However, a good process is no guarantee for a successful project. So, we have to evaluate (to audit) projects from time to time to adjust their execution or even to abandon them sometimes, and to learn in order to improve future projects.

We will finish our discussion of the decision making process by briefly commenting on the procedures that have to be followed.

Firstly, we distinguished several phases that were described in this book in a logical order. We call this the *conceptual* structuring of the decision making process.

Next to the conceptual structuring we can identify the *operational* structuring, i.e. the sequence of phases which are applied in a specific situation to solve a specific problem. Please bear in mind that conceptual and operational structuring may diverge. Sometimes it may be necessary to change part of the sequence of phases, or to work on phases simultaneously. It is even possible to reopen the discussion of a certain phase because it appears after some time that the wrong choices were made. So, conceptual structuring is completely linear, whereas operational structuring is partly circular, depending on the specific situation in which this procedure is applied.

This is relevant for instance for the relation between design phase and choice phase. Often, only a small number of alternatives will be generated and evaluated in the design phase. Afterwards, in the choice phase, we assess what alternative is acceptable.

If we have judged an alternative acceptable, we will continue the decision making process with the implementation phase. But it is also possible that we have to return to the design phase because not a single alternative comes up to our standards.

As the reader will remember, some pages ago we made a distinction between two different approaches, the blueprint approach and the process approach. We can conclude now, that the blueprint approach relates to the strict identification of the conceptual and the operational structuring of the control cycle, whereas the process approach advocates a well-considered disconnection between these two structuring modes, contingent upon the specific circumstances.

Of course, neither approach is suitable for all possible situations. As far as some more general advice may be given, we recommend the blueprint approach if future circumstances can be predicted rather well, which indicates the presence of structured decisions (see also section 4). Otherwise, the process approach should be applied.

Secondly, the distinction between several phases does not mean that they can all be separated and executed with time lags if necessary.

We will illustrate this point of view by looking at the phases 'observation', 'identifying' and 'interpretation'. As a rule, in daily practice these three are strictly related. Nevertheless, we distinguish between these phases because of the opportunities of information systems to support the activities to be executed and the conditions that should be fulfilled.

Thirdly, with our model of the process of decision making, and the distinction between several phases, we try to shed light on the dominant activities in this process, activities that have to be addressed in order to design information systems for decision and management support.

We will return to this topic in more detail in Chapter IX.

In the fourth place, we have to be aware that in the process of decision making generally more than one person is involved, either simultaneously or one after the other. As a result, additional conditions, facilitating the decision support capacities of information systems, must be met. This topic will be discussed in Chapter IX too.

4. Some more concepts

We will finish this chapter with a number of concepts that are relevant for the information policy of organizations; starting with six interrelated concepts:

signals/input data/output data/information/knowledge/wisdom

Signals are the triggers, or messages transmitted by others which make us attentive to certain events, developments, etc., which could be important to notice.

Before continuing with the five other concepts we want to illustrate things with an example.

Suppose a company trades in unprocessed wood; tree-trunks. The main process of this organization is buying tree-trunks, processing these trunks in a relatively simple way by removing bark and branches. The machine used in this process has a limited processing capacity, which means that only trees within specific tolerance limits as to girth can be processed.

One day, the company catches the signal that a parcel of forest which contains about ten thousand trees is for sale somewhere in Sweden. Naturally, our company is always interested in such an offer. However, before definitely deciding to buy the wood it wants more information about a number of things, such as the kind of wood, its condition, the expected return of wood, the selling price, etc.

At this stage of the process we want to recapitulate some things.

As said before, the company picks up a signal: 'forest in Sweden'. Essentially, signals have to do with communication. In addition, signals are composed of a number of symbols that we call *input data*. Indeed, the message 'there is a forest for sale' consists of a number of input data. We can define these input data as follows:

the symbolic representation of a specific characteristic of the real world

In the example just mentioned the units of representation, the symbols, are made up of letters.

Additionally, we speak about a *specific* characteristic because the real world has many characteristics. And one of these characteristics, which is particularly relevant for our wood company, concerns the presence of trees or forests.

The next step is the interpretation of input data. This is only possible if we have enough professional knowledge – not to be confused with 'knowledge' which will be discussed later on – meaning:

the complex of insights concerning a specific professional domain

The interpretation of input data generates *output data*. In other words, we can define output data as:

interpreted input data

Now we are getting nearer to *information*:

information is present if these output data contain news for the recipient, the user

In our wood example the presence of information is quite clear because our company had not been aware of the Swedish offer before.

If we can *use* the information in the decision making process to attain the company's goals, this information is *relevant*. Otherwise, we speak about *irrelevant* information; a topic that is also important for the design of information systems and will be discussed in greater detail in Chapter VII.

In the case at hand, the potential wood buyer has great use for the information because he has to decide whether to reject the offer or take the offer into consideration.

If this latter alternative is preferred, our company has to gather additional information. Unlike the information available until now, which was qualitative, this information will be *quantitative*.

In obtaining quantitative information, the same sequence input data/output data/information is relevant as before, although now knowledge and wisdom are involved as well.

In the remainder of the book, if we use this terminology – input data, output data and information – without further specification, we are always referring to the quantitative interpretation.

Continuing with our tree example, we restrict ourselves to information needs about the total wood volume, assuming that the kind of tree, the quality of the wood, etc., are acceptable.

To determine the wood volume of a forest all we have to know is the girth of the trees. Data about this feature can be transformed into wood volumes by using tables based on specific formulas. So we only have to measure circumferences.

We assume that the company uses a representative sample of one hundred trees to ascertain the girth of these trees. We are not going to enter into the backgrounds of sampling theory here, but we will assume that the company is able to apply this theory properly.

This approach generates one hundred results; (quantitative) input data. Therefore, these data can be defined as:

the symbolic representation of a specific characteristic of an object, or of a collection of objects, expressed in some unit of measuring

As to our tree example the sample generated the following collection of results, that is girths in centimetres (measuring units) of trees (objects) expressed in figures (symbols):

76	100	97	83	72	96	88	69	87	95
95	82	101	98	71	102	95	83	89	79
				etc.					

When all is said and done, such an enumeration registered in the order of observation, is rather meaningless to the average human being. Without a transformation of these data we are not able to determine the wood's volume.

Therefore, the next step is interpreting the collected input data, in a form that is easy for the decision maker to handle. Interpretation means that input data is processed somehow, resulting in output data.

If the company is only interested in the *total* wood volume of the Swedish wood, it is sufficient to determine the arithmetic mean of the input data.

However, in our example it goes without saying that the company also wants to know the variation of tree circumferences because of the specific tolerance limits of the machine that is used for the processing of tree-trunks (removing bark and branches). Trees that are too thick or too thin are waste, with less value than trees that can be processed.

That is why a second category of output data is important, concerning the variation of tree circumferences. Such a variation will usually be calculated by means of the standard deviation.

For the interpretation of the collection of data in terms of arithmetic mean and standard deviation, professional knowledge in the statistical domain is required again.

The arithmetic mean and standard deviation enable us to establish the total wood volume by approximation.

Regardless of the size of the sample, these two output data, resulting from the transformation process of input data, will suffice.

After this transformation process we meet the term *information* once more. We are interested again in the news value of the output data. Information means that the decision maker is informed about something he did not know yet by means of output data.

When we compare the definitions of output data and information, the following differences can be identified:

information	*output data*
– objective	– subjective
– concrete	– abstract
– concerning the past	– concerning the future

Output data are objective because everyone who is acquainted with the codes that have been used – for instance figures, characters or bar codes – is able to observe what kind of output data we are dealing with; in our case a collection of numbers called a sample. However, information is subjective. It is only in the relation between user and output data that information will be generated. What is new to some person (information), is familiar for another and for the latter it does not imply any information because he already knew it.

Output data are concrete due to the fact that everyone is able to observe them. For instance this holds for a table of numbers registered on paper. Information is abstract because the activity of assigning informative meaning to output data happens in our mind and this cannot normally be observed by others.

Output data are always based on registered facts. And facts are the results from events that happened in the past. Therefore, output data concern the past. Information, on the other hand, is meant to play a role in the process of decision making. And decision making always relates to the future course of events, regardless of – the lack – our interventions.

Returning to our example of the wood trader, our definition of information implies that the output data, extracted from the sample, contain information if the company did not know them before, which is obviously true in this case.

Our interpretation of output data and of information is important for the meaning of information systems. If the relation between user and (output) data is crucial for information, then this applies to information systems as well. In other words, in our view it is only justified to speak about information systems if the user is also taken into consideration. If he is ignored we are dealing with (input) *data* systems, instead of information systems.

The definition of information systems, as formulated earlier in this chapter (section 2), is rather popular, both in theory and in practice, but it ignores the position of the user. Therefore, we must adapt this earlier definition in the following way

an information system is a cohesive combination of processes, concerning the collection, transformation, storing and retrieval of (output) data which contain news for the user, regardless of the technical means applied

With respect to this definition we will make five observations.

Firstly, the distinction between data and information systems is not only necessary because of consistency in our use of language but it also reminds us of our obligation to centralize the position of the user when we design information systems, in order to build systems that are really acceptable; a notion that was quite unknown in the past (see Chapter VII).

Secondly, our definition is also relevant for the *management* of information systems, especially with respect to the clearing of databases that only contain obsolete data because their news value has completely evaporated.

Thirdly, a large part of the organization's information processing activities – some people speak about 85% – is beyond the reach of ICT, and that of information systems as well (Davenport, 1993).

Fourthly, to be able to speak about *information* systems not only the news value of the data involved is essential but also the user being an integral part of such information systems.

Fifthly, information systems defined this way are not limited to the use of ICT. In fact, any exchange of information within the organization is part of an information system. Thus information systems are interpreted in a *broad* sense.

Our adapted definition of information systems makes it also possible to define ICT more clearly as:

the combination of hardware and software that is able to process and to store data completely automatically, without human intervention

As a matter of fact we are dealing here with electronic storing, processing and retrieval devices.

Normally, if we are speaking about information systems in daily practice this latter (narrow) definition is meant. Nevertheless we prefer our broad definition, because of the five reasons mentioned above.

Knowledge, as we define it here, not be confused with professional knowledge, relates to:

> *the capacity of organizational participants to use information for the purpose it is gathered for: for the tasks assigned to these participants*

This definition of knowledge directly leads to a distinction between relevant and irrelevant information, as was indicated before. As was stipulated there, relevant information is information concerning organizational roles and tasks. Therefore, knowledge is a precondition for relevant information.

As mentioned above, the distinction between relevant and irrelevant information is important for the design of information systems, and will be discussed in more detail in Chapter VII.

Knowledge in this context, as far as our wood example is concerned, means that the company can do something with the information to facilitate its functioning, i.e. to take a decision about the purchase of the Swedish wood. And that is a rather obvious assumption.

Finally, in this context we distinguished 'wisdom'. By wisdom we mean:

> *the use of information for our decision making, taking moral and ethical values into consideration as well*

As to wisdom, our wood trader could decide not to buy the Swedish wood because the cutting down of trees on such a scale in that region would be an intolerable act according to conservation principles (Smith and Hasnas, 1999).

It is evident that wisdom does not play any role of significance in the design of information systems. Indeed, the considerations just mentioned are highly contingent, either for the decision maker or for the situation. Value judgments will differ from situation to situation and from decision maker to decision maker.

If an organization has need of specific information it is advisable to answer the question first what data sources are publicly accessible, before spending a lot of money on expensive research activities.

In this section we will pay attention to the identification of such sources, using a number of specific criteria. A first categorization will be made based on the following distinctions:
- internal/external and
- primary/sccondary.

Internal data sources are found inside the organization and *external* sources are outside of it. Furthermore, by *primary* we mean sources recorded on paper, magnetic disk, etc. These coded sources, coded in the legal sense, are directly accessible, at least for everyone who is authorized. *Secondary* sources, however, contain non-coded data. These data are stored in the memories of people.

If we combine these two pairs of characteristics, the following four categories emerge:
- primary/internal data sources,
- primary/external data sources,
- secondary/internal data sources,
- secondary/external data sources.

Before discussing these sources we note that, on account of the huge number of data sources, the enumeration of the sources below is not exhaustive but is only meant as an illustration of the many possibilities organizations have.

In the category primary/internal data sources we meet the results of any form of registration within the organization, not only formal but also informal. Examples of this source are computerized databases, internal memos and work orders. Of course, the most prominent internal/primary data source is the organization's collection of bookkeeping records, registered on paper or otherwise.

The category of primary/external data sources is huge and heterogeneous. Hence it is important to split up this category further, using the following criteria:
- general/specific and
- local/regional/national/international.

By *general* data sources we mean sources that are in principle relevant for all organizations, regardless of their size, branch, business location, etc. Unlike these sources, *specific* sources are only of interest for particular categories of organizations.

Local sources are relevant in the local field meaning that these sources contain data about a limited geographical area. *Regional* data sources relate to a wider area than local sources, whereas for *national* sources this area is even wider: a whole country. Finally, *international* sources contain data about a number of countries ranging to the entire world.

If we combine these two kinds of characteristics – general/specific and local/regional/national/international – we can identify eight categories, to be illustrated each with an example:
- local/general: Commerce Chambers,
- local/specific: local departments of branch organizations,
- regional/general: regional development institutions,
- regional specific: regional departments of branch organizations,
- national/general: the national statistical bureau,
- national/specific: institutes of branch organization at the national level,
- international/general: Organization for Economic Cooperation and Development (OECD),
- international/specific: International Labour Organization (part of the United Nations).

As said before, secondary sources may be found in the memories of people and therefore internal/secondary data sources may be located in the memories of organizational participants. We have a variety of techniques at our disposal to reveal these data, such as brainstorming, the Delphi technique and nominal group technique. Also, exit interviews – interviewing participants who are leaving the organizations – are a useful instrument.

External/secondary sources refer to data stored in the memories of people outside the organization. For instance, we may think of the experiences of the buyers of our products, especially if they have complaints. If we have a sophisticated system for handling the complaints of our clients with care, the – negative – information we get will be used adequately and complainers will feel satisfied, so they will become goodwill ambassadors for our products instead of making negative publicity.

We will continue this section with some remarks about the structure of problems; a subject which is important with respect to the opportunities to use information systems, if necessary combined with ICT. This latter topic, however, will be discussed in more detail in Chapter IX.

Following James March and Herbert Simon it is usual to distinguish three categories of problems, on the basis of the structure criterium (March and Simon, 1958):

- completely structured problems,
- semi-structured problems and
- unstructured problems.

Before discussing this distinction in detail, we want you to note that the concepts 'process', 'problem' and 'decision' will be used interchangeably. This is because *problems* are the inputs of a *process* which transforms these inputs into *decisions.*

Completely structured problems are problems whose structure is totally fixed, i.e. the solution procedure of such a problem can be described in a finite number of steps that will be taken in an unambiguous order. We are able to do this because in the course of the years we have acquired a great deal of experience in handling these problems, and our decision rules are continually sharpened. Actually, these are problems problems which can be solved more or less mechanically. No creativity is required from the person who applies the decision rules. On the contrary, it would be counterproductive if he used his own specific ideas and conceptions, and this would result in less efficient decision making processes.

Ordering raw materials or spare parts for several products if some minimum stock level is reached, is a good example of a completely structured decision. We see that many companies have automated the control of their stocks and ordering systems because such systems can be programmed in computer software (Simon, 1970). Therefore, completely structured decisions are also called *programmable* decisions. The category of information systems that is relevant here is called Structured Decision Systems (see Chapter IX). This does not mean that the transmission of orders to the supplier has been automated as well. In doing this, we have to use electronic data interchange in addition to the information system just mentioned (see Chapter IX again).

In most cases, the bulk of completely structured problems occur at the operational level of organizations.

By semi-structured problems we mean problems that have some structure; but this structure is not sufficient to solve them 'automatically'. This category is very broad because all problems that do not coincide with one of both ends of our 'structure' scale – completely structured or unstructured – belong to the category 'semi-structured'. In fact, the structure of semi-structured problems can only be described unambiguously at *meta* level. This means that we are able to establish some procedures in more or less general terms. If we want to enter into more detail, it is not possible to describe the process, i.e. the solution procedure of the problem at hand, in a finite number of steps. The decision maker's judgment is therefore inevitable.

This situation may be illustrated by the decision about a new production plant. Such a decision has a very long planning horizon. This means that it is impossible to make good predictions about the future outcome of the project. Therefore, a sensitivity analysis will normally be used, in which the computation process is gone through many times, depending on the number of variables whose impact is investigated and the values attached to these variables. After the selection of a specific combination of values of variables in the investment model and its results, the decision maker has to decide how to continue his computations; a sequence that hardly can be planned in advance.

Semi-structured problems are chiefly found at the level of the tactical control of organizations.

The category of information systems that can be helpful in supporting the solution process of such problems is called decision support systems and will be discussed in detail in Chapter IX.

Unstructured problems are problems of which we have no experience. Because the experience of others may sometimes be helpful, we distinguish between *conceptual* unstructured and *operational* unstructured problems.

Operational unstructured means that the organization does not have any kind of experience with the relevant problem, but other organizations do. By consulting those organizations or reading publications about this problem, it is possible to learn something about the aspects to be paid attention to.

Merger is an example of an operationally unstructured problem if the organization concerned does not have any experience in this field. In the past many mergers between organizations were carried out successfully. By consulting the organizations involved, or by reading about the merger process, we are able to use the experience of others.

Conceptual unstructured problems are problems that have never occurred before in any organization whatsoever. In this situation experience is completely lacking. As an example of this category of problems we can think about the organizations that merged for the first time in the history of the world.

By using the zooming-in procedure, we can look at the structure of problems in a different way.

To explain this approach we give the following example in the field of the tactical control of organizations: the decision to install a new production process in an organization.

This is essentially a capital budgeting problem which can be described in general terms with the following basic ingredients: the lifetime of the investments, cash receipts, expenditure, and minimum acceptable return on investment. These ingredients are related in a certain way, and they can be combined in a generally applicable investment model, or investment formula, such as the net present value method (see Chapter X).

At this level of problem formulation the structure of the problem is unambiguous.

In the next step we attempt to specificy this investment problem more accurately, by zooming in on the specific characteristics of the investment by quantifying the ingredients of the overall investment model, i.e. by decomposing the relevant variables in order to calculate the net present value.

In this phase of the process, however, we are usually faced with a lack of data because the developments in the future period which are relevant for the realization of the project are not entirely certain. In other words, dependent on the possible course of future developments, for instance in the market place, the data to quantify the ingredients of the investment model are different.

The qualification 'structure' of problems now relates to the question at which level of zooming in on the relevant problem uncertainty becomes relevant. If there is no uncertainty even at the lowest level of problem specification the problem is completely structured.

In all other situations, the application of the zooming-in procedure means that somewhere on the way down we will be confronted with uncertainty. In that case on the next-higher level we will find the lowest level at which the problem is still structured.

If we are able to describe this structure in quantitative data, such problems are semi-structured. If, however, on every – even the highest – level, the only description that is feasible is one in qualitative terms, which means that no more than a description in *process* terms can be reached, the problem is unstructured.

It is very important to understand this zooming-in approach and its consequences for the structure of problems. This is because of the opportunities to use specific categories of information systems in the support of problem handling by organizations. These opportunities will be discussed in Chapter IX in more detail.

In this section we will pay attention to the phenomenon 'uncertainty'. Uncertainty is relevant for almost every organization because it is related to the predictability of future developments and with the way organizations are able to anticipate those developments. The more uncertainty there is, the more difficult it will be to make predictions and to deal with the future adequately.

This is especially relevant for turbulent circumstances; circumstances most organizations are confronted with today.

This raises the question what variable(s) can be identified as the fundamental cause of uncertainty.

To answer this question we start with the example of a machine, such as a clockwork, composed of a number of parts with unambiguous mutual relations, inclusive of time lags or response times that are relevant for their effect on each other.

From a given starting position taken up at a specific moment, it is possible to predict the state the mechanism will be in some time later; a prediction which is one hundred percent reliable.

In view of our definition of complexity in section 2 of this chapter, the mechanism in the above-mentioned example is not complex. This is because future states of the system can be predicted with certainty.

As soon as the system has some degree of complexity, however, the actual relations between the elements of the system are no longer unambiguous and predicting may become more difficult. However, this is not the whole 'story'.

In addition to complexity, there is a second cause for the presence of uncertainty: the rate of response or rate of reaction between the elements of the system, resulting in a certain response time. If this response time is zero, then the elements do not react to each other, and future states of the system can be predicted with perfection. For uncertainty to be present, next to complexity, some response time is also required. If the system's elements react to each other at an increasing speed, while all other things – especially the system's complexity – are equal, predicitons about future states of the system become more and more difficult, that is, less reliable.

In conclusion, complexity alone is not sufficient for uncertainty to occur. The factor response time must also be present. If the latter is absent, it will take the elements an infinitely long time to react to each other, and there is no uncertainty. Conversely, an (infinitely) short response time (the elements respond to each other immediately) does not cause uncertainty if there is no complexity, as has become clear from our clockwork example.

Thus, complexity and rate of reaction are *together* responsible for the presence of uncertainty. This conclusion is of vital importance for the information policy of organizations. As we will see in the next chapter, it is possible to deal with uncertainty fundamentally; not by gathering more information, which might seem natural at first sight, but by reducing uncertainty, especially from the point of view of complexity.

This approach takes place via the complexity angle, instead of via response time or both, because it is very difficult or even impossible to influence response time.

Response times are highly dependent on physical and mental opportunities, or barriers, in our society, which are more or less given for a single organization. This is relevant for instance for developments in the field of ICT which are important for response times on the physical level.

Individual organizations on the other hand are able to influence the other component of uncertainty (complexity) by reducing it by means of appropriate measures, measures that will be discussed in the next chapter.

A topic we also pay attention to in this section is the distinction between efficiency and effectiveness.

By efficiency we mean the relation between the results we achieved and the means we used. Effectiveness is about the relation between the results that were realized and the intended results.

By applying efficiency we then try to reduce our costs as much as possible, given the target that has to be met. Effectiveness makes clear whether that target is reached while ignoring the means that were used.

As Peter Drucker formulates briefly and to the point (Drucker, 1990):

efficiency: doing things right
effectiveness: doing the right things

Thus, efficiency and effectiveness are rather loosely connected; it is possible to be efficient without being effective, and it is also possible to be effective without being efficient.

If I want to travel from town A to village B for instance and I arrive at metropolis C using the shortest way, then I am efficient indeed, but not effective. If I later on were to leave C for B, which was the goal of my trip after all, then I am – finally – effective but not efficient, because I did not take the shortest way from A to B.

Only if the trip goes directly from A to B efficiency and effectiveness are both present.

In spite of the mutual independence of these two concepts there is still a strong relation between them, which is that efficiency focuses especially on the resource side while effectiveness focuses on the goal side of problem solving activities.

The distinction between efficiency and effectiveness is particularly important for information systems and ICT, with a view to the opportunities to apply this technology.

If information systems aim at improving the efficiency of organizations, these systems will be used to *replace* people. If we intend to improve the organization's effectiveness by applying information systems, we are talking about *supporting* systems.

In close connection with efficiency and effectiveness we distinguish the following two concepts: information intensity and information content.

Information content relates to the application of information systems, c.q. ICT, in the production process, whereas information content concerns the amount of ICT embedded in the product as such.

For instance, control of the production process by means of ICT applications, such as numeric controlled machines, increases the information intensity of this process.

The so-called 'cruise control' in motor vehicles is an example of the increase of the product's information content (by using a piece of ICT). The services of banks which enable people to take a look at their financial accounts at home by using ICT, also illustrates the increase of the information content of their product.

Generally speaking, the application of ICT in the process will raise the information intensity of the process, and as a result the efficiency of the process increases as well. The use of information, or ICT, in the product, increasing the information content of the product, has a favourable effect on the effectiveness of the organization.

In both cases the organization's competitive position is improved. Therefore, decisions about information intensity and information content are made in the context of the strategic policy of organizations and of the positive effects information systems and ICT may have on their competitive position.

A final concept that is of some importance in this section concerns the innovative potential of organizations.

By this concept we mean generating completely new applications of information systems or ICT. New applications can be found in the product as well as in the process. This statement also sheds light on the relation between innovative potential and efficiency or effectiveness: if innovative applications take place in the process, the efficiency increases. On the other hand, by means of product innovation using ICT, the organization becomes more effective.

Innovative applications of ICT play an important role in business process redesign, a topic that will be discussed in Chapter IX.

We finish this section with a discussion about the organizational flows of information that can be distinguished, starting with the following classification:
- internal vs. external flows of information,
- horizontal vs. vertical flows of information,
- top down vs. bottom up flows of information.

The mutual relations between these various flows of information can be schematically represented as follows:

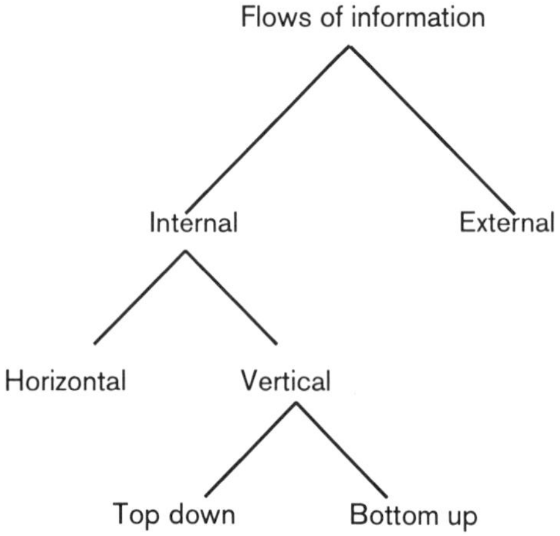

Internal information flows contain information that is transferred within the organization. External flows of information relate to the exchange of information between the organization and its environment.

These external flows of information are caused/triggered by:
- legal obligations and
- environmental turbulence.

For instance, every private organization is obliged by law to pay taxes. In order to determine the amount of taxes that have to be paid the fiscal authorities need information from the organization, which generates an information outflow from the organization's point of view, which results from a legal obligation.

Because of environmental turbulence organizations must continually be aware of the developments in the world around them, and this leads to information inflows.

Moreover, organizations must communicate their reactions to changes in the environment. Such communication concerns new products for example which have recently been developed in response to changing consumer needs; this generates information outflows.

Internal flows of information are caused by the organization's structure. To clarify this statement we pay attention to a Tayloristic organization structure in some detail.

Such a structure is characterized by the following principles:

- complete tasks are split up in a large number of very small parts and
- strict separation between thinking and doing.

We are interested in such an organization structure, not because of the reasons for which Taylor advocated this structure, but because of the far-reaching effects it has on the organization's internal flows of information, because (over)specialization is still very popular within organizations.

Due to the first principle – splitting up complete tasks in many parts – it is necessary to coordinate the activities that are carried out in order to fulfil these tasks, because people are working together to realize some common goal or target, for instance the production of an aeroplane. And coordination requires the exchange of information between them.

As long as the tasks can be carried out as planned, an exchange of information once per period is enough.

However, the connections between the tasks are important sources of potential disturbances. And quoting Murphy's Law (If anything can go wrong it will), many problems will arise; problems with effects on a many other tasks. Therefore, additional information is necessary to inform those tasks so they can adapt adequately. And the larger the number of tasks to be coordinated (and mutual connections) the more goes wrong and the more flows of information are needed.

On account of the second principle – separation between thinking and doing; or in other words: the separation between control and execution – processes on the workfloor are designed in every detail by 'thinkers', at a higher organization-hierarchical level, so that the 'doers' can do their job. But as soon as something goes wrong at the operational level (remember Murphy's Law again), the doers will have to make contact with the thinkers. In its extreme, a Tayloristic organization structure may imply that, if the execution deviates from the planning, every higher level in the organization will have to be involved until the level is reached that is authorized to take a proper decision. Meanwhile the function of the intermediate levels is restricted to passing information through, which carries the real risk that this information is damaged and/or delayed.

This extreme form of centralization of authority causes many flows of information between those levels.

Summing up what has been said before about organizational structures based on Tayloristic design principles, we come to the conclusion that these structures are characterized by a high degree of complexity combined with simple tasks and tremendous flows of information.

Of course, we are aware that for the description of most organizations such structures in their pure sense are a caricature of the real situation. But nevertheless, as said before, many organizations have far too much specialization; functionally as well as hierarchically, with negative consequences for the flows of information. As we will see in the next chapter, we meet here the point of impact to solve information problems fundamentally.

As can be concluded from our scheme, the distinction between horizontal and vertical flows of information is only relevant for the *internal* flows.

Horizontal flows of information are defined as the exchange of information between employees who do not have a hierarchical relationship with each other. For vertical flows of information a hierarchical relationship is essential.

Furthermore, a vertical component of horizontal flows of information can be identified. If employees are always obliged to involve their – common – boss if they want to exchange information with others, the horizontal flow of information follows the vertical pattern of the structure of the organization; therefore we speak of the 'vertical component of horizontal flows of information'. This phenomenon can be illustrated by means of the diagram below.

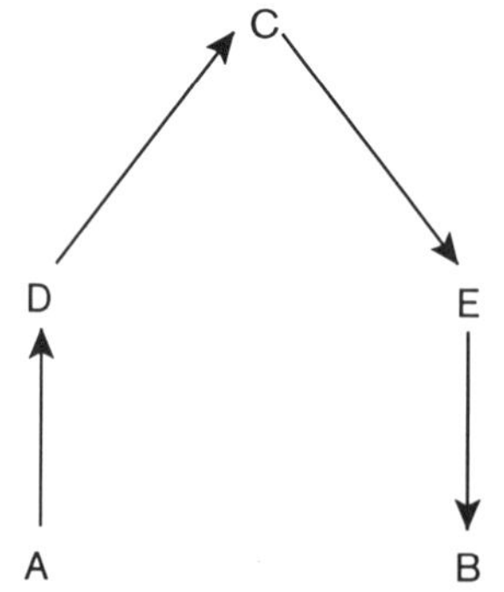

Employee A wants to send a message to colleague B. When he does so, the message goes up along the hierarchical lines, transmitted by boss D, until the first common boss (C) is reached (all higher bosses are also common, but this is not relevant for the information processing procedure). This is the turning point, which means that the flow goes down now: C informs E and finally the latter transmits the message to B.

It is clear that this whole procedure has a number of disadvantages, such as:

- in the process of transmission from person to person there is a chance that the original message will be eroded,
- the transmission process may take (too) much time, meanwhile delaying the opportunity for B to react if necessary,

– a great deal of the time of supervisors is spent on functioning as a communication channel instead of doing work with really added value.

Finally we can make a distinction between top-down and bottom-up information. This distinction relates to the direction of the information flows; bottom-up means a boss receiving a message from one of his subordinates, while top-down is a message from boss to subordinate.

It is not only the direction of these two flows which is different but also its contents. Top-down flows of information are about orders, the delegation of authority, etc. All these activities are part of the planning process. Bottom-up flows of information concern the actual execution of tasks; the realization of plans.

So far, these examples of top-down and bottom-up exchanges of information belong to more or less regular organizational procedures or activities. But, in addition, top-down and bottom-up flows of information may also be generated by ad hoc events if the planned tolerance limits in the execution process are exceeded, and corrective action is necessary. These latter flows of information will only occur if the subordinates are not entitled to take action without informing their bosses beforehand.

Ad hoc flows of information are sometimes caused by employees who wish to consult their boss although they have the authority to decide independently.

III THE IDENTITY OF MANAGEMENT INFORMATION SYSTEMS

1. Introduction

In this chapter we discuss 'management information systems' as a scientific discipline. We need an insight into this topic in order to adequately determine the nature of information problems and to indicate other solutions that are possible apart from ICT ones.

After discussing this subject in section 2, we will explore (more) fundamental solutions to information problems in section 3; information problems defined as a gap between the supply of and the demand for information. Section 4 deals with the reduction of internal flows of information while section 5 is about the reduction of external flows of information.

We continue this section by discussing some opinions about 'management information systems'. Two of these opinions are especially relevant here; one concerns a sort of system and the other concerns an academic discipline.

Starting with this first interpretation, we quote Davis and Olson, who define management information systems as follows (Davis and Olson, 1985):

> *an integrated user-machine system for providing information to support operations, management, and decision making functions in an organization. The system utilizes computer hardware and software; manual procedures; models for analysis, planning, control and decision making; and a database*

Of course, many other formulations of management information systems are conceivable, and they can be found in all sorts of (text)books and periodicals, but essentially this is the most familiar interpretation of this field of interest, in the sense that it is about information *systems* in a wide range of managerial applications.

The second interpretation that will be discussed here relates to management information systems as a scientific or academic discipline. Before defining this interpretation, let us take a short historical trip.

Since after the Second World War, a process of globalization and intensifying worldwide relations has been going on at the level of individual companies and at nation level. Therefore, companies are confronted with an increased number of diversified markets, competitors and institutional relations. These developments have resulted in such an explosion of data that organizations are frequently prevented from handling these data in a well-considered way.

Almost simultaneously with this data explosion another important development has occurred: the commercial application of ICT, originally in the form of mainframe computers. Because these machines have an enormous computing speed and/or processing speed, are able to store and manipulate many data, and provide users with almost immediate access to these data, computers were applied to cope with the data explosion after some time.

Computers in their turn intensified this explosion, since these machines produced many more data than there were before. Soon the term 'information system' came into use for these computer systems (combinations of hardware and software); initially, especially for administrative applications like bookkeeping.

Buying computers was a decision with great impact, on account of the amount of money that had to be spent and on account of the consequences for the employees involved. In respect of this latter point we must bear in mind the purpose an organization had in acquiring computers in those days: replacing people by machines. The application of ICT was therefore restricted to the field of efficiency. Such replacements are also called 'automation'. Therefore, laymen still persistent in using this term for the application of ICT, although the *support* function of this technology has become increasingly important.

We may conclude that computers, apart from their economic effects, also had a far-reaching social impact on organizations.

In order to take well-considered decisions about the purchase of computers, organizations consulted established scientific disciplines like economics, sociology, psychology and computer science. Economics was helpful, for example, in making cost/benefit analyses. Sociology, which studies the behaviour of *groups*, shed light on the impact of computers on group processes, whereas psychology, which studies the behaviour of individual persons, was able to clarify the reactions of employees to the introduction of computers, especially with respect to the threats – real or not – they perceived of losing their jobs. Of course, from computer science we can learn something about hardware and software.

After some time, a field of study came into being which consists of the many aspects of automation, called management information systems. This field is in fact a collection of individual disciplines applied to a specific class of problems, that of buying and using computers. Depending on the degree of mutual integration between the disciplines involved, this leads to an interdisciplinary or a multidisciplinary approach.

Such an approach, which consists of a combination of disciplines aimed at a specific problem (automation) is called a *problem approach*; as opposed to the *aspect approach* which is discussed in the next section, which deals with 'management information systems' as a scientific discipline.

2. The identity of management information systems as a scientific discipline

In this section we discuss the identity of management information systems as an academic, or scientific, *discipline*. Such an approach is very important, not as an essential principle for handling information problems, but in order to achieve fundamental solutions for these problems in organizations; solutions which are not exclusively based on ICT; something which the traditional problem approach is unable, or insufficiently able, to do. (Prakken, 1992).

We usually specify the identity of a scientific discipline by means of the concepts *object* of study and *aspect* of study, also called *locus* and *focus* respectively. By object of study, or empirical object, we mean the complex of phenomena that is studied by a scientific discipline.

From this definition we can deduce that not every science has an empirical object. Pure mathematics for example does not have such an object. We distinguish *formal* sciences, sciences without an empirical object, and *empirical* sciences, which do have such an object.

The empirical object of the management information discipline can be described as follows:

organizations

If the empirical object were the only criterion used in the identification of academic disciplines, it would often be impossible to describe a unique position, since many scientific disciplines share – part of – the same object of study, like management sciences, organizational psychology, organizational sociology, etc.

Therefore, a further limitation is necessary to achieve an unambiguous identification of scientific disciplines; and this is relevant for the management information discipline too. This limitation can be realized by using the aspect of study. This means the angle – or point of view – from which the discipline involved studies its empirical object. With regard to the management information discipline, the aspect of study can be described as:

the information aspect of the control of organizations

Such an aspect approach means that a scientific discipline is interested in a specific question about its object.

By defining the *information* aspect in greater detail we can formulate this question as follows (Campbell, 1979):

who *needs what* information *at what* moment *and in what* form?

The crucial concepts in this description are:
- who,
- information,
- moment and
- form.

In terms of the systems theory that was explained in Chapter II, we are dealing with an aspect system here, the information aspect system of organizations, while the problem field approach mentioned in section 1 refers to facet systems, i.e. systems as concrete parts of organizations.

Unlike the problem field approach (i.e. the collection of relevant aspects of a specific problem field), the scientific management information approach is an aspect approach, which means that only one specific aspect of all problem fields of organizations is paid attention to.

As said before, we opt for this aspect approach not only for fundamental academic reasons. Our most important objection to using the problem field approach is the fact that it assigns a dominant role to automation and/or ICT. Because of this central position in solving information problems of organizations, there is an almost automatic tendency to use this technology; just as someone who possesses a hammer perceives any problem as a nail.

By the way, this tendency does not only occur with information problems. Usually, organizations try to solve problems with a frame of reference which consists of solutions that were known to be successful in the past; although they are not always suitable for the future. And if problem and solution differ too much they try to achieve a convergence of problem and preferred solution by adapting the former (Mason and Mitroff, 1981). It goes without saying that, by using an approach like this, problems will not be eliminated, they will only fade into the background for a limited period of time.

That is why it is necessary that organizations, if confronted with problems in general and with information problems in particular, have a disposition which helps them formulate problems in a correct, i.e. fundamental, way which leads to real solutions.

The tendency of organizations to perceive information problems wrongly by using an important element of their frame of reference, called 'ICT', has at least two drawbacks.

First of all, problems are formulated, or reformulated, to fit the solution that was intended in advance; however, the underlying problem will often persist. What we need therefore is an approach to solve (information) problems fundamentally.

Secondly, ICT applications are often very expensive, and have far-reaching effects on the organization. This is another major reason to look for alternative solutions for eliminating information problems fundamentally. This topic will be discussed in more detail in the next section.

As conclusion to this section, we observe that (concrete) organizational problems in general, and information problems in particular, are always characterized by a number of aspects. Therefore it is of the utmost importance to distinguish between the information *aspect* on one hand, which can be identified in dealing with all organizational problems, and information *problems*, on the other hand, which are characterized by a number of aspects that have to be taken into account in order to reach well-considered decisions, but where the information aspect is paramount.

3. A (more) fundamental approach to information problems

In providing for an arbitrary need we can distinguish between a supply-side approach and a demand-side approach. Therefore, we have two possible lines of attack for solving information problems:

- meeting the information needs of organizational participants by supplying enough information and
- reducing the information needs by influencing the demand for information.

In view of what we said in the preceding section about the way in which organizations generally deal with (information) problems, it is obvious that they are in favour of a supply-side approach, preferably in combination with ICT instruments.

Apart from our objections against the dominant position of ICT, it is always advisable to consider information problems at a more fundamental level than at the 'disguise' level at which they appear to us at first glance, or in the shape they have when presented to us by others. It should be clear that, in order to reach – more – fundamental solutions, we especially address ourselves to the demand side of information problems.

By using the demand-side approach, we can remove the disguise from information problems and study these problems at a higher level of abstraction. The effect of this approach is that it opens our mind to other solution categories. Actually, in doing so we are zooming out on the problem (Winograd and Flores, 1986).

As an example of such a zooming-out approach we take, as done before in Chapter II, a look at the problem of buying a car to transport us from home to work and back.

If we formulate the car problem in this way, the number of possible solutions is limited to the question which brands and types are useful for getting rid of the problem.

By zooming out, that is, considering the problem at a higher level of abstraction, the car problem may become a transportation problem. And these problems can be solved in different ways. Other categories of solutions, such as using means of public transportation or a bicycle, are alternatives now.

An even higher level of abstraction is possible if we define the original problem as two activities – for instance living and working – which are not carried out in the same geographical location. From this point of view we are confronted with a problem of bilocation; and this problem can also be formulated by looking at solutions which join the locations together instead of bridging the gap; this can for instance be achieved by moving house or by looking for another job in the neighbourhood.

Such a zooming-out approach enables us to investigate a larger number of categories of alternatives, which might in some cases lead to solutions that are more fundamental.

If in our example, in spite of the zooming-out procedure, a new car is still preferred, the approach at least has the advantage that different categories of solutions have been considered. We then make sure that we choose an alternative with a favourable price/quality ratio.

We can also imagine that, as a result of this procedure, the solution category that was originally intended might be abandoned completely. A solution might be achieved which is better-considered than a choice which is based on the first problem formulation that came into our heads, without a critical analysis.

Now we have to answer the question how the zooming-out approach can be used to cope with information problems. In fact, at the beginning of this section, a first zooming-out round has already taken place when we explained that information problems or information needs can be formulated from two different angles, that of satisfying the demand for information or of calling this demand into question.

If the latter option is preferable, and what precedes will have made that evident, we must address the cause which underlies the demand for information. This cause is uncertainty. After all, the more uncertainty, the more people ask for information.

As we showed in Chapter II, uncertainty is based on the simultaneous presence of complexity and response time. We concluded that individual organizations lack the ability to influence the response time of phenomena which react to each other; this response time is relatively autonomous. Therefore, attempts to reduce uncertainty and, as a consequence, the need for information must start with an attack on complexity; a concept we defined in Chapter II as the number of potential states of a system.

The opportunities to reduce complexity can be identified by looking at the several flows of information in organizations, as we pointed out in Chapter II, especially with regard to the reasons why these flows are often so voluminous.

Before discussing concrete measures to reduce flows of information, we pay attention to two different angles that are relevant here:

- reducing the number of information relations and
- using an adequate model of the real world, so that organizations and their individual employees are aware of the developments they must observe or may ignore.

This first category of measures is explored in this Chapter, whereas the second category will be discussed in Chapter VIII under the label 'mental models'.

4. Measures to reduce internal flows of information

With resect to *internal* flows of information, the causes are already familiar to us and rather obvious: (too) much specialization, functionally (horizontally) as well as hierarchically (vertically). In order to reduce the resulting flows of information, we must take organizational measures which stimulate horizontal and vertical integration.

In principle, we have the following measures at our disposal (Galbraith, 1976):

- slack,
- lateral relations and
- autonomous tasks, or task groups.

These measures can be associated with several others. For instance, autonomous task groups are related to job enlargement and job enrichment, whereas lateral relations and quality control circles also show some similarity.

Another opportunity to reduce flows of information is 'parallelisation of orders'.

Our extended list of measures now looks as follows:
- job enlargement,
- job enrichment,
- lateral relations,
- slack,
- parallelisation of orders,
- quality control circles,
- autonomous task groups.

We will discuss these measures in more detail and look especially at how they affect the internal flows of information.

Job enlargement
Tasks consist of a number of components. Job enlargement means the increase of this number (Guest, 1957). Originally, job enlargement was used to raise the motivation of employees, because their jobs became less boring with greater task variety.

However, by taking measures in the field of task enlargement, complete tasks are split up over fewer employees. The number of connections between these tasks will therefore diminish. As a result, the exchange of information within the organization decreases as well.

The impact of job enlargement is restricted to the *horizontal* flows of information, which can be reduced substantially.

As to the practicability of job enlargement, depending on the technological shape of the production process, it may be necessary to restructure this process drastically. In such a situation a detailed cost/benefit analysis is required.

Job enrichment
If job enrichment is applied, employees get more responsibilities in doing their jobs (Herzberg, 1968). Instead of having to ask permission in advance they have the authority to take certain decisions on their own.

Like job enlargement, job enrichment was originally used to stimulate the motivation of employees. This positive effect is chiefly realized by their capacity to act independently, without continuous interference by the boss. In this way an important reason for the frustration of employees during their work is eliminated.

In addition, job enrichment has an advantage in the field of information processing: the extended responsibilities of employees, and the decreased involvement of management in their day-to-day activities reduce the *vertical* flows of information.

Unlike job enlargement, job enrichment usually requires only a modest change to the organization's structure, and/or to organizational rules and procedures, which are simple to introduce in most cases.

Lateral relations
Lateral relations refer to the permission of employees to exchange information directly among each other without communicating along the hierarchical lines of the organiza-

tion (Galbraith, 1976). Employees are still obliged to inform the management afterwards, but this may coincide with periodical reporting activities.

Generally, organizations have three reasons for allowing lateral relations:

- employees on the shop floor are often better informed and in a better position to solve any problems that may occur than their bosses,
- interference of managers sometimes causes unacceptable delays to problems getting solved,
- if managers of several hierarchical levels are involved in the communication process, the chances increase that the original message gets mixed up.

The effect of lateral relations on flows of information can be identified as the elimination of the *vertical* component of the *horizontal* flows (see also section of Chapter II).

Just like job enrichment, the application of lateral relations requires only a minor change to organizational rules and procedures.

Slack

Slack means the deliberate creation of some idle capacity, especially within the primary process; idle capacity that can be used if stagnation occurs somewhere in the production process. This idle capacity isolates the stagnation, and prevents it from spreading immediately through the entire production process. If it does, the other parts of the process have to be told to slow down or even stop their activities too.

An example of slack in the form of idle capacity is the creation of intermediate stocks at certain points between the tasks in the primary process. This is done by dividing this process into a number of segments which operate relatively independently as to production speed. This is especially important in the case of disturbances, quantitatively or qualitatively, in specific parts of the production process.

To illustrate this slack principle in more detail, we look at a production process that is split up into three segments, A, B and C, and two stocks between these segments, T_1 and T_2. We can represent this situation graphically as follows:

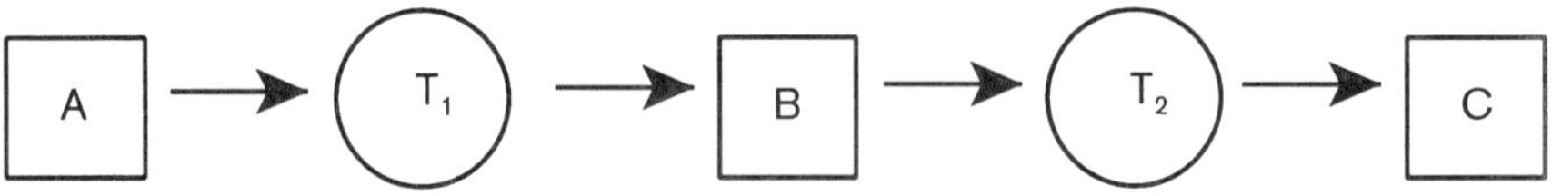

When stock T_1 has been exhausted, for instance due to a stagnation in segment A, segment B will have to halt its activities completely for some time.

The necessity of a temporary stop of activities is also present if stock T_2, because of stagnation of segment C, reaches its maximum limit. Until this limit has been reached, however, segment B can continue its activities.

After it has stopped its activities on account of problems in segment A or segment C, segment B will start up its production activities again if stocks T_1 and T_2 are within their predetermined tolerance limits. This means that stock T_1 is more than zero whereas stock T_2 has to be less than a specific maximum level.

Not only stagnation, but speeding up or slowing down of the production activities in one segment or another can also be absorbed in this way.

We are especially interested in the effects of slack on information processing. If the segments are loosely coupled (unlike a fixed coupling between the segments, which is a coupling without slack), variations in the level of activities will not immediately affect the other segments, in so far as the tolerance limits of the stocks between the segments have not been reached yet. Therefore, it is not necessary to exchange information about these variations.

We can even identify variations in the stocks between the segments as signals (information) for the other segments to adapt their production activities, without the necessity to exchange information by using the oral communication channels between the segments.

When the minimum or maximum position of the stocks between the segments is approached, such communication is necessary in order to give the other segments the opportunity to slow down their activities smoothly.

Thus, using slack effectively reduces the *horizontal* flows of information.

As we have said before, slack requires the creation of some idle capacity (a part of the total capacity which is only used in case of emergency). This measure causes costs that may be substantial. Therefore it is crucial to have a thorough cost/benefit analysis before using this instrument.

Parellelisation of orders

Imagine a production process, for instance the production of automobiles, which generates several types of products, and which is also characterized by a number of parallel lines of production or assembly lines. If in such a situation orders are allocated based on the in-turn principle, each line has to change types again and again. Apart from the costs of adjusting the line, this approach requires the exchange of information about the specific types that are to be produced at a given moment.

Parallelisation means the grouping of orders in such a way that each production line produces only one type, or a limited number of types. By applying this principle the exchange of information can be reduced, because it causes a reduction in *horizontal* flows of information.

If, like the company in our automobile example, the company has a number of parallel production lines, the parallelisation of orders causes almost no additional costs. The measures that have to be taken only have an organizational character.

If, on the contrary, the production process consists of a single production line, using the principle of parallelisation of orders could require far-reaching technical measures and large amounts of costs as well.

Quality control cycles

Influenced by people like Deming and Juran, a movement was started some decades ago in Japan to increase the quality of production *processes* (Juran, 1994). This was a new topic because in former days we only paid attention to the result of the production process: the *product*. However, we became aware of a major condition for the quality of the product: the quality of the process.

Because of the Japanese successes in the field of quality management, the interest in this subject increased in the eighties in the United States and in Western Europe.

An important means for ensuring sufficient attention for the quality of the production process consists of so-called 'quality control circles'. These circles can be described as follows (McMillan, 1985):

> *A quality control circle can be defined as a small group of workers who voluntarily carry out an analysis of job-related quality problems*

After some time, the scope of quality control circles was broadened to include other topics than the quality issue.

In actual practice, quality control circles consist of six to ten employees who carry out the same sort of activities and who function at the same hierarchical level in the organization. Group meetings usually take place once a week.

Because this attention to quality takes place in a group, quality control circles facilitate the direct exchange of information between the members as a positive side-effect. They generate horizontal flows of information. Essentially, the effect of quality control circles on information processing is very similar to that of the 'lateral relations' instrument: the impact of quality control circles is restricted to the elimination of the *vertical* component of *horizontal* flows of information as well.

However, some differences can be identified between these two measures. Quality control circles imply fairly frequent meetings, while lateral relations are activated on an ad hoc basis. Moreover, lateral relations usually involve two persons while quality control circles consist of a larger amount of members.

The effects of the introduction of quality control circles on the structure of the organization are not far-reaching, because the members of such groups are volunteers. Their activities in the field of quality are strictly informal and they take place exclusively outside the – formal – structure of the organization. Organizational rules and procedures do not have to be adjusted.

In addition, quality control groups often meet in leisure time, so labour productivity will hardly be affected by work interruptions.

Autonomous task groups

Autonomous task groups form a substantial part of the so-called 'sociotechnical' organization structure, also called 'integrated organizational renewal' (Van Eijnatten, 1994). A central concept of the sociotechnical approach is the number of responsibilities of workers, based on Ashby's Law of Requisite Variety, saying that (Ashby, 1969):

> *the variety of the moves, or regulative capacity, of workers must be equal to the variety of the environment with which they are confronted*

Too much regulative capacity is inefficient because employees are charged with superfluous responsibilities. On the other hand, if this capacity is insufficient for them to be able to react independently to unexpected events when carrying out their tasks, they will become frustrated instead of motivated. Due to frustration, the participation and involvement of workers will decrease, which leads to a loss of efficiency and other negative effects, such as:

- much labour turnover,
- a great deal of sick leave,
- low product quality,
- lack of creativity and ideas for innovation and renewal,
- low productivity.

If organizations want to avoid these negative effects, they will have to guarantee sufficient worker motivation.

On the basis of many research results we may conclude that the motivation of workers will be stimulated by (Hackman and Oldham, 1976):

- task variety,
- task identity,
- autonomy,
- feedback,
- responsibilities,
- task indispensability.

In view of these requirements, we might wonder whether it would suffice to combine job enlargement with job enrichment, supplemented if necessary with task rotation. By task rotation we mean charging employees with different tasks within the same department in the course of time on the one hand, and having employees take turns in different departments on the other hand.

However, such a combination has the disadvantage of being directed towards the individual workers who happen to be employed at a given moment, while the organizational context in which they are operating does not get enough attention. Moreover, because the existing situation is taken as starting point, there is the risk that only ad hoc solutions will be thought of instead of more fundamental ones, and there is the risk of freezing the – more or less – coincidental present position.

The major characteristic of the sociotechnical approach is that the *structure* of organizations is based on fundamental units which do not contain one individual task but rather a number of tasks, i.e. *group* tasks. Therefore, this approach makes room for job enlargement as well as job enrichment, and it designs organizations in a completely different way by grouping individual tasks together. This results in organizational units with group tasks that are geared to the production of complete products.

Autonomous task groups, also called self-steering teams, can be defined as follows:

> *a group of people, in a solid work relation and of constant composition, consisting of members with several skills, responsible for the planning, execution and improvements of a well-defined complete production task, possessing sufficient means of production*

Because self-steering teams are, in spite of their degrees of freedom, not free to do what they want in every respect (for instance they have to realize predetermined output norms expressed in product quantity and quality), it is preferable to use the term *semi*-autonomous task groups.

We conclude that, unlike Tayloristic principles, the sociotechnical approach leads to simple organization structures combined with complex and challenging tasks.

After all, we are especially interested in the sociotechnical approach because of the influence of self-steering teams on the flows of information of the organization.

It is evident that, due to the responsibilities assigned to such groups, the *vertical* flows of information are limited. After a process of negotiation and agreement about the task for the future production period the group has to solve all its problems itself, unless they ask the boss for consultation.

About the exchange of *horizontal* information in such a situation we can make the following observations. On account of the fact that complete (production) tasks are assigned to the self-steering teams there is no need for communication between the teams about their work; unlike the situation within the teams where the members cooperate to execute the group task.

However, an important condition for self-steering teams is the possibility of relying exclusively on *informal* exchange of information. This condition implies that the teams must be of limited size. If groups are too large, at least a part of their exchange of information will have to be formalized. Formalization of the communication between the group members has two disadvantages. In the first place, the flexibility of the group will decrease, and therefore also the flexibility of the organization. And secondly, formalization of information relations within self-steering teams requires the design of information systems, and as a consequence the expenditure of buying them. Therefore the number of members belonging to these teams should not exceed the maximum number which is feasible for informal communication.

If this condition, combined with the requirement of complete tasks, cannot be fulfilled, we have two possible alternatives:

- splitting up the complete task over more than one team; this measure requires the exchange of information between the teams involved,
- extending the team beyond its maximum size (maximum with respect to informal exchange of information), which leads to the – partial – formalization of the flows of information.

In choosing between these two alternatives a cost/benefit analysis must be made in order to determine which alternative is preferable.

What we may conclude from the above about the effects of the sociotechnical approach on information is that we now have an almost ideal organization structure, i.e. organization theory. However, we must still answer the question to what degree such a structure is also characterized by one or more disadvantages. This question is valid because the process of increasing specialization which started with the Industrial Revolution many years ago, is reversed drastically.

This question can only be answered satisfactorily if sufficient experience with the sociotechnical approach is accumulated in day-to-day business practice. Fortunately, there have been experiments with this organization model all over the world; from Sweden to Japan, and from the Netherlands to the United States. Recapitulating the results, we can sum up the following advantages of the sociotechnical approach:

- decrease of production processing time to 70%,
- decrease of sick leave by an average of 50%,
- reduction of costs by an average of 60%,
- failure reduction by an average of 50%,
- complaint reduction by an average of 40%,
- reduction of overhead costs (including costs of information processing) by an average of 25%,
- increase of productivity by an average of 15%.

This last figure in particular is very important because advocates of the principle of specialization (and assembly line production structures) believed that no other production system could be more efficient.

These figures prove that organization structures based on the design principles of the sociotechnical approach are not only favourable for organizational information processing, but for other fields as well.

Because of the importance of this organization structure, we will discuss it more profoundly in the next chapter.

From this section we may conclude that there is a number of organizational measures available for reducing the complexity of the structure of organizations, and the ensuing information burden created by man. In this way, we will be able to attack information problems radically. It is only when these measures are not sufficient that the information problems which remain may be solved by means of information systems, generally on the basis of ICT. So the starting point of the information policy of organizations is:

(re)organize first, then informatize/computerize

However, there is a second reason for this principle. Computerizing means that existing information structures – including the production and control structure which lie behind them – are temporarily frozen. This also applies to any inefficiencies which already exist. That is why it is important to review the production and control structure, and to adapt these if necessary, before the information structure is implemented.

Until now, we have paid attention to the impact of the organization (structure) on the information policy and on ICT. However, a relationship the other way around can also be identified: the impact of ICT on the organization. With regard to this impact we distinguish two variants: a relatively passive and a relatively active one.

The rather passive variant refers to the possibility that the information structure may be changed by the use of information systems, ICT respectively, because they affect the organization's structure as far as its degree of centralization, or decentralization, is concerned.

By (de)centralization we mean the degree of concentration of authority on the higher hierarchical levels, or the delegation of authority to the lower levels.

With regard to the phenomenon of (de)centralization caused by ICT, some students perceive more centralization, whereas others emphasize exactly the opposite (Markus,

1984). As so often, the truth lies somewhere in between. ICT as such, is neither favourable to centralization nor to decentralization. Both are compatible with ICT.

Actually, if the management of the organization wants to centralize authority as much as possible, this tendency can be supported by ICT. However, it is also possible for managers who are characterized by a fundamentally democratic attitude, to stimulate decentralization and employee autonomy. By using ICT, management gets the opportunity to delegate responsibilities, without losing control of activities at the lower levels. They can keep their grip on the latter by the use of more sophisticated monitoring techniques.

We have shown that ICT is strictly neutral with regard to centralization or decentralization, and that it may be used to strengthen tendencies in either direction which already exist within organizations.

The rather active impact of ICT on the organization refers to the opportunity to (re)design the organization which is offered by ICT. Organizational changes are no longer a side-effect of new information systems, they are the purpose, whereas these systems are the means. This approach will be discussed in more detail under the label business process redesign in Chapter IX.

5. Measures to reduce external flows of information

Before analyzing the opportunities to reduce external flows of information, it is relevant to make a categorization, using the following two couples of criteria:
- information inflows vs. information outflows,
- flows of information that are required by law vs. 'other' flows of information.

This first couple of concepts hardly needs any explanation, because it is about flows of information entering or leaving the organization.

Flows of information that are required by law occur because of legal rules. As we know, some companies, such as limited liability companies, are obliged to report periodically about their financial position; information that is publicly available.

The *'other'* flows of information do not have a legal basis but are initiated because of the organization's need to exchange information with its environment.

When we combine the two couples of criteria, four categories of external flows of information result:
- entering/legally based flows of information,
- leaving/legally based flows of information,
- entering/other flows of information,
- leaving/other flows of information.

These four categories will be discussed in more detail below.

Just like other tax payers, organizations receive information from the fiscal authorities (entering/legally based flow of information) on a regular basis, for instance once a year, in the form of an assessment about the amount of taxes they have to pay.

Information about all sorts of legal rules, rights and duties, can be relevant for organizations as well. For instance, organizations are interested in changes to subsidy rules, etc. These rules are also examples of entering/legally based flows of information.

Leaving/legally based flows of information refer to all information provided by organizations which is based on legal requirements. Aside from the example of periodic company reports above, organizations have to inform the fiscal authorities about the composition of their income, costs, etc. in detail. Product information to customers also has a basis in law.

In order to preserve its viability, now and in the future, the organization needs information about its environment. On the one hand, organizations must be informed about the appreciation of their products in the market. And on the other hand, organizations have to be aware of all societal developments in order to use their opportunities to create new combinations of products, markets and technologies. These entering/other flows of information are numerous and extremely heterogeneous. Therefore, making a good selection is crucial. We will return to this issue when we discuss strategic flows of information in Chapter IX.

Leaving/other flows of information are mostly operational in nature and their purpose is to inform suppliers and clients. If suppliers are informed, it is chiefly about ordering raw materials, etc. We also have to inform clients, potential as well as actual ones, about the products of the organization and about any changes that have been realized. Advertising is a well-known example of this latter category.

In so far as organizations try to reduce external flows of information, it is only the category 'other' flows which offers some opportunities. This is obvious because we cannot shirk our fiscal obligations.

What remains is the possibility of reducing the information burden of organizations by means of the category other/entering flows of information. Just like internal flows of information, the direct cause of these flows is uncertainty; a phenomenon that can be split up into complexity and response time. Our well-known thesis is also relevant here: if complexity and/or response time increase, uncertainty increases, and people ask for more information as a first reaction.

As we know, an individual organization has hardly any influence on the response time. This also holds for the response time of phenomena in the environment. Therefore, the point of attack for reducing flows of information is complexity again; complexity of the organization's environment; (external) complexity defined as the possible number of relevant future states of the environment.

The larger the variety of products sold by the organization on a larger variety of markets, the larger the number of potential states (it rises exponentially). Therefore, it is advisable that organizations restrict their activities to core competencies, not only because of their lack of knowledge about other activities, but because such narrowing also has positive effects on the external flows of information.

In the slipstream of a reduction of other/entering flows of information, leaving/other flows of information will decrease also, on account of a smaller number of products and/or markets.

IV THE SOCIOTECHNICAL APPROACH OF ORGANIZATIONS

1. Introduction

As we have seen in the preceding chapter, the sociotechnical approach is a very powerful instrument for solving information problems at their root. In fact, using this approach information problems are not solved by meeting information needs but by eliminating them permanently. Put another way, quoting Ackoff (1978), information problems are dissolved. So we have a strong preference for sociotechnical structures of organizations.

And not only does the sociotechnical approach have an overwhelming impact on the organization's information structure, leading to numerous benefits by saving a lot of money in the field of information systems and ICT, but it is accompanied by other advantages too, such as more motivated people and higher flexibility.

Not surprisingly, we embrace the sociotechnical approach as an almost ideal organization concept in many different ways, but especially for information problems. And for this reason we think it is unavoidable to explore the ideas behind this concept in a separate chapter, more thoroughly.

Discussing the sociotechnical approach, two angles can be identified. The first angle relates to the sociotechnical *structure* of organizations; the organization's sociotechnical blueprint. Here we meet a number of relevant *design* principles lying behind this blueprint. The second angle emphasizes the sociotechnical *process*. This process has two sides. On the one hand, we pay attention to the way organizations can be turned into a sociotechnical organization, the *implementation* of the sociotechnical structure, and on the other hand the functioning of sociotechnical organizations, the *exploitation*, will be discussed.

These topics are the subjects of the following three sections (2 to 4).

In the beginning the sociotechnical approach has been developed to structure a specific kind of organization and a specific organizational layer: the shop floor of business firms producing physical goods. But can the sociotechnical approach be applied to other organizations and other organizational layers as well? This question will be answered in section 5. Finally, in section 6 we pay attention to the principle of 'dialogical control' of organizations and so-called 'set based concurrent design', to improve the functioning of sociotechnical organizations.

2. The sociotechnical structure of organizations: design principles

The sociotechnical theory of organizations can be seen as a reaction to more classic organization theories in general and to the ideas of Frederick W. Taylor in particular, which are still rather popular in many organizations today. Therefore, to catch the essential properties of this former theory, at the start of this section we pay attention to Taylor's organization theory.

In the early years of this century millions of people lived in great poverty, especially in the industrialized areas of our society, many coming from more agricultural areas. Under such conditions, according to Maslov's need hierarchy, people's most important concern is to stay alive and to satisfy their basic needs. Thus, their participation in organizations is exclusively motivated by earning money. With this problem in mind, Taylor looked for opportunities to improve the situation, by restructuring the organization, as mentioned before (Chapter II, section 4) on the following basic principles:

- splitting up complete tasks into many different parts and
- separation of operational activities from control.

Applying this first principle, (blue collar) workers have very simple tasks, that can be easily learned and executed efficiently. The second principle means the exemption of workers from indirect productive tasks, leaving control tasks to the management as much as possible. Taken together, these two principles led to a tremendous increase in labour productivity and to greater worker welfare.

The ultimate consequence of Taylor's approach is the assembly line system where workers are reduced to – mechanical – human parts of machines; a system that, at first glance, looks more efficient than any other.

However, Taylor's production system also has a number of disadvantages:

1. lack of product flexibility,
2. lack of control,
3. lack of quality orientation,
4. lack of innovative potential,
5. lack of labour quality,
6. lack of cooperative labour relations,
7. information burden.

We will now discuss these seven properties briefly.

1. As long as Henry Ford's slogan – 'you can get any colour if it's black' – is broadly accepted by consumers, product flexibility is not an issue at all. But, due to increasing incomes, changing consumer needs and product diversity, product flexibility – changing from one product to another and meeting the consumers' individual needs – becomes more and more important.
2. If a specific part of a process based on Tayloristic design principles slows down, for instance because of engine trouble, consequences for all the other parts of the process will emerge. Of course, the tight mutual coupling of process parts can be decreased in particular by introducing stocks. But this is a very expensive solution.
3. As we have seen before it was Taylor's intention to increase the output quantity of workers in order to increase their wages too. But by overemphasizing quantity,

the quality of products will be neglected and many products exceed the tolerance limits; products that have to be rejected or recycled. And if an effective quality control system is lacking, there is no feedback about the poor quality achievements.
4. Because workers are only responsible for a very small part of the total process and of the product as well, their scope is also limited. As a consequence, innovative ideas, as far as such ideas come forward, are useless most of the time, because they do not fit well in the larger whole of the production system. And if people's ideas are often rejected, their motivation to stick one's neck out considerably decreases.
5. One of the conerstones of Taylor's production system relates to the continuous repetition of a limited number of activities. So people's tasks are not challenging. Rather they feel bored and alienated. Often, executing a routine job, their mind is elsewhere, contributing to poor product quality. High labour turnover and sick leave are normal phenomena here.
6. Though people have to cooperate, their only concern is their own job, and sometimes also the jobs of their shift members. So, between shifts and between departments, walls, sometimes literally, can be identified, preventing people from working together. As a consequence, there may be a misfit between the product one department produces and another department uses.
7. As is already pointed out in the preceding chapter, the two basic principles of Taylor's organization structure cause, combined with Murphy's Law, many coordination problems and huge flows of information, horizontally as well as vertically. Actually, the Tayloristic organization structure can briefly be characterized as complex, containing simple and boring tasks.

A number of these disadvantages can be cancelled by measures like job enlargement, job enrichment and job rotation. However, as we have seen before (Chapter III, section 4) their focus is limited to individual tasks and existing organizational relations. Moreover, these measures are rather static, meaning that it is very difficult to enlarge, enrich and rotate jobs variably depending on changing worker preferences.

Finally, again looking at Maslov's need hierarchy, if people earn enough money to fulfil their basic needs sufficiently (Taylor's goal), higher needs, especially social needs (contacts with colleagues during the job), become relevant. And these needs are satisfied only haphazardly by the measures just mentioned.

To take social needs into consideration the organization structure has to deal with these needs explicitly.

Applying the sociotechnical approach, these – and also a number of other – problems, accompanying Tayloristic organization structures, can be solved effectively.

Looking at the structure of sociotechnical organizations, three basic substructures can be distinguished:
- production structure,
- control structure,
- information structure.

Originally, the design of these structures was thought to be a linear process, starting with the production structure, followed by the control structure and finally the information structure. However, as was demonstrated in the preceding chapter, between these structures interdependencies can be identified. If, for instance, production orders are assigned randomly based on the principle of time a production team has been waiting already, then the teams have to switch many times from one product to another. Thus every time they have to be informed about the relevant product specifications.

A second example relates to the size of the sociotechnical teams and their information processing capacity. If, as was also discussed in the preceding chapter, the team's size, because of the requirement of *complete* production tasks, to be assigned to sociotechnical teams, exceeds a critical limit, then the information relations between the team members have to be formalized using some sort of information system. The alternative solution, based on informal relations within the team, requires a less complete task for the team. In other words, we have to look for a balance between the three structures.

So between these three substructures, mutual dependencies exist, as illustrated in the scheme below.

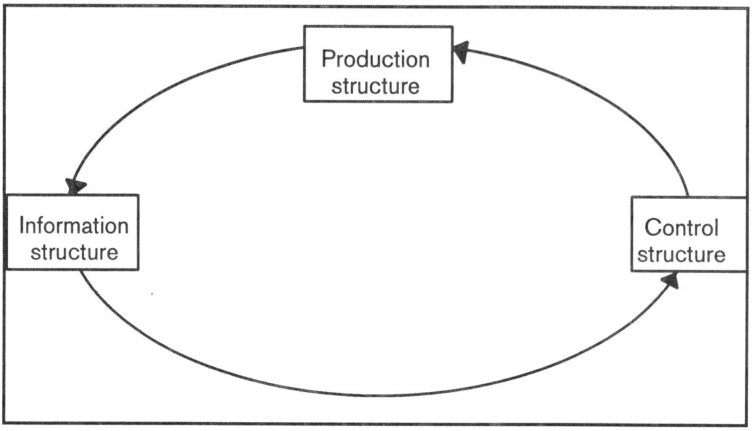

Notwithstanding these interdependencies, we have to start somewhere with the design process and normally this is the production structure. But the design process will not be finished until the three substuctures are fine tuned to each other in an interactive process.

The production structure

For the design of the production structure two principles are dominant: segmentation and parallellisation.

Segmentation and *parallellisation* mean dividing and clustering the product flows into homogeneous task domains. For instance, looking at an organization producing motorcars, the product flows can be divided into one flow for each type of car, assigned to a number of task groups. Therefore, segmentation leads to separating things which are different, whereas parallellisation leads to combining things which are similar.

The control structure
The sociotechnical control structure too is dominated by two principles: integration of tasks and integration of authority.

Integration of *tasks* is a reaction to one of Taylor's two major starting points in respect of extreme specialization. From the sociotechnical point of view tasks have to be *complete*, so workers are able to identify themselves with the products they make, among other things reducing alienation and increasing worker involvement.

Integration of *authority* is a reaction to Taylor's other major starting point: separation of operational activities from control. As opposed to such a separation the sociotechnical approach advocates the delegation of enough authority to the shop floor level. The rules governing the degree of delegation will be discussed later in section 4 of this chapter under the heading 'requisite variety'.

The information structure
In fact control means the coordination of activities, belonging together but, because of operational considerations, assigned to a number of people and thus having become more or less separated. In order to coordinate these activities, information has to be exchanged in advance to plan activities properly and during the operations, because deviations from plans, due to incompletely controllable factors, have also to be communicated to the people involved. In other words, if many people are – closely – working together and if the number of factors getting out of control is high, then a lot of information will flow through the organization. By integrating tasks the sociotechnical approach is able to reduce these flows considerably.

So far, we are actually speaking about *horizontal* flows of information, because until now nothing is said about the degree of involvement of managers. Depending on this degree of involvement, the *vertical* flows of information will have some size. Compared with horizontal flows of information, for the vertical flows of information the sociotechnical approach has similar effects. As we have seen before, one of its basic priciples is delegating people extensive authority, meaning that making appeals to managers does not happen frequently, leading to limited flows of information in the vertical sense.

With our discussion of the three sociotechnical basic structures, we are still not finished yet. As we have learned from a number of experiences in the field, the integral character of the sociotechnical approach does not only relate to the integration of tasks and authority (on the shop floor level), but to all the other organization's aspects as well. For instance, the organization's reward system is a crucial factor for the success, or failure, of the new structure. Traditional organizations are designed starting with individual tasks. And so their reward systems are oriented individually too. However, instead of individual members, teams are the building blocks of the sociotechnical organization. Thus, the reward system has also to be redesigned in such a way that individual and group rewards are balanced sufficiently.

Another example of an important aspect which is crucial for the sociotechnical organization's success concerns the organization's information systems. Though meant to facilitate primary processes, formalized information systems often come to be viewed as administrative burdens, imposed by the information department, and often they actually are (Mohrman, Cohen and Mohrman, 1995). This is because the major client of this department, looking at traditional structured organizations, is the corporate management. But within sociotechnical organizations teams on the shop floor are not less important. Hence, instead of being authoritarian for this latter organizational layer, information systems have to be facilitative.

Probably, for some departments, to the extent that they are not liquidated if organizations are redesigned, a sociotechnical structure perhaps causes quite a culture shock. Also the possibility of such a shock requires careful attention from the organization's management and/or of the change agents from outside.

Though sociotechnical design principles can be used for a wide range of organizational entities, in some situations they are not fully appropriate. Generally speaking, a sociotechnical structure – containing all the basic characteristics of job enlargement, job enrichment and job rotation – is not well-suited for tasks requiring high skill professional capabilities. In that case it takes a lot of time to learn to perform those tasks, and rotating them between the team members is not feasible.

The same holds for teams executing tasks of different levels of education, meaning that between workers of these levels work rotation is out of the question too.

An illustration of both elements is provided by an operation team working together in a theatre of a hospital. On the one hand the doctors belonging to this team all are specialized differently, whereas on the other hand the team's nurses have lower qualifications, preventing them doing a doctor's job. Thus the opportunities to take over the other members' tasks are very limited here, or even absent.

Of course rotating work is only one specific, though important, requirement of sociotechnical teams, not met by a hospital theatre team, perhaps meanwhile fulfilling other requirements such as self control. So this section actually contains the message that, if organizations intend to apply the sociotechnical principles, they have to be well aware of the teams' idiosyncracies, sometimes leading to the rejection of one or more of these principles, meanwhile applying other ones (see also sectioen 5).

3. Paving the way to the sociotechnical organization: the implementation

If the organization's structure has to be changed drastically, which is the situation if a more traditional structured organization with an emphasis on hierarchical relations is turned into a sociotechnical organization, then the change process is more than pushing a button. In fact, the organization has to grow from one structure to another. Indeed we are dealing here with a – sometimes far-reaching – change process that has to be handled with care. Though we primarily pay attention to the structure aspect of this process, the culture aspect is important as well. In this section we will focus on the process leading from a traditional structured organization to a combination of mature sociotechnical groups. In order to have this process smoothly developed, four stages can be distinguished with the following labels (VanAmelsvoort and Scholtes, 1994):

- collection of individuals,
- group,

- team,
- open team.

Collection of individuals
In this phase the increase of technical and professional skills is emphasized. Actually, we are speaking here about job enlargement. Increase of these skills is necessary because of the desire to stimulate the organization's flexibility and to offer its members more work variety.

Next to this attention at the individual level there is also room for adaptation of the technical conditions in order to facilitate the group process. For instance the machines are set up in such a way that the group members are able to communicate with each other easily.

Finally, a 'collection of individuals' is characterized by task rotation and work deliberation at their own discretion.

Group
In addition to a 'collection of individuals' a 'group' has two other characteristics: integration of task elements and integration of authority.

As to integration of task elements, tasks in the field of planning, maintenance and human resources are added to the team's job. Moreover, the team gets, partly as a consequence of the extended task, more authority or autonomy.

Team
Looking back at the 'group' phase we may conclude that for a sociotechnical team, its foundation, relating to the organization's structure, is mature. However, are the team members ready too? For instance, deliberations about work may cause a lot of stress and disagreement. And are they able to handle conflicts? Thus, in the team phase attention has to be paid especially to social abilities of the team members and how to get on with each other (see also below). Team building is an important topic here. As a consequence, the team learns to function effectively.

Needless to say that, so far, the measures taken to improve the team's functioning have a strong team internal orientation.

Open team
In fact in this phase we are dealing with a mature team in every relevant respect. In this situation the team deserves it to be called a 'team', but the team is also 'open' to the world around it. The team perceives itself as a supplier, and as a client respectively. And it tries to meet the customer's wishes, not because of the orders of the boss, but because of an intrinsic need to create added value, as much as possible. Therefore, the team will, on its own initiative, start improvement activities concerning the product and the process as well. Open teams are able to operate very independently, without losing sight of the larger whole; the organization they are part of.

As has already been mentioned in this section, to function as a team the team members should have specific skills, going beyond the skills required in traditional organiza-

tions, to be successful. The skills to be present can be listed as follows (Mohrman, Cohen and Mohrman, 1995):
- technical or functional skills,
- cross training skills,
- interpersonal and conflict resolution skills,
- decision making skills,
- learning skills,
- leadership skills.

Technical or functional skills
In any organizational role people have to be technically competent to do their job properly. However, in team based organizations the team members must also have some additional capabilities, particularly in respect of their willingness to keep up with the technical changes in their professional field. As we will see later on in section 5 this requirement of technical skills holds especially for teams on the shop floor of organizations. As soon as teams contain – very – specialized knowledge (see the example about a hospital theatre team mentioned at the end of the previous section), then it is absolutely impossible for the team members to have expertise in more than one field, though some knowledge about the other members' expertise, to facilitate the team's internal communication, would be very helpful.

So far, we focused on individual characteristics, but from the angle of the team other properties can be identified. For instance, the team as a whole must have the collective skills to produce the team's product or service adequately.

Cross training skills
In order to get complete advantage of – shop floor – team structures it is necessary for the team members to be cross-trained on a full set of team skills, as much as possible. This requirement holds for a number of reasons. Firstly, to be able to discuss team relevant issues the team members must have enough understanding of the skills of their teammates. Secondly, work rotation is only possible if the team members have skills to do different tasks. Thirdly, in case of illness people with sufficient skills are able to replace each other.

Interpersonal and conflict resolution skills
To work with other people effectively, open communication is an absolute prerequisite. People must have an open mind listening to each other and must have the opportunity to discuss relevant topics without creating hard feelings. If they do so, conflicts will be prevented most of the time. If conflicts do break out the team must have abilities to solve them adequately. Managing conflicts is a topic that will be discussed in more detail in Chapter VIII.

Decision making skills
In contrast to workers within traditional – hierarchical – organization structures sociotechnical teams have much more authority. As a consequence they have to take many decisions themselves. So they need decision skills to function effectively. These decision skills, meaning that teams behave in a systematic way, relate to things like collecting data, evaluating alternatives and determining outcomes.

Learning skills
As mentioned above, when discussing technical and functional skills, team members have to be willing to acquire new knowledge in their field. But this is not enough. Working with people, especially people from other disciplines, requires a capacity of different ways of viewing the world. Not only is this a necessary precondition for effective communication between the team members but also for stimulating the team's idea-generation abilities to solve problems, not only reactively but especially proactively.

Leadership skills
Team members have to play several leadership roles. An obvious one is the role of team leader or captain (see below). But also other leadership roles can be identified, such as technical mentor of junior team members, systems integrator and liaison officer. These latter two roles will be discussed in section 5. To play leadership roles effectively specific skills have to be required, such as informal influence, meeting management, communication and conflict resolution abilities, to mention a few.

As opposed to the other skills discussed so far, leadership skills are less easy to learn. Moreover, to function as a team in the sociotechnical meaning it is not necessary for any member to take the leadership role temporarily. But on the other hand it is important that this role is not limited to a minority of the members, because of the danger of creating – informal – hierarchical levels within the team this way.

In addition to these skills, other skills may be required if specific teams are focal. If for instance we are looking at management teams, to be discussed in section 5 below, skills in the area of organizational design and change are necessary too.

4. The sociotechnical organization; its exploitation

As mentioned before, teams are the building blocks of the sociotechnical organization structure, organizing their own activities. Because of this characteristic sociotechnical teams are designated variously as self-contained, self-managing, self-directing, self-regulating, self-organizing, self-steering and (semi) autonomous work teams. Self-organization is based on four principles (Emery and Thorsrud, 1976; Ashby, 1969; Herbst, 1974; Argyris and Schon, 1978):

- redundancy of functions,
- requisite variety,
- minimum critical specifications,
- double loop learning.

Redundancy of functions

In a Tayloristic organization every worker only has very specialized knowledge about a very small task, resulting in very limited skills. Thus, workers are not able to replace each other immediately, though to learn the other skills involved does not take much time. However, limited skills are detrimental for worker flexibility.

As opposed to this Tayloristic situation, sociotechnical team members basically have all the skills needed to do the team's job. In other words, the members are able to execute different tasks and can replace each other immediately, if necessary.

Redundancy not only relates to operational activities but to planning and control as well, meaning that the team members also have the capacity to replace each other in planning and controlling roles. So, these latter activities are also part of the team's system of rotating work.

Requisite variety

The principle of requisite variety is based on Ashby's Law of requisite variety; in our own words: only (internal) variety can destroy (external) variety.

What do we mean by that? If teams have tasks, characterized by changing circumstances (external variety), sufficient authority (internal variety), also called discretion, has to be delegated to them to handle this external variety effectively. Too little authority causes frustration because teams are confronted with problems they are not allowed to solve independently and are not able to control, whereas too much authority is inefficient because they are responsible for something they do not need.

Minimum ctitical specifications

Within Tayloristic structured organizations, workers have very precise orders about the execution of their activities in respect of *what* and *how*. Hence, their room to manoeuver is almost zero. Obviously, this was Taylor's intention because thus they are able to function almost automatically, whereas things they would really have to think about, fall under the jurisdiction of their bosses and do not require the 'waste' of valuable blue colour worker production time.

In a sociotechnical structured situation, however, people are self steering, among other things meaning that most of their problems they have to solve by themselves. Of course they also have to follow orders. But with the boss they globally agree about things that really matter. In other words, only the least possible number of critical specifications will be determined, in order to create as much room as possible.

Double loop learning

As was explained in section 2 of Chapter II we distinguish between single loop learning, also called first order learning, and double loop learning, or second order learning. This distinction is particularly relevant if organizations are confronted with environmental turbulence. Because if they are functioning in a fast changing world, then adaptations of their frame of reference from time to time to remain viable are required. These adaptations can be seen as the result of double loop learning.

Due to the fundamental role of sociotechnical teams within the total organization, for its survival in the future, double loop learning is crucial. Actually, learning

– particularly in this latter sence – is the essence of sociotechnically structured organizations.

An important aspect of the good functioning of teams concerns the team's roles that have to be defined carefully. Within the team two sorts of roles can be identified: operating roles and coordinating roles. Operating roles are the roles played by people responsible for direct productive activities of the team. As to the operating roles two questions arise:

- in what way are these roles assigned to the members?
- who takes care of the mutual coordination between them?

Answering these questions we start with noting that the tasks, concerning both questions, belong to the team's coordinating role. And just like all the team's roles the coordinating role too changes from time to time, on the team's own initiative, as we have seen above. In other words, as a starting point all the members need to have enough competences to play operational as well as coordinating roles, and also will do so. As a matter of fact, using the metaphor of a football team, the member with the coordinating role is the team's captain, but still having the same rank as the other players.

Next to the captain's role, another role can be distinguished, played by the boss who, within the traditional organization structure, has a rather dominant position. However, in a sociotechnical setting his role is comparable with the role of the coach of a football team. An important task of the coach is to instruct the team members sufficiently, to take care of the members' abilities and to change the team's composition if necessary. But during the game he has to keep his mouth shut. And this is exactly the role of the hierachical manager in a sociotechnical structure. Before and after the work is done he interferes with the team, but during the production process the captain takes over.

Instead of controlling and giving orders, the role of the manager in a team based organization is especially facilitating.

Of course for some traditional managers such a role is difficult to play. Therefore, the change process here, to grow from a traditional structure to a sociotechnical one, requires careful attention; a topic already discussed in the preceding section.

Illustrating coordinating roles – charged with the allocation of operating roles – the football team metaphor does not hold anymore. As is well-known, the members of a football team have a clearly defined position, depending on their specific expertise, similar to the roles of the hospital theatre team members. Role allocation is not an issue until the training of the team members, to execute operating roles, can rather easily be acquired or if the differences between these roles are gradual. Only then does task rotation take place, and will be discussed during some sort of negotiation process. Normally this process will be managed by the coach, leading to a long term agreement, containing items like: which team members play what series of roles for how long.

5. The sociotechnical structure; a universal principle?

In its early years the sociotechnical approach has been limited to organizations characterized by mass production. In this situation the concept 'team' had only one meaning, already defined in the preceding chapter and concerning groups of blue collar workers on the shop floor of organizations producing physical goods; the so-called *production* or *work* team. However, because of the convincing successes this approach brought about, designers of organization structures looked for other applications of the sociotechnical approach, i.e. other parts of organizations producing physical goods and organizations not producing such goods as well. It is even much easier to apply sociotechnical principles to other organizational units than the shop floor level because then only organizational measures are required instead of an accompanying redesign of the production process architecture. Indeed, if on the shop floor tasks are grouped differently (sociotechnically instead of functionally) then the physical equipment has to be adapted too.

So after some time the team concept was broadened considerably. And not suprisingly, this concept is sometimes interpreted as the abbreviation of Together Everyone Achieves More.

Nowadays, next to production teams, three other kinds of teams can be identified (Mohrman, Cohen and Mohrman, 1995):
- management teams,
- improvement teams,
- integrating teams.

Management teams
Evidently management teams in traditional organizations already have more or less sociotechnical characteristics, in so far as they are charged with a complete task and sufficient authority. Nevertheless, in an organization-wide sociotechnical setting, management teams have additional properties. For instance, the tasks within traditional management teams are assigned functionally, based on the members' specialization or preference. Not surprisingly, this structure prevents an integral approach to organizational issues. Therefore, sociotechnical management teams should, if specialization is necessary, be organized along different products or selling areas, similar to the team structure on the shop floor. And if functional specialization is present, regular task rotation could be helpful.

Improvement teams
Apart from the organization's structure on the shop floor, and the absence or presence of production teams, within other parts of the organization it is possible to use team structures, based on specific categories of teams, such as improvement teams.

Improvement teams are established to improve the organization's capability to produce (more) effectively. Of improvement teams a number of examples can be listed: organizational redesign teams, process redesign teams and quality improvement teams (Ledford, c.s., 1988). Because of the scope of such teams to realize significant improvements, often reaching far beyond departmental borders, these teams should be composed cross functionally and cross departmentally (Hammer and Champy, 1993).

Integrating teams
A third category of teams that can be used apart from team structures on the shop floor concerns integrating teams. As a matter of fact if a team's task can be executed separated from the task of other teams, then there is no coordination needed. This is especially relevant for teams charged with structured tasks, such as most production teams. However, if the team structure is not only applied to the organization's core transformation process but to other processes as well, for example to the product design process, teams are often – mutually – dependent. Hence their activities have to be integrated. Integration can be realized by using a number of instruments. One of these instruments relates to the integrating team, meaning that this team is composed of a number of members of the teams involved, charged with integrating roles.

Until now we discussed teams belonging to the overall category of *real* teams, meaning that the team members work together in the same place and at the same time. Finally another sort of team, different from the real team, can be identified, the so-called *virtual* team. This sort of team can be defined as a group of people, geographically dispersed, working together, sometimes also at different moments, made possible by using ICT. In fact the concept of virtual teams can easily be combined with the other ones if the team's task does not require the members' immediate nearness. Only for production teams is this usually a prerequisite.

Teams can be classified using a number of criteria like (Mohrman, Cohen and Mohrman, 1995):
- mission,
- relationship to the formal organization structure,
- duration.

Mission
As we have seen above, describing different teams, teams may be established for different purposes. Depending on their specific assignment teams have a mission that has to be determined unambiguously. For instance, a work team's mission is to produce and to deliver goods or services to clients, inside or outside the organization. Also for other sorts of teams, their purpose has to be made clear beforehand, because one of the issues, particularly relevant for knowledge teams (see below) is their ability to achieve shared understanding internally and aligning this understanding to the organization's goals.

Relationship to the formal organization structure
In fact two possibilities can be distinguished here. On the one hand teams can be part of the formal organization structure and appear on the organization chart as independent organizational entities with relationships to other entities. Normally work teams belong to this category. On the other hand teams can be used as 'overlay' structures in addition

to the formal organization structure, meaning that the team members have a double loyalty; a loyalty to the team involved of course, but a loyalty to the other entity, or entities, they are part of too. Integrating teams are an example of such an overlay team.

Duration

Some teams are rather permanent, whereas others are temporary. This distinction can not be isolated completely from the previous criterion (relationship to the formal organization structure). If teams are meant to be permanent they should have a clear organizational position as a part of the formal organization structure. Again work teams are an example.

Teams, established to do a job with a limited time horizon, will be dissolved if their task is finished. Such teams can be illustrated by the project teams functioning in the framework of a project organization with the assignment to execute a specific project during a predetermined period of time. Teams charged with the design of an information system fit this description well. These teams' position vis-a-vis the organization's structure is determined by this structure's properties, particularly as far as it is based on the project principle or not. If for instance an information system has to be designed, normally two companies are involved; the selling and the buying company. To meet this target a team is composed. Usually this team will not be formally integrated with the existing organization structure of the buyer, unless this structure, as only rarely happens, is explicitly designed from the point of view of projects. However, the selling company probably has a different point of view because the majority of such organizations is permanently working in teams with a limited time horizon. Therefore, these organizations prefer to make clear links between their teams and the formal organization structure; in particular in case of double memberships. Double memberships occur if, for example during the design process of information systems, the designers are members of the design team – within the client organization – and of teams within their own organization.

As mentioned above, a number of different teams can be distinguished, not only in regard to the shop floor of organizations producing physical products and containing blue collar workers. Actually all these 'other' teams are executing tasks in the field of knowledge work. So the next step in this development of the sociotechnical approach is broadening its concept to organizations, such as consultancy agencies, producing knowledge as the main result of their core transformation process and to other teams within organizations based on shop floor work teams as well. But before we discuss this topic we have to answer the question in what way the sociotechnical approach could be favourable here.

More and more, it has been recognized that the fit between the organization's strategy and its design enables it to create a competitive advantage (Galbraith, Lawler, and Associates, 1993; Mohrman, Cohen and Mohrman, 1995). As a matter of fact properly designed organizations reveal a number of advantages; for instance they execute better, they learn faster and they change more easily. And increasingly, appropriate organizational design and team based organization structures are being perceived as two sides of the same coin.

Moreover, team based organizations are, compared with traditional organizations relying on hierarchical structures, claimed to have advantages relating to speed, cycle time and time-to-market (Myer, 1993). An important explanation lying behind these properties has to do with the organization's ability to process information efficiently and effectively (Czerniawsky and Potter, 1998). Increasingly, competitive advantages depend on the way organizations are able to get information from their customers, to design products coming up to their needs without losing much time. And organizations able to launch more products more quickly than their competitors will win. So, organizations should have internal procedures, based upon their structures, that shorten their response time considerably. As is well-known hierarchical structures are not suited for this purpose, whereas team based structures are.

As was stipulated in section 1 of this chapter a sociotechnically structured organization not only reduces its information burden tremendously but is also characterized by increased flexibility, due to delayering the organization and to more autonomy for the participants. Actually, these properties are almost universal, meaning that irrespective of the nature of the organization, advantages can be realized by applying a well-considered combination of sociotechnical design principles, depending on the organization's idiosyncracies.

Thus not surpringly, the interest in team based organization structures is still growing and after the successes of production teams (producing physical goods) other sorts of teams are taken into consideration.

As was said before, in this section we are especially interested in the application of sociotechnical design principles for knowledge work based – parts of – organizations. In the remainder of this section we discuss the opportunities and threats of such an approach.

Without pretending to be exhaustive, knowledge work is claimed to be:

- highly specialized,
- interdependent,
- dynamic.

Highly specialized

Looking at this property its content seems to run counter to the 'ideal' properties of team based work according to Pasmore. In this author's opinion sociotechnical teams are most suitable for work that is stable, containing routine tasks with members having relatively equal levels of skill, skills that can be learned rather easily from each other (Pasmore, 1988).

Therefore in order to apply sociotechnical principles to knowledge work, a number of precautions have to be taken to eliminate the threats emerging from its characteristics listed above.

As has already been demonstrated in section 1 of this chapter, using the example of a medical team operating in a hospital theatre, the more specialization, the less work rotation is possible between the team's members. But in spite of this restriction, a number of other design principles, described under the labels of the four stages of the team building process explained in section 3, is still valid.

Interdependency

Inderdependency, as a major property of knowledge work, is particularly about the relations of the teams' tasks with those of others'. Because of this interdependency we meet an important area of tension composing knowledge work teams. On the one hand a basic sociotechnical design principle is autonomy with a limited number of relations with entities outside the team, whereas on the other hand, from the point of view of informal mutual contacts, the team's size should not exceed ten to twelve members. So, if we have to deal with a lot of interdependenies, either the team will be expanded beyond its maximum size, or we have to deal explicitly with interdependencies. Choosing between these two alternatives, generally speaking, the latter option is preferable. This is because the other option will cause teams to fall apart in a rather coincidental way. Thus, we have to integrate the work of different teams to make sure that the work of various parts of the organization fits together. To integrate the work of these teams, three instruments are available (Mohrman, Cohen and Mohrman, 1995):

- liaison roles,
- overlapping membership,
- cross-team integrating teams.

The instrument of *liaison roles* means the appointment of a specific team member to be a liaison officer with one or more other teams. *Overlapping membership*, meaning that some participants are a member of more than one team, is a second instrument to cope with interdependencies adequately. Finally we can use a specific team, called *cross-team integrating team*, to integrate the tasks of teams. Which opportunity will be preferred depends on the degree of interdependency. With only modest interdependencies it suffices to appoint a liaison officer or to use overlapping membership. As a positive side effect of this approach the flexibility of individuals, as opposed to teams, has to be mentioned. However, if the degree of interdependency is high, it may be necessary to charge a *team* with integrating roles, instead of single persons executing those roles in addition to other – regular – tasks.

Dynamic

The third and final property of knowledge work we listed above is its *dynamic* character. If the team's task is rather stable then its composition and tasks can be agreed upon for quite a long time. But, as soon as dynamics is a major issue teams become more fluid in respect of these two dimensions (composition and task). So compared with teams executing (physical) production tasks, knowledge teams offer a less certain work setting for their members. As a consequence some participants may get feelings of alienation, whereas other participants perceive such a work setting as challenging. For instance, the higher educated people are the more this latter attitude is present.

We will finish this section with a real life example concerning a consultancy agency, active in the field of bookkeeping systems as an illustration of succesful organizational redesign based on sociotechnical principles.

This organization's consultants are grouped in rather autonomous teams along the lines of a number of branches of industry with specific book keeping requirements. In order to charge the clients, the consultants have the duty to register the hours they worked for them by filling in a form to be sent to the agency's bookkeeping department at the end of the week. However, the consultants are very reluctant to do so, mainly perceiving it as an administrative burden, preventing them from executing higher qualified work. Often they fill in the forms not more than once a month, and per project they do not calculate the hours really worked but the hours the project in their opinion could be charged with, and then throw the form 'over the wall'.

Wondering how the consultants could be stimulated to fill in these forms more accurately, the agency's management decided to buy a computerized information system enabling the consultants to do this job at home and to send the forms electronically to the bookkeeping department.

After some time of experimenting with this system the management came to the conclusion that the consultants' behaviour of filling in the hour forms had not been improved to any extent. So the author of this book became involved as an external expert to solve the problem effectively.

After some time of investigation it became clear that it was not in the consultants' interest to fill in the forms because their involvement in the bookkeeping department was almost zero. Hence we looked for ways to make the consultants feel responsible for that part of the administrative process. Perceiving the problem from this angle, its solution was rather obvious: enlargement of the consultant teams' tasks with sending clients a bill and expanding their number of participants by adding a member of the bookkeeping department; a very simple and cheap measure compared with the new information system. And rather soon the problem appeared to be eliminated.

However, the new information system seemed to be redundant now. Thus, the question arose what to do with it? After rejecting some options the agency came to the conclusion that it could be used very well as some sort of intranet, facilitating the communication between the consultants, who were outside the agency's physical location most of the time.

Not only does this example illustrate the way sociotechnical teams could be designed effectively but it also demonstrates one of the main issues of this book, particularly discussed in the previous chapter, that fundamental solutions of information problems often not should be looked for in the – narrow – field of information systems, but are a matter of organizational redesign.

6. The principle of dialogical control

As we have seen above more than once, sociotechnical teams are self-controlling, meaning that they have to answer a number of questions; to mention a few:

- which tasks are asigned to whom?
- in what order will the tasks of the team be executed?
- who is the team's captain, for how long and who is the next one?

To answer these questions, and perhaps many others, the team members have to negotiate with each other. One of the aspects of this negotiation process is about the way the participants propose and select alternatives to come to an agreement. Two basic approaches can be identified here:

- point based concurrent design and
- set based concurrent design.

If the team has to reach an agreement, for instance about the tasks to be executed by each of them in the next planning period, then the members have to choose between a – large – number of alternative configurations. In the situation of *point based concurrent design* every member is supposed to determine for himself in isolation what task he prefers to do, just like all the other members. With these options in mind, the negotiation process between the team members will be started. If all these individual options do match, this process will quickly be finished. However the chance of such an initial match is almost zero. If, for example, the team has eight members and eight tasks – together summing up to a complete job – to be allocated among them, then a configuration matching the members' wishes immediately has a chance of .003%. So in almost any situation one or more members have to change their position. And such a process often takes a lot of time because they feel personally involved sometimes, and perceive it as a defeat to withdraw from their initial position (Ward, 1995). Although the team members are talking together we can hardly see this as a dialogue; on the contrary, most of the time they only try to make clear their own position without really listening to each other. Here we meet one of the major disadvantages of the sociotechnical organization structure. And it may be even worse if the negotiation process is not only time consuming but results in the outburst of conflicts, harming the groups' mutual relationships tremendously.

Fortunately, an alternative approach to the negotiation process is available, called *set based concurrent design*. Applying set based concurrent design the members of the team do not select one option – a single point – beforehand but start the negotiation process with a number of options which are more or less equally satisficing; a set. During this process, the team has to find out what combinations do match. And even if such a combination cannot be found, for the team members it is much easier to change their intitial position compared with point based concurrent design. Now, during the negotiation process a real dialogue takes place. So set based concurrent design can be seen as a synonym for 'dialogical control'.

As far as set based concurrent design has been practiced the results are very positive. For instance Ward reports, referring to the Toyota case where set based concurrent design has been applied to the product development process, a shorter development period with more successful products (Ward, 1995).

As can be easily demonstrated, set based concurrent design may – in addition to its role in facilitating the allocation of individual tasks among team members – be very helpful too if we are, as is usual in knowledge work settings, confronted with teams which are interdependent. To coordinate the tasks of different – mutually dependent – teams a negotiation process also takes place. And by 'keeping your options open' before starting the process of mutual coordination, this process will be more efficient and more effective as well.

V INFORMATION POLICY

1. Introduction

Generally speaking the policy of organizations, as was indicated in Chapter II, is composed of three crucial concepts:
- means,
- ways and
- goals.

Between these concepts the following relationship can be defined:

> *policy relates to the means used and the ways being followed to reach the organization's goals*

According to this definition, information policy, as a specific field of policy, is:

> *the policy of organizations concerning information systems, irrespective of the technological means that will be applied*

It is very fundamental to be aware that in our opinion information policy is about *all* sorts of information, and not only information supported by ICT, as is assumed – sometimes tacitly – by a lot of students.

Dropping such a restriction is of the utmost importance, looking at the storing of data within organizations. For instance, research at the end of the eighties reveals a division of data over a number of storing devices in the following way (Canning McNurlin, 1989):
- 95% on paper,
- 4% on microfilm, magnetic disk, etc.
- 1% on line in computers.

Though, in the meantime till now, a shift towards the second and the third category probably has occurred, it would surprise us very much if these two categoies have doubled today and sum up to ten percent.

Therefore, if we should restrict our attentention to the part of the organization's information processing activities supported by ICT, then an unacceptable narrowing of our focus would be the result.

In this introduction, the concept information *policy* was used. Alternatively, this field of knowledge is also called 'information planning' and 'information management'.

Remembering the control cycle from Chapter II, it is clear that the concept information *planning* does not cover all relevant control phases. Not only planning but also execution and check up are essential parts of information policy.

The danger of the concept of information *management* is its emphasis on the role of management; an undesired restriction of the field of knowledge involved.

Of course, it is absolutely necessary to embed decisions, made about every issue within organizations whatsoever, in a broader policy framework (Teo and Ang, 1999). Based on practical experiences with information policy, in addition to this more general requirement, a number of specific reasons can be formulated, such as (Theeuwes, 1986):

1. information policy is insufficiently attuned to the information needs of organizational participants,
2. the fine tuning between subsystems in the field of information policy is missing,
3. the phenomenon of more or less continuous changes of organizations and of their control,
4. the lack of clear criteria for capital budgeting decisions in the field of ICT,
5. obsolete – automated – systems are still functioning,
6. top management is insufficiently involved in the organization's automation policy,
7. unclear responsibilities in the field of information processing activities,
8. reorientation of the organization's strategic position,
9. a lack of awareness of the opportunities offered by new technologies.

We will briefly discuss these reasons in more detail now.

ad 1.
Remembering what is said in Chapter I, the poor correspondence between the information needs of the users and the information systems of the organization should not surprise us at all.

ad 2.
Especially because of miniaturization in the domain of ICT and the amateurism of participants everywhere within the organization, the information policy of many organizations is the sum of a lot of different parts, often incompatible with each other.

ad 3.
Because of turbulent developments of their environment, organizations are continually changing. The structure of organizations, and their information structure too, may be a restricting factor in adapting smoothly to the environment.

As a matter of fact, structure is necessary to give the organization some solidity. But too much structure causes rigidity. Therefore, structures must give sufficient solidity, but they must also tolerate sufficient mobility. As a consequence, they have to be revised form time to time, due to the acceleration of changes in the environment, in order to create more fluidity.

ad 4.
Clear evaluation criteria are missing for making capital budgeting decisions about ICT projects. Of course, organizations have extended knowledge to evaluate 'normal' capital budgeting proposals. But capital budgeting decisions in the field of ICT are of a specific kind, due to the difficult predictability of revenues and often unforeseen capital outlays increasingly combined with qualitative results, once the information system is in its design stage or even after implementation.

It is clear that with this book it is the author's intention to decrease the danger of numerous and unexpected expenditures afterwards. A number of methods to clarify the consequences of information projects is available; methods that will be discussed in combination with more sophisticated evaluation procedures in Chapter X.

ad 5.
Using obsolete – automated – information systems is related to points 3 and 4. On the one hand, using systems no longer coming up to standards will impede the organization's functioning, especially considering the necessary flexibility of the organization. On the other hand, a lack of clear criteria for adequate replacements has a paralyzing impact on the decision making process.

Moreover, a third reason why organizations hesitate to replace automated information systems, can be identified. Most of the time buying and exploiting such systems cost a lot of money. And if at sequential moments organizations are forced to spend money again and again, they are building a psychological threshold, becoming bigger and bigger, which prevents them from admitting that they are moving in the wrong direction. In fact they are trapped in a self enforcing process; once the information expenditures of an organization are set about in a certain way, then the pressure to follow this way becomes higher and higher.

ad 6.
Due to the amateurism accompanying the application of ICT in organizations, developments in this field are left to persons of good will without any policy framework. Moreover, the other organizational participants don't have enough incentives to take an active position, because of the hesitant role of the organization's management. We pay attention to this topic, discussing project management in the next chapter.

ad 7.
Closely connected with a lack of policy framework, unclear responsibilities in the field of information processing and information policy exist. This question is related to the role of one specific department, called computer centre or information centre, at a central level, occupied with the organization's information problems.

ad 8.
In formulating the strategic policy of organizations, the role of information, and ICT as well, becomes more and more important, drawing the consumers' attention. Therefore, it is absolutely necessary for information policy to be embedded in the organization's strategic policy.

Information and ICT are often decisive as to future competitive relations between organizations. In particular innovative applications of this technology create opportunities to beat competitors effectively.

ad 9.
To create competitive advantages, a lack of insight into the opportunities of ICT is disastrous. Only if organizations and their participants have sufficient creativity in applying this technology, instead of imitating others, can we expect organizations to be able to make it a substantial part of their innovative capacity.

After this introduction, in the next section we take up the issue of the levels of information policy. Section 3 is devoted to the historical development of information policy, using Richard Nolan's stage model. Though this model is more or less outdated we discuss it because it is still used as a tool by consultants, and by criticizing it we get a better insight in the growth process of ICT applications. In section 4 we pay attention to the position of the information centre of organizations; a rather crucial department, shaping the organization's information policy.

This chapter is finished with section 5, discussing the topic of outsourcing of ICT. Outsourcing will be discussed in this chapter because it is the logical next step in the information policy of organizations and the role of the information centre as an independent organizational unit whose income is no longer guaranteed by the organization.

2. The levels of information policy

In order to shape the information policy of organization, its embedment in the organization's strategic policy is not enough. It is also necessary to distinguish between a number of *levels* of information policy. This distinction is not only relevant because of theoretical arguments, but has practical implications too. Distinguishing and applying the 'level' concept, information projects will have a greater chance to succeed.

Just like the distinction of policy levels we made in general and discussed in Chapter II a similar distinction of information policy is possible:
- level 1: information strategy,
- level 2: tactical information policy,
- level 3: information projects.

A fourth level that can be added relates to the execution of single information projects, once the policy at level 3 is determined.

Information strategy
If within the framework of the organization's strategic policy the decision is made to give ICT a certain position, then this position must be interpreted at the several levels of information policy, starting with the first level. At this level the following questions are relevant:

- should information or ICT be used to improve the production process, increasing the information *intensity* of the process, or to improve the product, increasing the product's information *content*, or even both?
- in what parts of the organization in particular do we want to use information or ICT?
- will information or ICT be used to streamline the production process, aimed at cost reduction (efficiency approach), or to respond better and quicker to the demands of the client (effectiveness approach)?
- is the application of ICT restricted to what others, especially competitors, do (imitation behaviour), or do we have the intention to create complete new applications (innovative behaviour)?

Tactical information policy
At the second level – the tactical level – of information policy, also called information *(infra)structure* or information *architecture* level, we have to identify the categories of information systems being needed, in order to realize the applications determined at the former level. Also the relations between these systems have to be studied.

Moreover, at this policy level we have to know what data should be collected, etc. In doing so, we are shaping the *structure* of the organization's information policy.

Information projects
To move from the existing to the new one, defined at level 2, we have to identify the road to be followed, called the migration path. At this level, the planning of the necessary projects takes place in a mutual dependence, because of limited time and resources.

Also, at this level it is important to determine what projects can be executed simultaneaously, what projects have to be executed serially and in what sequence.

The execution of single projects
Using the three former information policy levels, we make use of a thorough procedure to plan the organization's information policy. As a matter of fact, the organization is very much prepared because it has taken the necessary precautions.

But finishing the information control cycle the organization must put its plan into practice by executing single projects. On this – fourth – level, project management, discussed in the next chapter and the design methods of Chapter VII play an important role in assuring satisfying outcomes.

The control cycle, as discussed in Chapter II, can be applied to all sorts of policy and so to information policy. Such an approach refers among other things to a distinction between planning, execution and check up, at the different levels of this policy.

Starting with *planning* this phase of the control cycle is about the design of an information *plan*. The point of departure of this plan is a clear policy vision as a fundament for the organization's information policy, resulting in a collection of information systems with sufficient mutual consistency.

Incidentally, this does not mean for the organization the obligation to try to realize one integrated overall information system, as has been formerly advocated (Blumenthal, 1969). Apart from the maintenance problems of such a complex system, its design process is very difficult and almost impossible to manage adequately. But moreover, one big system for the whole organization is completely unnecessary. Many organizational information systems only have local significance, and coupling them with other systems is out of the question.

Only if information systems have a supra local impact is it necessary to link these systems. Together they form a so-called local area network (abbreviated LAN).

Shaping the organization's information policy we make a distinction between circularity and recursivity. Circularity means a process of going through the different levels of this policy in a non linear way. If a process were linear, then at each single level the decisions we make are absolutely definite and form the constraints for the further elaboration of our policy at the next level. However, because of the many uncertainties we are confronted with, it is often necessary to return to former levels, to revise our policy there in order to plan adequately.

A second form of circularity refers to the organization's hierarchy: shaping the information policy top down as well as bottom up. More concretely this approach starts with the organization's top management determining the contours of the information policy and communicates them top down along the hierarchical line of the organization. The next step is a discussion at all lower levels in the organization about a more detailed interpretation of the contours in a bottom up process. Such a process of circularity has at least two advantages:

- because of the democratic character of this process people are really involved and feel responsible for the final outcome,
- everyone in the organization gets the opportunity to make a contribution to this policy making process; so, many ideas are generated that otherwise would not have been picked up by the top management.

In this section, we also mentioned recursivity. This concept means the identification of the same sequence of steps for any single step of the cycle. In other words, the step concept is also applicable to each of the cycle's steps separately. For instance, if we are making a plan (planning) as the first step in the control cycle, we must plan this planning activity, then we execute the planning activity and finally we have to make a check. This *nested* control cycle procedure can be applied to each single step, again and again: being a chief executive officer of my organization I plan that I must plan that a planning meeting must be arranged to discuss our information policy. Planning of the planning process is necessary in order to assure that the procedures, the organization agreed upon, are not violated. If they were, this could be very detrimental for the outcomes of the policy making process.

In the same way, this nested approach holds for the execution step and for the check up step as well.

Though the nested planning procedure can go on almost infinitely, never resulting in execution or even check up, we make this distinction, not because of its theoretical sgnificance, but because we must be aware of the necessity to be careful and thorough in the field of policy making.

3. Nolan's stage model

After several years of observation Richard Nolan concluded that applying ICT, especially database technology, a number of stages can be identified. If the development of the expenditures of organizations on ICT are studied over time, then the resulting pattern can accurately be described by using a so-called sigmoid or S shaped function; after a wavering start in the introduction period, these expenditures increase quickly, called the expansion period. Finally, they slow down in the stabilization period.

Originally, within these three periods Nolan distinguished four different stages (Nolan, 1973; Gibson and Nolan, 1974):

- initiation,
- expansion or contagion,
- formalization or control and
- integration.

In the initiation stage a new technology is introduced, i.c. ICT. Only a small number of users – freaks – is involved, meeting basic organizational needs. This stage is further characterized by a lot of amateurism, the applications are limited to a number of 'computer islands' within the organization without any compatibility. The acquisition of these technological means is hardly planned and the control is decentralized.

Due to the success of the early experiments with computers other organizational participants are also stimulated to use these tools and the proliferation of ICT – the stage of expansion and contagion – sets in.

Because of the quickly rising expenditures on computers, resulting in a chaotic unplanned collection of computers, a crisis within organizations in this field originates.

Therefore, in the next stage – formalization or control – the organization's management becomes well aware of the necessity to interfere in this process; first of all to control the costs, temporarily preventing the attunement of computers to the real needs of the organization.

In the integration stage the integration of (computer) applications come forward, and also the alignment of information systems to organizations is an important target. Meanwhile, the interest of organizations shifts from computers to data and data bases.

In a subsequent article Nolan expanded his model from four to six stages, adding (Nolan, 1979):

- data administration and
- maturity.

In the data administration stage, next to the integration of computer systems already realized in the former stage, the management of databases is emphasized and its use is facilitated and stimulated. Also the design of companywide databases is an important activity in this stage, together with the creation of some slack resources to encourage the development of systems, making a contribution to the competitive position of organizations.

Finally, in the sixth stage – the maturity stage – an integrated policy can be identified, leading to an application portfolio of information systems satisfactorily matching the objectives of the organization.

However, in the extended version not did only the number of stages increase, but also instead of one sigmoid development pattern of ICT applications, Nolan now distinguished two such curves; the one succeeding the other, due to a technology shift between stage 3 and stage 4.

More recently a third development of Nolan's model emerged. Originally, he paid attention exclusively to database technology, but in an article in 1991 he broadened his view by distinguishing three categories of ICT instead of one, including the relevant patterns of expenditures (Nolan, 1991):
- database technology,
- work stations such as personal computers and
- computer networks.

The expenditure pattern of these three categories, taken together, shows, as opposed to the single categories' pattern, a sigmoid image.

Nolan makes the following assumptions about the usefulness of his stage model to control the organization's policy, especially applying ICT (Davis and Olson, 1984):
- organizations are able to learn from experiences in one stage permitting them to move to another easily,
- stages cannot be skipped because the experiences in one stage are a necessary condition for moving to the next; just as human beings become adult over a number of years, so do organizations using ICT,
- although organizations are confronted with growth processes, ruled by some sort of 'natural' laws, the activities in Nolan's stages can be controlled in order to move effectively and efficiently from one stage to another.

Obviously, in Nolan's stage model the concept of the 'learning' organization is rather dominant. As we said before, as with human beings, it takes organizations, passing through the several stages, time to become mature in the field of ICT. Attempts to accelerate this process, for instance by shortening or even skipping stages with the help of adequate measures will, in Nolan's view, have unacceptable consequences for the next stages.

In other words, Nolan assumes a development process to which organizations are inevitably submitted. Notwithstanding this 'natural' condition, it is helpful to have some insight in this process, because it makes the future of ICT less unpredictable. Though the future cannot be manipulated, the chance to make wrong decisions decreases. This insight, referring to ICT, is especially important because the growth process will start again and again everytime a radical innovation in this field is generated. (Davis and Olson, 1984).

If the management of the organization uses this growth model, Nolan distinguishes two different basic attitudes; called 'slack' and 'control'. On the one hand slack means an organization where departments are rather free to experiment with ICT approaches.

On the other hand control leads to very tight supervision. Depending on the specific stage one of these attitudes will dominate. For instance, in stage 5 (data administration) some slack is present to encourage the development of systems, contributing to the creation of strategic advantages for the organization, whereas in the preceding stage (integration) control is emphasized.

After some time Nolan's model has acquired a solid position in the practice of consultants.

As to its validity, Nolan's stage model can be criticized in several aspects. We will discuss the following:

1. lack of empirical support,
2. mechanistic organizational learning process,
3. one-sided image of organizations,
4. universal character of the model.

ad 1.

A number of students has examined the model's practical relevance and criticized it that way (Benbasat c.s., 1984). Also, Nolan himself tried to confirm his model; and with success, we believe. However, he is not willing to make his results public because of supposed commercial interests.

None of the other students, however, found sufficient support in their field research. The weak spots of Nolan's model refer, as far as its empirical background is concerned, to the characteristics of the different stages, the causal connections between them, and the causes of moving from one stage to another.

Incidentally, this lack of support does not mean that in our opinion Nolan's model should be dropped in the dustbin. First of all, in spite of the absence of data to confirm the model it is not falsified either. Secondly, it is often difficult to give situation dependent (contingent) models, like Nolan's, a solid empirical basis. Thirdly, growth processes show more or less continuous development patterns without spectacular changes from one stage to another. Fourthly, it is very unlikely that the departments of an organization are in the same stage together, making a unique identification of the organization's overall position rather difficult.

ad 2.

On the road to maturity, looking at human beings, we can observe a process of growth. Such a growth process is relevant for organizations as well. Growth is manifest in two fields: physical and mental. To grow in a physical way people and organizations need sufficient time, and it is almost impossible to pass over or even to compress stages. Like people organizations can be characterized by a life cycle, consisting of four different stages: introduction, expansion, stabilization and coming to an end.

As to mental processes, where the accumulation of knowledge and experience takes a central position, people and organizations are fundamentally different. An important characteristic of people is learning by having all sorts of experiences, rather than learning from others. Therefore, it is impossible for human beings, on their road to maturity, to pass over some stages (a metaphor Nolan uses for the learning process of organizations in the field of ICT).

As opposed to human beings, organizations do not have to discover all sorts of things themselves, because they are able to learn from others, for instance by using consultants, attending conferences, reading periodicals, hiring new personnel, etc.

So organizations are able to accelerate some of their growth processes and even to pass over certain stages. For example, the acquisition of licenses from other organizations in the technical field is, among other things, advantageous because assimilation – embedding the new technology in the own organization – costs are about half the costs of self generated inventions. Also time can be saved. For instance, the imitation period is only seventy per cent of the time necessary for the maturing of the original invention (Mansfield, 1981).

Therefore, the learning process in the field of ICT, as described by Nolan, is too compulsive. In other words, here the metaphor of the learning organization has been taken too far (Morgan, 1986).

ad 3.
As we have seen before, in Nolan's model, the metaphor of the learning organization takes a central position. This metaphor implies for organizations, in the field of ICT, that they will show growth mainly resulting from former experiences organized as a collective learning process. However, what is good for the organization as a whole, can be detrimental for some of its individual participants. This is because ICT may disturb the existing balance of power.

Therefore, looking at information and ICT we are not dealing with neutral phenomena; on the contrary, they absolutely will have impact on the decisions about this technology with results being rather difficult to predict (see also Chapter II and Chapter VII).

ad 4.
Nolan sees his model more or less as universally applicable, for instance by not differentiating between specific types of organizations. In several ways an organization typology may have some impact. For example, the intended degree of integration is heavily dependent upon the *structure* of organizations.

To illustrate this point of view, if we are confronted with a divisional organization structure, it is, as opposed to more centralized organizations, rather obvious that we should not seek integration at the corporate level.

This difference justifies the assumption that the growth process of a divisionalized organization structure at the corporate level will stick at the control stage. So we recommend in this situation to apply the Nolan model to the divisional level only.

Moreover, the concept 'integration' as such can be conceived in more than one way. Nolan sees it as a – stringent – coupling between a number of information systems within the organization. But we can imagine seeing integration on the *policy* level as well. This means that the organization has an integral policy vision not necessarily leading to a tight coupling of single information systems.

These four objections raise the question to what extent Nolan's stage model has still some practical relevance. Notwithstanding our criticism, in our opinion this model, if it is used carefully, can make a contribution to the acceleration of the learning process in the field of ICT. Applying it, organizations may save much time and money, meanwhile avoiding a lot of frustration.

Though, as demonstrated above, Nolan's growth model is useful if handled with care, we will also discuss other growth models. One such model, being less detailed, assumes that the application of new technology, and therefore also ICT, can be characterized by four stages (Bemelmans, 1987):
- initiation,
- diffusion,
- consolidation and
- integration.

This stage model is not only relevant for the introduction of complete new technologies but also for the improvement of existing ones. Therefore, organizations do not pass these stages once, but again and again. As a consequence, in a world with an increasing speed in the field of technological developments, a last stage of maturity, as the Nolan model supposes, will never be attained.

The advantage of this model, as opposed to Nolan's, refers to the possibility of making more general predictions, due to its more global character. Just because of its fine tuning, Nolan's model has lost some of its practical significance.

4. Task and position of the information centre

Within many organizations a central department, often called computer centre, occupied with the design and management of information systems, can be identified. In particular, this involvement is embodied in ICT components of these systems. Next to this task, the department has a role in formulating the organization's information policy on the several levels we distinguished in Chapter III.

In the beginning, actually in the sixties of the previous century, in such a department the organization's centralized computer system (normally a mainframe computer) took a very central position. Therefore, originally the term 'computer centre' was used. These centres had a number of tasks, to be summarized as follows:
- registration of data on tape or cards,
- input of tape and cards,
- operating computer systems,
- taking care of the output of data,
- installation and maintenance of computer hardware and software,
- developing software for the users.

Originally, computer centres were closed bulwarks of technical computer knowledge, shielded from the users.

Because of increasing miniaturization of computer technology and decreasing prices, at the beginning of the seventies of the previous century the first sign of deconcentration became visible, formed by terminals that facilitated the use of central computers at distant locations.*

And very soon, this tendency was followed by the deconcentration of computers, due to the development of mini and micro computers (also called personal computers; abbreviated: PC's). This process was accompanied by the circulation of knowledge in the field of computer software and hardware at many different locations within the organization, leading to an important loss of influence of the computer centres and eroding their power base.

Almost synchronous with this development, a change in the application of computers could be observed. In the beginning the storage and processing of data was emphasized especially by making large computations. But after some time the accent was shifting to the application of computers for management information systems.

One major characteristic of this category of information systems is more or less automatically providing managers with information about relevant issues at predetermined moments. This change in computer application also caused new requirements as to the functioning of computer centres; a change in the direction of the *design* of information systems. And with this shift, problems accumulated rapidly.

On the one hand these problems especially related, and still relate, to the background, education and culture of the computer centre's employees and to the characteristics of the users of information systems on the other hand. A number of these problems is already discussed in preceding chapters, for instance in Chapter I. Therefore, a summary suffices:

- communication gap between designers and users,
- the purpose, to develop information systems that users and designers have in mind,
- the designers' mechanical image of the world around them.

Originally, computer centres had hardly any incentive to behave in a client oriented way. At least three reasons for this attitude can be identified.

First of all every department within the organization was obliged to do business with the computer centre. So, competitive pressures were completely lacking.

Secondly, the application area of ICT changed drastically: after a period of applications to stimulate efficiency this technology became more and more a weapon on the competitive battle field. As opposed to efficiency applications, a cost/benefit analysis of competitive applications is very difficult. And as we will see later on in Chapter X this situation impedes the economic evaluation of such investments. As a result, a

---

* Related to this subject it is useful to point out the difference between the two pairs of concepts 'centralization/decentralization' and 'concentration/deconcentration'. Centralization/decentralization is about the location of control: higher or lower within the organization. Concentration/deconcentration refers to the location of computer hardware: one central location or several decentral locations.

Connected with this distinction a third pair of concepts deserves some attention: 'not ditributed/distributed' data processing. Here the location of data storage and processing is relevant: at one location or a number of locations.

careful analysis, before starting and after finishing investments in information systems, often was avoided and misfits were not detected.

Thirdly, it is, especially in larger organizations, common practice to determine budgets for a number of investment categories, such as ICT projects. This procedure implies the weakening of the competition between these categories to allocate scarce resources, meanwhile discouraging a thorough capital budgeting analysis. Also this approach hampers the possibilities to reveal the disfunctioning of computer centres.

In the course of the eighties of the previous century a change could be observed, due to three developments.

Primarily, organizations became more and more critical about the economic impact of expenditures in the field of ICT and about the role of computer centres stimulating these expenditures.

Secondly, a movement to delayer organizations, together with the liquidation or privatization of staff departments, including computer centres, emerged.

Thirdly, organizations revealed a strong tendency to restrict their activities to core business (Peters and Waterman, 1983). In such a vision, computer centres have hardly any position.

In addition to these three reasons, for computer departments that survived, the question became relevant whether the term 'computer centre' was still compatible with its drastically changing role. As to this issue nowadays the term 'information centre' is normally used. We pay attention to the position of the information centre in the nineties of the previous century below..

Due to the growth from computer centre to information centre, and as a consequence from a technical bulwark to a client oriented department, this department underwent a dramatic change of position. In this section we especially pay attention to the question in what way the institutionalized relations between information centre and clients, i.e. the position of the information centre in the structure of the organization, impedes or stimulates a more client orientated attitude.

As to this organizational setting we can distinguish between a number of possibilities:

1. organizational departments are obliged to do business with the information centre based on fixed budgets each period,
2. organizational departments are obliged to do business with the information centre, but now only the tariff structure is fixed,
3. organizational departments are free to do business with an information centre, inside or outside the organization, based on tariffs that can be negotiated.

ad 1.

In fact, from the organization's point of view, this situation hardly differs from the original position of the computer centre. The rest of the organization has the obligation to make use of the information centre's services. And so they will, not only due to the available resources, but also because of the possibility that parts of the budget, not being used, will not be added to the next year's budget. It is even possible that, not completely exhausting the budget in one period results in a budget reduction in the next period.

To the extent that the organization is not content with the services of the information centre, and the departments, in consultation with each other, are not able to solve this problem, the only way is to lodge a complant with the organization's management, because of its responsibility for the proper functioning of the information centre.

It may be clear that this organizational embedment has only limited impulses for a client oriented attitude for the information centre.

ad 2.

In this situation, as opposed to the former situation, the rest of the organization is no longer obliged to spend a fixed amount of money on ICT. In fact ICT expenditures have to compete with expenditures in other fields directly. As a result, a thorough analysis of the alternative uses of scarce resources must be made. In spite of the fixed tariff structure in this situation, there will be an impulse for a more client oriented approach of the information centre, because of the direct competition between ICT and other possible investment categories.

Not only has such an approach psychological effects but it will also force the information centre to make attempts to identify the real wishes of its clients, meanwhile increasing the quality of its products considerably.

Nevertheless, as to this element of client orientation we should warn against over high expectations. Though in this situation there is some sort of competition, this competition relates to fields that are often very difficult to compare with each other; for instance a choice has to be made between expansion of the machinery and new information systems. And because of the hyped character of some of the expenditures in this latter category we can srongly doubt the process of carefully identifying pros and cons.

ad 3.

In this situation the information centre has to compete directly with the suppliers of similar products outside the organization. And just like all sorts of competition between organizations, the information centre must adopt an attitude based on market conformity, i.e. it should offer products with an acceptable price/quality rate as perceived by its customers.

This is a position of the information centre that will be realized in an increasing number of organizations: partial or total privatization.

And here the former behaviour of the information centre is a major road block. Because of a lack of client orientation in the past many users of information systems developed a hostile attitude towards the information centre. As a consequence, as soon as organizational departments have the authority to decide with whom they can do business, the inside information centre has a rather low priority.

This strengthens the tendency to buy ICT products outside the organization. In fact, guaranteeing the quality of products is not only a matter of generating a good product, nor a matter of keeping the quality of the previous process, but especially a matter of mentality, of quality consciousness.

In so far as the information centre in this situation does not have a specific strategic meaning for the organization, it will disappear after some time, because it is not viable without support from top management.

Such a development, however, may raise a number of problems if top management has the opinion that it is desirable to have some expertise within the organization in the field of ICT. To realize this, there is no other way than to provide the information centre with some minimal resources in order to guarantee its survival and a limited number of critical ICT functions. In this situation it is, because of the need to keep the expertise on a satisfactory level, obvious that small budgets are allocated to the several departments, c.q. they get some drawing rights, corresponding with this minimum package. Additionally, or alternatively, the information centre can be charged with the design and management of information systems at the organization's central level, called concern systems.

In the latter situation of limited budget allocation, combined with departmental drawing rights, some mix between situation 1 and situation 3 is actually present, though the departments are free not to use the capacity they are entitled to. However, if they abandon this right of 'costless' services, then they have to pay external suppliers for it. This is also a matter of the price/quality rates that can be offered by both.

We will finish this section by a remark about the way the changes in the task and position of the computer centre, or information centre respectively, are able to make a contribution to cover the failure factors in the field of information systems, identified in Chapter I. The tendency of this development can be seen as an increase of the information centre's client orientation . And this orientation is an important guarantee for the users to get what they really want. In doing so, a major cause of the short fall of information systems will be eliminated.

5. Outsourcing of ICT

As has already been mentioned in the preceding section, organizations reveal a tendency to return to their core business. As a consequence, this tendency means laying off a number of tasks and activities. If laying off concerns the organization's primary process, then we are dealing with the so-called 'make or buy' decision. If, however, laying off refers to facilitating or supporting processes, then the concept *outsourcing* is used. Therefore, outsourcing of ICT means (Beulen, c.s., 1994):

> *the transfer of the exploitation and management of a combination of ICT devices, based on a long term contract containing the specification of the products/services involved and the price that has to be paid*

As to ICT, we distinguish three outsourcing models as far as the degree of the transmission of activities in this technological field to other companies is concerned:
- body shop outsourcing,
- project management outsourcing,
- total outsourcing.

Body shop outsourcing
Body shop outsourcing relates to solve short term problems mostly realized by hiring personnel from outside ICT agencies on an ad hoc basis.

Project management outsourcing
Project management outsourcing is more radical than the former model, meaning that complete ICT projects are executed by others; the exploitation of these projects, however, is an internal affair.

Total outsourcing
In its most radical form, complete ICT systems with all its parts are managed by experts from outside the organization, called 'total outsourcing'.

Outsourcing not only has advantages, but has a number of disadvantages as well. Speaking about advantages we must especially think about:
- decreasing costs of the application of ICT; because of large scale economies which the ICT company is able to realize, the costs forgone by the buyer are less than the costs generated by the supplier, leading to a net advantage for both,
- closely connected with this first advantage, outsourcing offers the opportunity for the organization to get rid of inconvenient additional activities and to concentrate on core business; this starting point also leads to a decision not to outsource ICT if the relation between this technology and core business is too close,
- outsourcing (of ICT) creates the opportunity to take advantage of the newest developments in the field of ICT; the monitoring of these developments is one of the fundamental tasks of the supplier.

Outsourcing of ICT also has some disadvantages, such as:
- the organization has to pay for the services and products it buys from outside,
- outsourcing, especially if it is far-reaching such as total outsourcing, often is an irreversible process; if the road of outsourcing is covered considerably then it is hardly feasible to turn back; this weakens the organization's negotiation position if the contract has to be renewed,
- in addition to the costs for services rendered, just like other forms of rights and duties that are laid down in a contract, a specific category of costs can be identified: transaction costs.

With this latter disadvantage we meet the problem of weighing up the pros and cons of market and hierarchy, applying ICT. If an organization has disposal over ICT means of its own, then it is able to guarantee the quality of these services, using direct supervision; meaning that coordination takes place by the hierarchy principle. If ICT services are taken over by others, then the possibility of direct supervision is missing and the market, i.e. the price mechanism, is used as a coordination device.

Because outsourcing is a rather complex matter referring to the transaction costs involved, this topic will be discussed in more detail below.

Finally, outsourcing may have a specific disadvantage, becoming more and more important. This disadvantage is related to a dominant reason why organizations use outsourcing: return to the core business. If organizations, as can be illustrated with a lot of examples, want to improve their processes and/or products radically, then for most of the time ICT plays a dominant role. Thus, to get competitive advantages, this technology is of increasing strategic importance. And outsourcing has to be handled with care if ICT can be considered as a part of the organization's core business.

To shed more light on this matter we pay attention to the reasons why organizations did outsource ICT in the past and what attitude vis-a-vis this phenomenon will be required in the future.

Until recently, one of the most important considerations to outsource ICT was cost reduction. However, based on research in the United States in only 39% of the cases has this target been realized, whereas in 4% the costs were even higher than before (Blejie, 1998). Other considerations to outsource this technology refer to the point of view that its strategic role was unimportant or even absent and that it did not belong to the organization's core business.

This first consideration especially is a very dangerous one because the advantages of outsourcing ICT are not so much lower costs (efficiency) but higher income (effectiveness), to be realized by additional opportunities offered by the vendor of ICT services. So, looking back at the outsourcing models discussed above, we have to distinguish between a number of target levels organizations could intend to realize using the instrument of outsourcing:

- comfort,
- costs,
- control,
- change,
- competence.

Comfort

The quality of the present service level of information systems has to be improved, for instance by means of a helpdesk.

Costs

Here the organization's target is to reduce the cost/benefit ratio; among other things to be realized by standardization.

Control

Now it is the organization's intention to increase its internal control using the outsourcing instrument.

Change

In order to improve its flexibility to react to market changes (time-to-market) outsourcing may be considered.

Competence

At this level the organization aims to use ICT as an important instrument to innovate its products and transform business processes. To be well informed about recent developments and the ability to use them adequately is very important here.

With these five target levels in mind organizations are able to make well-considered decisions about the role of outsourcing of ICT adapted to there specific situation and the preferred model to be used to make it more concrete.

An important aspect of outsourcing refers to transaction costs. Generally speaking, these costs can be split up as follows (Williamson, 1985):
- costs of looking for a supplier (market survey),
- costs of contract negotiations,
- costs of monitoring the way the contract is executed,
- costs of reinforcement of the contract terms that have been agreed upon.

That market surveys cost money, just like negotiations about contracts, is probably not astonishing for anybody. However, the cause of the other two cost categories is perhaps less obvious.

As a matter of fact, the transaction cost theory assumes that the parties, contracting with each other, will try to minimize their duties as much as possible (opportunistic behaviour), or by creating a wrong impression using false information (this is a case of information asymmetry) about fulfilling their obligations. As to this topic the buyer takes more risks than the supplier because he has to make clear in detail what he expects from the supplier. The supplier, however, is in a favourable position because it suffices to formulate the customer's compensation using an unambiguous yard stick: money.

Moreover, if one of both parties discovers disperformance by the orther one, costs sometimes have to be made to force him to do what has been agreed upon.

As to their size, transaction costs are influenced by:
1. the degree of transaction specific investments,
2. the degree of uncertainty,
3. the transactions' frequency,
4. the degree of competition between potential suppliers.

ad 1.
Because of the specific wishes of the customer the supplier has sometimes to make specific investments. Normally, these investments only have limited value for other customers. Therefore, the customer who asks for transaction specific investments has to pay the whole amount, leading to increasing transaction costs.

As an organization transmits more activities in the field of ICT to others, the necessity to make transaction specific investments also increases. This feature will considerably diminish the customer's propensity to outsource its ICT projects. To the extent that, from this point of view, outsourcing takes place it is at a minimal level, i.e. body shop outsourcing instead of project management outsourcing or total outsourcing.

ad 2.
As a transaction is characterized by more uncertainty, the chance of information asymmetry and opportunistic behaviour will increase, also leading to more transaction costs

and a decrease in the propensity to use outsourcing. Rather simple ICT activities such as body shop outsourcing are less uncertain than total outsourcing. Also this feature means that, just like the preceding one, outsourcing has to be low profile.

ad 3.
If organizations agree upon long term contracts, then contract negotiations will occur less frequently. Moreover, this frequency influences the experience to be acquired in the past as to these contract negotiations if other potential suppliers are considered. From this we may conclude: the less frequently contracts are effected the more effort has to be made to come to an agreement with other suppliers and the bigger the chance to get stuck with the present supplier.

Also this feature has a relation to the degree of outsourcing in such a way that the more radical the form of outsourcing the longer the contract period will be.

ad 4.
If customers only have one supplier they will have the propensity to invest more effort in concract negotiations compared with a situation with a number of potential suppliers. As a matter of fact, in this latter situation with other suppliers the need to settle the contract in every detail is reduced.

In addition to the considerations above we want to make some remarks about the influence of the culture of organizations in respect of the phenomenon of outsourcing. A first aspect concerns the way organizations look at the issue of make or buy decisions. Particularly smaller organizations prefer, because of some mistaken pride, to do things themselves as much as possible. And these organizations especially could, because of their limited economies of scale, gain a lot if they hived off specific parts of the primary and/or facilitating processes.

A second consideration refers to the culture differences between suppliers and customers in the field of outsourcing, in particular keeping their duties and promises. Because even if contracts are very detailed, it is absolutely impossible for the contract to contain every contingency whatsoever. Therefore, both contract parties must trust each other. If one party is not trustworthy, then the other is always in a disadvantageous position. In this latter situation it would, because of the necessary symmetry in the relation, be better for both parties to have the same culture in this respect; either no one of them can be trusted or both are trustworthy.

We finish this section with a short reproduction of the results of two recent research projects in the field of outsourcing of ICT (DeLooff, 1996; IDC, 1998). We start with some figures from the first project (DeLooff, 1996). Outsourcing contracts have a mean term of three years and an amount of two million dollars. Technical support dominates (70%), followed by application development and network design.

The advantages of outsourcing are seen as:
- cost reduction,
- higher service level,

- concentration on core business,
- admittance to advanced technologies.

As opposed to these advantages, disadvantages are also mentioned:
- decreased worker motivation,
- the supplier lacks flexibility
- quickly increasing cost of ICT services,
- too much dependence on one specific supplier.

A remarkable result of this research relates to the tendency not to renew a number of contracts, because of the revealed disadvantages.

Additionally, decisions about outsourcing have some specific features, such as being:
- made in a short time,
- made by the top management,
- made without a thorough analysis.

Moreover, the research points out that long term relations with more than one supplier combined with outsourcing agreements about short term contracts as parts of a framework agreement are rather fruitful. Furthermore, for outsourcing it is important that organizations have sufficient knowledge about ICT at their disposal in order to control suppliers effectively.

The second research project concerns the hundred biggest contracts for outsourcing in Europe in 1997, together amounting to twenty billion dollars (IDC, 1998). This research indicates the following developments:
- increasingly clients prefer so-called 'selective outsourcing': instead of complete computer centres only specific parts – such as application management, maintenance of networks and helpdesks – of the information function are outsourced,
- based on the previous development mega contracts occur less frequently than before; more than 50% of the contracts already relates to amounts less than fifty million dollars,
- increasingly suppliers of ICT services cooperate to take advantage of the strengths of each other.

VI PROJECT MANAGEMENT

1. Introduction

After the information policy of organizations, as discussed in the preceding chapter, is settled down on the various levels that can be distinguished, it is necessary to be more specific about this policy, focussing on single information projects. Hence, this chapter contains a number of guidelines for elaborating the fourth level of information policy from Chapter IV.

In order to reach the desired result, i.c. information systems coming up to the expectations of the users, a number of methods and techniques is used to support the execution of information projects, to be divided into three categories:
- project management methods,
- general design methods,
- specific design methods.

This chapter focuses on methods in the field of project management. General design methods will be discussed in the next chapter. The next chapter also pays some attention to specific design methods. In this chapter we define the concept 'project' as follows:

a project is composed of a number of activities aimed at reaching a clearly specified unique target

Since the target is unique, the project organization involved is also a unique matter, and the project team will be dissolved as soon as the target is reached. For each single project, a new project organization will be formed, depending on the specific features of the project. The same is true for the composition of the project teams in terms of people and necessary expertise.

In shaping the project organization of single information projects it is of the utmost importance to be aware of the specific characteristics of these projects such as complexity and uncertainty. It is not very efficient, for instance, to use for a simple project a project organization, that was actually meant to deal with complex projects. Overshooting in the field of information projects should be avoided.

2. Organizing information projects

In project management shortfalls of ICT projects are often due to the following causes:
- the target of the project is too ambitious,
- the project's structure is too complex,
- support within the organization, especially from (top) management is insufficient.

To deal with these critical success factors adequately, project control, as a substantial part of the project organization, is absolutely essential.

As we mentioned in the preceding section, the design of information systems is a matter of single projects needing an ad hoc project organization; an organization *structure*. This structure facilitates *organizing* the project, i.e. leading it towards its target.

Before discussing the project structure in the next section, we identify the main project characteristics:
- projects are divided into a number of stages,
- at the end of each stage projects are evaluated,
- during the project execution the project management can mobilize additional people and/or resources,
- the target of the project becomes increasingly detailed during the project's execution period,
- the composition of the project teams usually exceeds the hierarchical and functional structure of the organization as the basis for the grouping of departments,
- the project leads with a limited budget within a limited period of time to a unique – globally specified – result.

Now we will discuss these characteristics of projects in more detail.

Project stages

Because of the necessary control of projects in terms of time and money it is important to split up projects in a number of parts that can be dealt with rather easily one after another. Hence, several stages can be distinguished. Such a phasing is especially relevant for big (and complex) projects. Due to this phasing all people involved are, as opposed to an undivided whole, confronted with well-organized, parts that are easy to control.

Systems Development Methodology is a project control method, especially developed for information projects, and will be discussed in section 3.

Regular evaluation

In addition to the phasing of information projects milestones have to be specified. Such milestones define semi-finished products to be realized at the end of each stage, in terms of:
- quality (specifications),
- time and
- money.

Therefore, milestones mark the end of a single stage and the beginning of the next one. Moreover, we only have a stage transition if all parties involved have accepted the semi-fished product, based on the characteristics just mentioned.

Finally, it is very important to finish a stage well-documented. So, it is possible to use this documentation if necessary.

Mobilization of additional people and/or resources
Within the regular structure of organizations people and departments have resources at their disposal more or less permanently, based on some sort of budgeting system: fixed, variable, mixed or flexible. In this situation most organizational activities can be budgeted accurately, based on many years of experience, and so they will lead to rather reliable forecasts for the near future.

In the situation of unique projects too, organizations normally have some experience with a number of similar projects in the past, which is helpful for the budgeting of new projects.

Because of the unique features of each project, however they are sometimes full of surprises. Therefore, the project management needs sufficient authority, of course within clearly defined constraints, to mobilize additional people and/or resources if necessary, in order to satisfy the milestone criteria and to reach the project's target at the end of each stage.

Especially for a realistic and credible project planning, it is very important for the client to limit unpleasant surprises to the absolutely minimum, and, if they are inescapable, to give an adequate explanation.

Moreover, in respect of the acceptance of the project when finished, we recommend creating possible choices between additional cost, less quality (i.e. limited functionality of information systems) and delayed delivery, to be discussed with the client very thoroughly.

Detailing the project's target
As we will also see in section 4 of this chapter, on Systems Development Methodology, project targets initially are rather global and will be detailed more and more, stage after stage. In the first stage, this global specification of the final product is compatible with a number of solutions in the field of information systems. But in the last stage these specifications must be detailed in such a way that a completely specified information system results. Because of a number of reasons this design strategy from global to detailed is a rather obvious approach.

First of all, the identification of the – future – needs of the users of information systems during the design process is important because of the interrelation between these needs and the technical opportunities to shape information systems.

Secondly, the potential user is often not completely aware of his information needs, especially when the design process is started; an issue to be discussed in more detail in the next chapter.

Thirdly, the procedure from global to detailed, has the advantage for user and designer that there is time available to get acquainted with each other.

Returning to the former characteristic of information projects, discussed above – the mobilization of additional people and/or resources – a 'target refining' procedure offers the opportunity to adapt the original project plan, if necessary, in a number of ways in order to maintain an acceptable expected price/quality rate.

Exceeding the normal organization structure
Apart from our remarks about the structure of (information) projects (see section 3 of this chapter) we notice that the composition of project teams is usually based on the need of a – limited – number of specific experts. In some cases it is also possible to recruit experts from outside the organization.

Thus, during the length of the project the project team members have to work in a completely different setting, as far as their boss, their collegues and their subordinates are concerned. Not surprisingly, the people involved must have the necessary capacity of adaptation. However, especially if some team members are not occupied full time, the danger of a loyalty conflict arises. In such a situation it is important to make clear arrangements about people's availability for the project.

As we will see below, in the next section, a double loyalty is especially relevant for the members of the steering committee.

Limited resources
In discussing the topic 'from global to detailed' we already mentioned the possibility of such an approach resulting in a change of the initial project planning that will not be wellcomed by the client, i.e. the project leads to more development time and/or more costs and/or a negative change of the information project's functionality.

It is a major task of the project management to watch over the use of the resources available in an efficient and an effective way.

This remark seems to be rather obvious. But, if we remember the results of a number of research projects about the success or failure of information systems and the development and management costs involved, as mentioned in Chapter I, then it is clear these problems need a lot of attention.

In discussing general design methods in the next chapter, we will return to this topic.

3. The organization structure of information projects

Apart from the meaning of the concept 'organization' as shaping the project, i.e. organizing, we can interpret organization as the project's *structure*. This issue will be discussed in the present section.

The whole of the people involved in the project, together responsible for the final result, is called the *project team*. So, it is possible for a project team to consist of more than one task group. And dealing with information projects, this is a normal situation.

A *task group* can be defined as a group of people, within the project (team), having a specific assignment.

At the top of the hierarchy of the project team, usually a *steering committee* can be identified. And this steering committee controls one or more *project groups*.

Finally, project groups can be assisted by *work groups*. Before discussing the role of these groups in more detail we can schematically represent the project's structure as follows (Figure V.1):

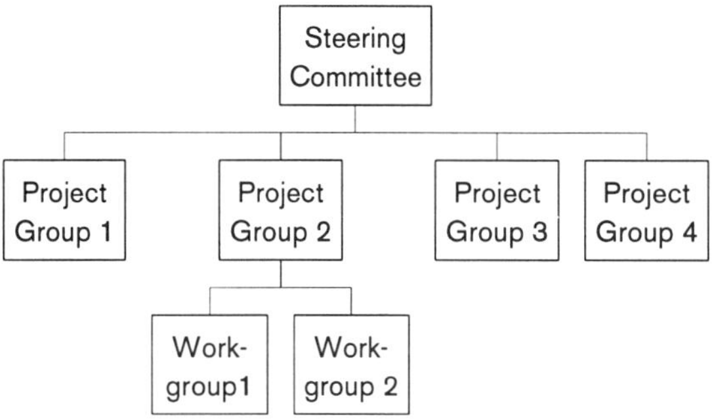

Figure VI.1

The steering committee

In Chapter V we spoke about a stepwise interpretation of the information policy of organizations, meaning that, after determining the organization's strategy and the role of ICT, seperate information projects cannot be executed until the information architecture and the information project planning are also specified.

Therefore, organizations have to take care of the fitting of information projects within the broader field of their overall policy. If not, organizations will develop probably a number of rather isolated – incompatible – information systems.

With this problem in mind, the most important task of the steering committee can be identified as: making a connection between a number of single information projects and the organization's overall policy.

Because of this task it is almost obvious that the steering committee must have its chair occupied by a member of the highest management; especially whoever is charged with the organization's information policy.

Next to this linking function of the steering committee, executed in particular by the chairman, two other reasons to charge top management with its chair are relevant. First of all, in doing so, decisions about changes in the intitial project design can be made quickly.

And secondly, involvement of the top managment is an absolute condition for the success of information projects, as the results of a lot of research point out (Doll, 1987).

In addition to its primary task – the mutual coordination of single projects and the linking of these projects with the organization's strategic policy – the steering committee has a second task: the coordination of the activities of the project groups. This coordination is necessary because of two reasons.

Primarily, the steering committee functions as a forum for the exchange of experiences of the project groups; so, they can learn from each other.

Secondly, sometimes it is necessary to make shifts between current projects as to their speed of development as well as to the people or the resources, or both, at their disposal. In other words, the steering committee is also charged with the determination of – political loaden priorities and posteriorities between the groups involved.

Besides its chair, the steering committee consists of a number of other members. For instance, the manager of the information centre, in some organizations called computer centre, has to be a member, just like the chairmen of the project groups.

As a rule, the members of the steering committee are not full time occupied with the committee's activities. Thus, perhaps the problem of a double loyalty may arise. To solve this problem in advance clear agreements about hours spent, and time available, for the committee have to be made.

The project group

Project groups are occupied with the actual execution of information projects. Therefore, not only designers but also – future – users have undoubtedly to be members of these groups.

Here the concept 'user' must be interpreted rather broadly, because the information system should not only come up to the needs of its direct users but has also to be compatible with already existing systems, including current – adminstrative – procedures.

In summary, next to the categories of people already mentioned, project groups will have to be composed by members of the information centre, the administration department, etc.

The project group is especially the place where external expertise can be mobilized; an opportunity that will certainly be utilized for a second opinion if internal experts are charged with the development of information systems.

And also if the project development is an external affair it does no harm if the project team gets independent advice about hardware and software.

As to their participation in project groups the members are usually occupied full time, so, they have no tension, referring to the problem of a double loyalty. Nevertheless, if a loyalty conflict would rise here, then clear agreements can help to solve it.

The work group

Under specific conditions it is sometimes necessary to do additional research in certain fields if the project group has too little expertise or lacks time. In such a situation the project group can use the work group model to clarify some matters.

As to the quality of the members of the work group, of course they must have sufficient expertise to solve the specific project group problem. Moreover, we also recommend adding to the work group some members of the project group in order to facilitate efficient communication between both groups.

As far as the membership of work groups is part time, and so a double loyalty may be possible, clear agreements are necessary.

4. Systems Development Methodology

In this section we return to the subject 'Systems Development Methodology' (abbreviated SDM), also called 'cascade' model.

We pay attention to this method here because of three reasons.

First of all, SDM was, and probably still is, a very popular information systems design method.

Secondly, SDM has a rather bad reputation, not because of its intrinsic qualities but due to the way it is often applied.

Thirdly, in connection with the two former points, SDM can, in our opinion, be very helpful in facilitating information systems' design.

Though SDM, as a project control method, is more broadly applicable, we will only judge its usefulness from the point of view of the requirements in the field of information system design.

To identify this usefullness we continue with a short discussion of SDM. Before doing so, we pay attention to the difference of organizing information projects (see section 2 and 3 of this chapter) and SDM.

The subject 'organizing information projects' is especially about the *structure* of these projects; in other words the relations between players in the field and the rules they have to obey. SDM, however, refers to the *process* that, combined with adequate design methods, helps to attain the intended result.

SDM is developed by PANDATA, an agency for information systems design, founded by a number of large companies.

After a version draft in the mid seventies, in 1985 a revised version was published, well-known as SDM-II (Turner, c.s. 1985).

The assumptions of SDM can be summarized as follows:

- information projects are planned and developed,
- information projects are controlled and organized by splitting up these projects into manageable parts,
- information projects are administered in detail, combined with an extensive systems documentation.

As to this second principle we emphasize that it is not the intended information system – the project result – that is split up in a number of parts, but the design process – the project road – which is divided into several stages.

According to SDM we distinguish between the following stages:

0. information planning,
1. definition study,
2. global design,
3. specific design,
4. realization,
5. implementation,
6. exploitation and management.

Apart from the stage of 'information planning', that actually does not belong to the design process and therefore has the code '0', as does the stage 'exploitation and management', we can, looking at this enumeration conclude that, after the identification of information requirements in the 'definition study' stage, step by step the specification of the intended information system becomes more and more detailed; particularly in the stages 'global design' and 'specific design'.

After these two stages the developers retreat in order to develop the information system in the 'realization' stage.

At the end of this stage the acid test is made, because now the question has to be answered whether the system really comes up to the needs of the users. Therefore, the realization stage is completed with an acceptance test.

If the test succeeds then the 'implementation' stage begins. In this stage three points of attention are relevant:

- the implementation of the information system as such,
- the transfer of the information system to the organization and
- a first evaluation of the information system.

As opposed to the acceptance test, in this – implementation – stage the users get their first experience with the information system operating in the organizational context.

After this short explanation of SDM we notice that this method explicitly pays attention to the stage *following* the implementation of information systems: application and management.

As we will see in the next chapter, this is a very important aspect of SDM because the design route of information projects is often not completely finished after delivering the system; on the contrary, delivering an information system refers to a specific moment during an ongoing design process at which designers and users agree that the result of the design process so far has sufficient functionality to be useful in daily practice.

In other words, the design process of an information system does not actually come to an end until the decision is taken to use it, or to replace it. And even then, in this latter case, the thesis of an ongoing design process still holds.

As we will see in Chapter VII, such a process like approach of the design of information systems is characteristic for most methods belonging to the category 'general design methods', such as prototyping, evolutionary design methods and Rapid Application Development.

In the several stages of SDM, attention is paid to a number of facets, in regard of the planning of information systems as well as their realization; for instance:

- the target of each stage, defined as semi-finished product to be reached, or the specification of the various milestones,
- the construction of an activity network, normally by using network planning, c.q. critical path analysis,
- the identification of the possible relations with former products, or information systems respectively.

Above we have, because of experiences with SDM in the past, spoken about rather negative evaluations of this method. An important reason for such evaluations is, as we call it, the confusion between the 'conceptual' and the 'operational' structuring of the design process of information systems, to be interpreted as follows.

If we describe methods in any field whatsoever, then we do this on paper or in any other medium. And if such a method consists of a number of stages, this description is based on some, rational, sequential order. This structuring in writing we call the 'conceptual' structuring of the method involved.

However, this conceptual structuring does not imply precisely the same following order of the method's stages if it is applied to solve a practical problem; the 'operational' structuring.

And that is exactly the mistake often made, when applying SDM in the past. Too often the description of SDM is interpreted as a blueprint for the design process of information systems, just like the use of a cooking book with recipes, which has to be executed in linear way, strictly following the steps and stages that have been described. In this situation we have a perfect identification of the 'operational' and the 'conceptual' structuring of the process involved.

Because of such an identification, shortcomings observed after finishing a specific stage can hardly be compensated, due to the blueprint approach, and will influence the final result, leading to negative consequences for acceptance by the users.

This is especially problematic if the detected mistakes cause an adaptation of the final product's specification. In such a situation we need circular design methods instead of linear ones. Circular methods are methods making possible the adaptation of the semi-finished products of former stages, if necessary. So, we are dealing with a circular design process.

Circularity of the design process is especially realized, using so-called 'general design' methods; methods that have already been mentioned in the previous section such as prototyping, evolutionary development methods and Rapid Application Development (see Chapter VII).

In addition to a lack of circularity, a second reason why SDM has failed in the past can be identified. As to this specific reason we have to think about so-called 'turn key' approaches designing information systems.

Such an approach has the following characteristic. After identifying the information requirements of the user organization in the stage of the definition study, the designers retreat to build the intended information system. And after some time the complete system is delivered. The user only has to turn the key in order to get the system operational.

Evidently, such an approach will only lead to an acceptable result if we can make the assumption that the information requirements can be sufficiently identified beforehand and that these needs do not change during the design process. As we have seen in Chapter II, discussing organic systems, this assumption usually is an illusion. The nature of the problem situation, i.c. the nature of the information requirements is, because of a number of limitations, only evident when one or more stages of the design process have been already passed (see also Chapter VII).

Both shortcomings mentioned – lack of circularity and turn key approach – raise the question in what way SDM still can be helpful in the process of designing information systems in the future.

First of all, we already warned against interpreting this methodology as a blue print of the design process; on the contrary, it is only meant as an enumeration of things to be remembered explicitly during this process, regardless of its sequential order. Using SDM this way, enough circularity is guaranteed.

Secondly, a turn key approach is not characteristic for the design process prescribed by SDM. Just like the so-called 'interactive' design methods to be discussed in Chapter VII, SDM offers the opportunity to involve, if necessary, the potential user permanently in the design process after the definition study in order to guarantee an adequate problem definition.

Thirdly, other categories of design methods are available: methods to which we will return in the next chapter, so-called general design methods, as a complement to more global project management methods such as SDM, offering opportunities to get the necessary flexibility for the specification of the user organization's information requirements.

Therefore, if we take sufficient precautions, as discussed above, we are sure that SDM in the future is very much helpful in designing information systems that really do what the user has in mind.

Finally, though meant as a project management method to facilitate the design process of information systems, with SDM we have a method also useful to manage large projects in other fields. For instance in the housing sector, especially referring to buildings, and other large projects. Remembering the exceeding of costs and time that often have been reported, SDM could be of great value.

VII DESIGN AND MANAGEMENT METHODS

1. Introduction

In designing information systems, a very important step is the identification of the information needs of the user organization, called information analysis. For instance this activity is in SDM located in the definition study stage.

In the past it was usually assumed that the identification of the information needs could be simply effected by asking the user organization. For instance this assumption explains the linear application of design methods like SDM (see Chapter VI). If designers are sufficiently familiar with the information needs at the beginning of the design process, there is no reason to return to this subject in the next stages, actually leading to a linear design process.

However, the identification of information needs by questioning users and/or by interviews assumes, among other things, a user sufficiently informed about the requirements the information has to meet. And this is an absolute misperception.

According to Davis and Olson users have three handicaps in this field (Davis and Olson, 1984):

1. concreteness,
2. recency bias and
3. anchoring.

ad 1.

People are bombarded by data every day, only a small fraction of which is used. And this fraction is heavily dependent on the data's *form.* As a matter of fact people tend to use data appealing in form. For instance, visually oriented people prefer data displayed in graphical form or pie charts, instead of data in a tabular form.

Such behaviour is relevant to the perception of information needs. Actually, these needs are heavily dependent upon the – selective collection – of data used in the past, due to the user's preferences. Some data, though not available in the form preferred, but still relevant to improving future performance, will not only be neglected but their significance, as far as information needs have to be identified, is clearly undervalued.

ad 2.

To the extent that events happened in the more distant future, people tend more and more to underestimate these events in regard of their present behaviour. Data used recently will, as opposed to data used some time ago, be perceived as more important.

So the identification of information needs based on data used by people in organizations is biased.

ad 3.
In Chapter II we paid attention to the phenomenon of 'mental models' in relation to the philosophical/epistemological trend of so-called 'constructivism'. These mental models actually offer an anchoring point for people to observe the world around them.

Consequently, such an approach means that some observations are valued very much, because they fit the image people have constructed about the real world, whereas other observations, conflicting with this image, usually are put aside as (hindering) exceptions, or are even neglected.

And in the same way our behaviour is shaped in formulating information needs. Only observations – data – confirming our image of the world around us are used for the identification of our (future) information needs.

If the world were rather stable, then it would be no problem. However, due to environmental turbulence mental models may become obsolete, leading to misperceptions of information needs.

To these three handicaps, identifying information needs by questioning people, two others can be added:

- the user's need for *ir*relevant information and
- the presence of controversies between users and designers/developers of information systems.

In Chapter II we distinguished a number of concepts such as relevant and irrelevant information. From the definitions we gave it is rather obvious that for employees in organizations and their functioning in well-defined structures, only relevant information comes to our minds.

Furthermore, the hierarchical position of people within these (formal) structures is the basis for their authority and power.

However, a major part of the organizational power of people is based on the informal power structure, directly coupled with the informal organization structure (see also Chapter VIII where the power phenomenon of organizations, related to information, will be discussed in detail).

Referring to the informal organization structure we do not look at the way organizational participants cooperate, according to the formal organizational rules, but at how the cooperative and informational relations are really shaped. So we can identify within organizations people who have an extensive (information) network; information networks only partly important for their well-functioning within the framework of the formal organization structure and the execution of the tasks they are charged with. For the rest these networks are especially important to strengthen the power basis of the people involved; actually, information is power (see Chapter VIII).

In so far as that information, though it may be of a pure businesslike character, is not directly useful for people's tasks and functional position, we are dealing with *irrelevant* information.

A second form of irrelevant information can be identified, too. Now, we have to think about information not being useful for tasks and/or functions as such, but creating some additional prestige, c.q. power. For instance, this refers to the gossips in organizations giving some status to people who are informed in advance, thus leading to a strengthening of their power basis.

Therefore, both categories of irrelevant information are more or less a goal of their own; as opposed to relevant information, to be seen as a means to reach another target, i.e. the execution of the tasks people are charged with.

For the identification of information needs, it is of the utmost importance to distinguish between relevant and irrrelevant information, especially as far as pure businesslike information is concerned in order to recognize the first category.

For designers of information systems this is normally not a simple instruction, because they need thorough knowledge about all the organization's tasks and functions, including the mutual relations.

Remembering what is said in the previous chapter about (information) project management and the composition of project groups, we suggest to consider the possibility of including also organization experts in these groups, if necessary.

The second category of irrelevant information we distinguish – irrelevant no-businesslike information – is easier to identify and can be handled according to the specific situation to be investigated.

Between users and designers, c.q. developers, of information systems, two controversies can be identified, both having repercussions for the final product after finishing the design process.

As to these controversies we must think about:

- a controversy in the field of communication between users and designers of information systems and
- a controversy in respect of the desired properties of information systems from the point of view of the user and of the designer respectively.

As far as the communication controversy is concerned, this is about the communication gap between both parties, described in many books and articles.

In their contacts with users, the designers of information systems have their own jargon, which users often do not understand sufficiently. And as far as this jargon contains concepts familiar to the users we sometimes come across a different meaning for the same words and concepts. As an example we can think about the concept 'information analysis' as used by the designers of information systems. As opposed to what might be expected here they do not mean the identification of information needs as such, but the data needs resulting from information needs.

Not until both groups – users and designers of information systems – speak the same language, will there be a basis for mutual communication in the real sense of the word.

The second controversy relates to the difference between users and designers as far as the goal of the new information system is concerned: the aspiration gap. Users often only look for ordinary information systems, helping them a little bit further in daily practice. Designers, however, have the intention of building advanced information systems in order to increase their professional prestige and/or to create possibilities to write articles for – scientific – periodicals, meanwhile without explicitly posing the question whether the user really benefits from such a system.

By the way, this technical orientation, instead of a more client-oriented attitude is not exclusively the domain of designers of information systems. In other fields, such approaches are also present. For instance, we can think about the big manuals that have to be studied before people are able to use their purchases in the field of consumer electronics effectively.

It should also not surprise us, remembering what is said about this subject in Chapter II, that the a priori identification of the desired characteristics of information systems is an almost impossible assignment.

In the chapter just mentioned we noticed: in a situation with complex problems, such as the design of information systems, it is not realistic to assume our ability to formulate problems sufficiently in the early stage of the decision making process.

And as yet, the list of problems to identify the information needs of the – potential – users of information systems is not completed. Not only is it very difficult, if not impossible, to identify the information needs before the design process is started, but afterwards, if the design process is going on, additional problems will be met. These problems are caused by the dynamics of the design process as such and by the dynamics of the world around us, particularly after finishing the design process, in which the information system has to function satisfactorily.

Because of the dynamics of the design process in practice the specification of the information systems' requirements, will change during this process.

These changes are especially caused by the confrontation between the user organization and the technical opportunities for satisfying a wide range of information needs, and by changing perceptions about already present information systems interfering with the intended system.

If – future – users are confronted with far reaching technical opportunities their phantasy generates new information needs, again and again.

Interference with existing systems could imply changes in the composition of the people involved (stakeholders) leading to changing requirements as well.

And also after implementation of the information system, in fact the design process is not finished. Due to organizational dynamics, information systems' requirements are constantly changing. Therefore, to the management of information systems we have to pay sufficient attention; an issue that will be discussed later in this chapter, in section 4.

Anticipating our discussion of a number of categories of design methods in section 3 of the present chapter, we explicitly distinguish between *designing* and *developing* information systems. By *designing* information systems we mean the complete process, starting directly after the origin of – provisionally determined – information needs, to be followed until the system is delivered to the user; therefore, also including implementation.

Developing information systems is a specific stage within this design process concerning the construction of these systems in terms of hardware and software.

We continue this section with a short discussion about the information needs of managers. In doing so, it is necessary to have some knowledge about the nature of the activities of managers in organizations.

Originally managers were thought by students of management behaviour to finish several jobs one after the other, just like a blue collar worker at an assembly line sequentially pays attention to every product passing by. However, since Henry Mintzberg, who did a lot of research in this field, we know better.

According to his findings, the characteristics of the activities of managers can be summarized as follows (Mintzberg, 1973):
- brevity,
- variety and
- fragmentation.

These three properties are mutually dependent. Most topics managers are dealing with only get attention for very short periods of time. This is because managers are interrupted very frequently.

Because of this characteristic managers are not able to finish several jobs properly, one after another but are busy with a number of jobs synchronously. This leads to fragmentation of their activities.

Moreover, because managers commute between a number of jobs several times their activities are rather varied too.

In regard of the media used by managers to exchange information, they have a number of instruments at their disposal:
- by post (documented information exchange),
- by telephone (verbal information exchange),
- by non calendered meetings (informal personal information exchange),
- by calendered meetings (formal personal information exchange),
- by walking around in the organizations and speaking with employees (visual information exchange).

Documented information exchange requires the application of a formal language and costs, compared with messages being transmitted real time such as e-mail, some transmission time. As opposed to this, verbal information exchange is much more direct, whereas non verbal communication can also be included; even if the telephone is used.

Because of these reasons managers obviously prefer verbal exchange of information. As a matter of fact research in this field indicates that 60 to 90% of managers' time is spent in verbal communication.

In terms of information sources we may generally summarize this section on managers' preferences, as consisting of:

> *ad hoc data concerning concrete and actual issues, instead of more routine based reports and acquired by conversations with others, especially co-workers*

Of course, differences in characteristics between managers based on their specific situation – so-called contingency factors – can be identified. For instance, we must think about:
- organizational dynamics,
- hierarchical level,
- specific function,
- personality traits.

In designing information systems for managers – so-called executive information systems or executive support systems – it is of the utmost importance to start with their information behaviour. To this topic we will return in Chapter IX, discussing a number of categories of information systems.

We wish to finish this section by taking a look at what can be expected in the remainder of this chapter. Because of the numerous risks characterizing information projects, we explicitly pay attention to this subject in the next section. In section 3 'general design methods' will be discussed. Using these methods, it is possible to handle information projects' risks with care; especially risks arising from or a – lack of – understanding information needs of the potential users of information systems at the start of the design process and thereafter during this process.

Of course, it is not, or hardly, possible to take into account *future* information needs, because these needs often change rather quickly. Therefore, in the exploitation stage it is necessary to apply management methods guaranteeing a fine tuning between information systems and information requirements. So, in our opinion this topic should not be discussed within the framework of information policy (Chapter V), but in regard of problems in the field of the relationship between – changing – information needs and information systems, now and in the – distant – future; problems belonging to the core of this chapter. Methods for the fine-tuning between information systems and information needs after implemenatation are dealt with in section 4 of this chapter.

Finally, we are actually not very much interested in so-called *specific* design methods in this book because they are hardly relevant to the information aspect of the control of organizations but belong to the technical domain of information systems. However, in our opinion it would be an omission not to mention these methods at all. Thus some room is given to this subject in section 5.

2. Information projects and project risks

As has been made clear in the previous section, information (and ICT) projects are rather risky. This characteristic has an impact on the way these projects have to be dealt with and executed, and on the final result in terms of acceptable information systems.

Therefore, it is necessary, before starting these projects, to make a thorough and extended risk analysis. With such an analysis we have two purposes.

First of all, it is important to have a good idea about all sorts of risks of information projects in order to make a well-considered decision, referring to the economic evaluation of these projects (see also Chapter X).

Secondly, using such a risk analysis we are able to identify the opportunities for manipulating these risks effectively.

As to the risk *dimensions* of information projects, we may distinguish project result and project path; to put it differently: *what* do we want to realize and *how*. It goes without saying that product and process are both important.

As to the risks associated with the project results sometimes a distinction is made between the *intrinsic* properties of the project result and the *meaning* of the project result for the project's environment. These two angles can be split up as follows:

Intrinsic properties of the project result, involving
- the size of the information system,
- level of ambition, c.q. aspiration level, of the project,
- organizational diffusion,
- homogenity,
- integration with other systems,
- complexity.

Meaning of the project result for its environment, involving
- priority of the information system,
- involvement of the (executive) management,
- involvement of the shopfloor,
- stability of the demands formulated,
- degree of innovation of the information system,
- consequences of the information system for the organization,
- location of the project in the process.

Four of these risk factors are particularly important: involvement of the (executive) management, size of the information system in connection with the complexity characteristics and stability of the demands having been specified, c.q. the project specifications. We will discuss these four factors in more detail below.

As we have seen in the previous chapter *involvement* of the (executive) management concerning information projects is of vital importance and has to be taken into consideration explicitly when shaping the project organization.

The *size* of information projects can be measured in many different ways, c.q. measured using many different criteria. As to these projects it is common practice to measure size using so-called 'function points' (Albrecht and Jaffney, 1983). When this method is applied, specific attention is paid to the following properties of information systems:
- number of inputs,
- number of outputs,
- number of data collections to be used,

- number of interfaces with other systems,
- number of retrievals.

After quantifying these properties, using some sort of procedure to assess their relative weights, we can sum up all these numbers, leading to the over all score of the intended information system indicating its size. Unfortunately, we are not able to translate these function points unambiguously into project development costs. As far as we should like to make such an attempt we can hypothesize that each function point approximately equals $ 400,- to $ 500,-.

Complexity we already defined as the number of possible states, referring to the system theory, of a system (see Chapter II). Hence, this concept is also useful to determine the complexity of information systems.

Though, as is demonstrated above, complexity and size can be clearly distinguished on a conceptual level, in every day experience these two phenomena usually are coupled rather strictly.

These two characteristics – size and complexity – deserve special attention, in regard of the design process of information systems, because of the following reasons.

Firstly, starting the design process the users of these systems want systems able to cope with any possible exception whatsoever, instead of especially adressing the main processes having to be supported. Dealing with this problem we have to remember Pareto's rule, for instance, saying that of all our clients only 20% are responsible for 80% of our sales. Therefore, this phenomenon is also called the '20/80' rule.

In just the same way in applying information systems, the bulk of their use refers to rather simple, daily returning, applications, c.q. retrievals, amounting to 80% of their total use.

If it is our intention to cover also the other 20%, then it is necessary to design information systems characterized by a multiple of their original size, design time, design costs, management costs, etc. Thus, we can conclude: with 20% of its design costs and design time we are able to realize about 80% of the functionality of an information system. The other 20% is extremely expensive and, based on a superficial cost/benefit analysis, will usually not be taken into consideration at all.

Secondly, the problem of the so-called 'nice-to-haves' can be identified. If the potential users are involved during the design process, they have the opportunity to formulate new demands, again and again, based on their experience with parts of intended system so far, without asking whether the additional needs are really functional, or even disfunctional.

Both causes are heavily pushing the size of those information systems upwards, resulting in more and more complex systems difficult to manage and to maintain.

The risks in respect of the project route can be divided into four categories:
- project size,
- project limitations,
- project organization,
- people and resources.

These four categories can be subdivided in the following way.

Project size
- processing time,
- costs,
- number of project team members.

Project limitations
- agreed delivery data,
- agreed budget,
- constraints due to other activities.

Project organization
- relationship with the principal,
- organization.

People and resources
- quality of the project team members,
- quality of the communication within and between the project teams,
- quality of the development tools,
- availability of advanced development tools.

Because of everyday experience with the design of information systems, four factors are especially important: processing time, costs, quality of the participants in the design process (combined with their availability) and modern development tools.

As was, among other things, stipulated in Chapter I, information projects often get out of control because of higher costs and longer development time. Therefore, within the project organisation we have to take precautions in order to control information projects satisfactorily (see also Chapter V).

Also, the quality of the participants, combined with their availability, is of crucial importance for the success of information projects.

As to this quality aspect we have to differentiate between designers and potential users. For this latter group it is essential to have an organizational position high enough to have the authority to take ad hoc decisions, for instance, about additional resources, meanwhile having sufficient feeling with the organizational level on which the information system has to function.

As far as the designers are concerned, attention should primarily be paid to their capacity to communicate with their clients (users) fruitfully.

Moreover, as to the users, it is necessary they have enough time for the project, because otherwise project delays are created beforehand.

Also the availability of advanced development tools is very important, especially in regard of the wish of both parties to have quick deliveries (releases) and reactions (see also the next section).

Overviewing the several risks of the project route, mentioned in this section, we may come to the following conclusion: their basic cause can be found in a lack of

knowledge about the required specifications of information systems before starting the design process. In other words, obviously we are unable to make a clear problem definition, due to the unstructured character of these problems (see also Chapter III). As most important reasons for this problem, summarizing what has been said before, we can list the following ones:
- the user is not able to formulate his information needs adequately,
- the change of – perceived – information needs during the design process, because of the confrontation of users and technical opportunities,
- changes of the number of stake holders, in combination with their information needs, during the design process due to initially unforeseen consequences for other information systems already operating,
- changes of information needs caused by changing conditions after implementation.

Therefore, we can make no other choice than to specify the problem definition *during* the design process. In order to do this we need general design methods in addition to project management methods, as discussed in the preceding chapter, facilitating the problem definition process of information systems.

Using these methods, we are able to deal with the risks of information systems in a responsible way; particularly by trying to identify information needs as well as possible.

3. General design methods

In this section we discuss the subject 'general design methods'; design methods especially meant to identify the information needs of (future) users of information systems, at least until the moment the systems involved will be implemented.

The methods can be divided into four categories:
- participatory design methods,
- evolutionary design methods,
- incremental design methods,
- participatory/incremental design methods.

In the remainder of this section we discuss these four categories, of which three are pure and the fourth is a mixed one. But before doing so we want to make a remark.

Sometimes it is rather difficult to categorize specific applications of general design methods unambiguously, because they contain combinations of characteristics of more than one method. Hence, we identified the fourth category: 'participatory/incremental' design methods.

Finally, Rapid Application Development is a method showing some resemblance with incremental design methods, but otherwise this method has a number of specific properties. Therefore, we will discuss it separately.

Participatory design methods
Using participatory design methods, the user of information systems has a dominant position. This does not mean that with participatory design methods it is primarily the intention to identify the information needs in a thorough way *before* starting the design process but more to involve the users in the design process from beginning to end.

The advantages of user participation especially relate to the formulation of their present needs and possible changes during the design process. These changes are, next to developments in the environment, particularly due to the confrontation between users and – parts of – the intended information system. Actually, every day experience teaches us that, if users are informed about the possible functionality of information systems they often formulate additional wishes generated during the rest of the design process, creating the risk of realizing 'nice-to-haves'.

Another advantage refers to the responsibility of the users for the information system. As opposed to a turn key approach, where the designers are solely responsible for the final product, participatory design methods create a shared responsibility of both parties involved. As a consequence, the users' attitude towards the system is more positive.

Of course, such a procedure also contains some drawbacks because users will not be confronted with the final system until the design process is finished. Unfortunately, they have to make their judgements based on *descriptions* of the intended information system. Not only does such an approach require users with sufficient imagination but also the contribution of participatory design methods to bridge the – communication and aspiration – gap between users and designers of information systems is rather limited.

Evolutionary design methods
As opposed to participatory design methods, evolutionary design methods are not used to implement complete information systems after the development process is finished but to implement them bit by bit; one piece after another. After each delivery the next round is planned, based on former experiences from earlier rounds.

Therefore, the project's planning horizon coincides with the moment the next part of the information system is released.

This approach has, compared with participatory design methods, the advantage of identifying the needs of the users based on parts of the information system that have proved to be really usable.

A second advantage of this method relates to the time users have to get acquainted with – parts of – the system; thus, facilitating the intended learning process. In fact learning occurs during the whole design period.

A third advantage of evolutionary design methods has to do with the communication aspect of information systems, because the developed parts are actually functioning as media facilitating the communication between users and designers, leading to a substantial contribution to bridge the communication gap between both groups.

Moreover, the development of the next part is not started until all participants agree about the present one. Thus rash decisions will be avoided.

However, evolutionary design methods are also accompanied with a number of disadvantages. For instance, in the beginning of the design process developed parts of the information system will fall short because of a lack of understanding of the needs of the users. Apart from user disappointment – and possible lack of motivation to cooperate in the design process – this may cost a lot of money.

To another disadvantage of evolutionary design methods we will pay attention in this section, discussing the subject 'aspect system approach/facet system approach'.

A third disadvantage, being relevant for any method characterized by user involvement, concerns the risk of realizing 'nice-to-haves', as mentioned before.

Incremental design methods

Just like evolutionary design methods, incremental design methods relate to the design of a number of parts of the intended system successively. Because of this resemblance both categories have more or less the same advantages and disadvantages.

The main difference between evolutionary and incremental design methods is the length of the planning horizon. As was mentioned before, evolutionary design methods have a very near horizon: the moment of delivery of the next part of the information system. However, using an incremental design method the complete planning period, including the several deliveries, is determined in advance. Once the planning is ready the execution of the project takes place, step by step.

Between the planning of the complete project and an incremental execution some tension may arise. After all, if the final product is specified in every detail, as is also usual if traditional linear design methods are applied, hardly any room for adaptation is present. Therefore, planning of the whole process has to be interpreted as the determination of the main lines of the information system, filling in the details later on, based on the experience gained during the design process.

If the design process is accompanied by more and more uncertainty – based on project result and project route – it will be difficult to specify the final product in sufficient detail, even in formulating the main lines. Here we meet the difference in applicability between evolutionary and incremental design methods. If we have to choose between these two categories then, as uncertainty rises, evolutionary design methods will be preferred more and more. Thus, the borderline between both categories has to be determined by looking at information projects' uncertainties.

Participatory/incremental approaches and prototyping

Participatory/incremental approaches are meant to combine the advantages of participative and incremental design methods. A well-known example of such a combination is prototyping (Naumann and Jenkins, 1987; Beynon-Davies, c.s., 1999).

Prototyping is literally related to the concept 'prototype'. Therefore, first of all we discuss a number of interpretations of this concept.

Among others, prototyping may have the following meaning:

- basic specimen,
- test specimen,
- standard specimen,
- model.

A basic specimen refers to a specimen that can be added with many different characteristics. For instance, in the automobile sector often some sort of standard car is used.

Next to this basic model, the customer can make a choice out of a number of options; thus, composing a car satisfying his individual whishes.

If we use the concept prototype in the sense of test specimen, then a specimen is meant with which we want to get more experience. Again this interpretation of prototypes is well-known in the automobile sector. If a new type of car is developed it has to be tested many times, under different conditions, before it is ready to be produced on a large scale.

Not only single products being tested, but also complete production plants for trying out new processes, are called prototypes.

The concept of prototype used as a standard specimen relates to a measure for other specimens of the same kind. For instance, our measure of length 'meter' is defined as a specific part of the circumference of our planet earth (one to forty million). And the meter exactly coming up to this requirement is kept in Paris, in gold, under constant regulated air conditions of temperature and humidity. In other words, this gold meter is the prototype of our meter used in every day practice.

Finally, the concept prototype has a fourth meaning: model. And a model can be definied as any representation of the real world. Models also are a simplification, because we are only interested in a limited number of characteristics, meanwhile neglecting other ones, if the world around us is represented.

When we are dealing with prototyping, the concept prototype is used in this latter significance, i.e. as a model; a model containing all the relevant characteristics of the intended information system.

A prototype is also an operating model, meaning that the user has the opportunity to experiment with the model of the information system during the design process.

Using prototyping as a design method, the following procedure has to be applied. After a first overall identification of the information needs of the users a prototype will be developed.

As has been said before, only the characteristics essential for the users are relevant to shape the prototype. And these characteristics especially relate to the system's interface; devices of a computerized information system for external communication, consisting of a screen (monitor), key board, mouse and printing facilities.

Due to this emphasis prototypes of information systems refer especially to the *datalogical* aspect – also called external aspect or syntactical aspect – of these systems, because here we have to answer the following question: which output data should a system produce and in what format?

However, prototyping is not limited to the datalogical aspect only, but is also helpful to identify the users' information needs, lying behind their data needs. Now we encounter the *infological* aspect – also called the conceptual aspect or semantic aspect – of information systems.

Moreover, prototypes can also be used to support the *systelogical* aspect of information systems: the purposes the information will be used for. Applying prototyping the user has to clarify, at least for himself, the reasons why information is needed. As we have seen before, this is een important issue for the design of information systems to control their size and complexity.

It is only the *technical* aspect, or internal aspect, of information systems that is beyond the reach of prototyping, because this aspect concerns the internal structure of information systems, such as the structure of the data base. And as long as this structure does not function as a stumbling block to come up to the needs of the user, he is not interested in this subject at all. Therefore, unlike the three other aspects the technical aspect is not an issue for the construction of prototypes.

In fact, the prototypes used to design information systems, essentially function as a communication medium for users and designers. In a number of rounds the users are confronted again and again with different – better – versions of the system. During this process users communicate with the designers making suggestions to change the prototype. In the next round the designers will check their interpretation of the users' wishes by offering a new version of the prototype. This process continues until the users are satisfied and the prototyping phase is finished. So the intended information system will be developed and implemented.

Based on experiences with prototyping, usually three to four rounds are necessary to reach an accepted prototype. However, to make this design method succesfull in essence a number of conditions has to be fulfilled.

Firstly, it is important that the users involved in the design process have enough time to evaluate a new prototype as soon as it is released. Before the start of the design process clear arrangements have to be made, because the rate of evaluating and giving feed back on new prototypes, applying this method, is essential for its success.

Secondly, in connection with this condition, it is important for designers to be able to contribute to the speed of the design process as well. Therefore, in order to produce new prototypes rather quickly, it is necessary to have resources helping them to generate new prototypes more or less automatically, such as CASE tools or I-CASE tools (the abbreviation of (Integrated-) Computer Assisted Software Engineering.

From our previous discussion of prototyping we can conclude that this method is incremental as well as participative. *Incremental* because in a number of rounds the information needs of the – future – users of information systems are identified. Hence, the development process of the intended system can normally be planned rather well in advance.

Prototyping is also *participative* because of the close involvement of the users during the design process.

The difference between prototyping and the other three general design methods especially relates to the moment at which the development phase is started; as opposed to these latter methods, when using prototyping this moment does not take place until the characteristics of the information system are sufficiently clear. Hence, all parties involved are well-informed about the final product, leading to a short development period, and minimalising the risk of deception.

A second difference between prototyping and the other three methods has to do with the status of the system parts compared with prototypes. Essentially, prototypes are no more than empty boxes, usually not being included in the information system, but are thrown away. Though, there may be exceptions to this rule, because sometimes it is possible to upgrade the final prototype, thus freeing the way to use it for the information system. Which alternative – throwing away the prototype or upgrading it – will be preferred only depends on the results of a cost/benefit analysis.

As opposed to prototypes, the various parts of the information system, using the three other design methods will always be incorporated in these systems, because they function as building blocks.

Rapid application development

Finishing our discussion about a number of general (non linear) design methods, we pay attention to a method called Rapid Application Development; abbreviated: RAD (Martin, 1991).

This method, being part of *Information Engineering*, shows, as said before, much resemblance with incremental design methods and also with participative methods (Martin, 1987). Notwithstanding this, RAD has so many specific characteristics that a special discussion is legitimate; particularly because prototyping is also a substantial part of this method.

As the name RAD suggests, as to the design process, the rate of producing several increments – system parts – is crucial for its application. However, this does not mean that RAD favors 'quick and dirty' procedures. On the contrary, this method is, as opposed to traditional design methods, especially characterized by procedures facilitating the realization of win/win solutions in regard of the following – incongruent – targets:

- higher quality,
- lesser design costs,
- shorter design periods.

Now, RAD can be defined as:

> *an integral system of:*
> - *methods, techniques and resources fitting together, combined with*
> - *management instruments, responsibilities and regulative capacity assigned to*
> - *multidisciplinary teams of users and designers, who have the authority to*
> - *mobilize technical and specialistic support.*

As to RAD the design teams have a very central position, whose size and composition are based on the following starting points:

- because small organizational entities are most favourable for group work, group size should not exceed more than four to five members,
- it is absolutely necessary for representatives of the user organization and system developers to be a member of the design teams.

In order to stimulate the well-functioning of the RAD teams the following requirements, concerning the individual team members, must be met:

- enough time for the project,
- enough expertise about the project,
- enough authority to take ad hoc decisions,
- enough credit in the user organization to function as a respresentative.

For the developers being a member of the design teams, an important condition is the broad range of their expertise. As opposed to the application of traditional design methods leading to mobilizing new experts, again and again, depending on the specific phase of the design process, RAD requires experts with more general knowledge. Thus, the team's composition does not have to change with every new stage in the design process, leading to a drastic reduction of coordination problems.

Notwithstanding this, in RAD there is still a role for experts, but at some distance from the design team. If necessary the design team has the authority to mobilize expertise in certain fields.

In the everyday experience of this method the so-called 'dynamic systems development' approach is used. This approach is based on a number of – thirteen – rules, such as:
- user participation during the *whole* development process,
- tight planning combined with frequent deliveries of products (time box management),
- design teams with sufficient authority,
- availability of advanced development tools (for instance I-CASE tools),
- application of a number of methods and techniques,
- synchronous systems development.

To some of these rules we will pay attention in more detail.

First of all the topic 'user participation'. Though user participation is of the utmost importance, this involvement is also accompanied with some danger. As is indicated in the previous section all sorts of 'nice-to-haves' can be formulated, meanwhile leading to a multiplication of design time and design costs.

Therefore, RAD is also characterized by Pareto's Law: the '20/80' rule: in the beginning of the design process one will explicitly try to realize only 80% of the total functionality of the information system, as intended by the users, thus costing no more than 20%, measured in time and money compared with the total functionality. To this topic we will return, when discussing the subject 'creeping' in a latter section.

Secondly, we wish to make some remarks about the design teams. As was said before, these teams should have suficient authority, because otherwise they need the approval of other persons outside the team for making decisions. This authority is especially a prerequisite for maintaining the speed of the development process (Castello, 1991).

Thirdly, teams, because of the development speed just mentioned, need to have – ICT based – development tools at their disposal: the already known I-CASE tools. As to these tools we are speaking about the so-called SWAT principle: Skilled With Advanced Tools.

Fourthly, RAD includes the use of some specific methods and techniques, such as prototyping and 'joint application design'. Within the framework of RAD it is, as opposed to prototyping, always the intention not to throw prototypes away but to absorb them in the final information system.

Moreover, joint application design is applied by RAD. This is a technique meant to clarify and to register the specifications of information systems in a workshop-like environment, in an interactive way.

Fifthly, using RAD it is, in respect of the required speed of the development process, possible to have more than one design team separately and synchronously elaborating on different parts of the system. In order to split up information systems for this approach and the integration later on, the use of I-CASE tools is very important.

Unfortunately, such a synchronous system development approach does not only have advantages; one of its major disadvantages, as opposed to a serial development process, has to do with the possibility of endangering the learning process about the identification of the system's functionality. In fact, different people, involved in the design process, may have different experiences with the prototypes of different parts of the system without gathering these experiences together.

Meanwhile, RAD has been applied in a number of development projects, leading to the following conclusions:
- the productivity of the design process can be improved, three to twelve times and
- it is seems possible to shorten the development period of information projects from between 1.6 and 7.6 times.

Choices between the general design methods, as discussed in this chapter so far, are heavily dependent on the characteristics of the intended information system, especially its uncertainty. If uncertainty is low, or even absent, then it would be a wise decision to use traditional design methods, such as the turn key approach, assuming the possibility of a complete identification of the users' information needs before starting the development process.

However, as our every day experience reveals, information projects are often accompanied with much uncertainty preventing us from identifying information needs before starting the design/development process. Thus, the clarification of these needs is a substantial part of the design process.

With this point in mind, the design process ought to be characterized by sufficient user participation and by circularity as well. As to these two requirements, participative design methods on the one hand and incremental, or evolutionary, design methods on the other hand, emphasize user involvement, respectively circularity, in a rather one sided way.

Looking at these two prerequisites, both other methods – prototyping and RAD – are a lot more balanced. Therefore, in the remainder of this section we restrict our attention to these two methods.

Essentially, shaping the confrontation between users and parts of the information system to be designed, we can distinguish two alternatives:
- the facet system approach and
- the aspect system approach.

Using the *facet* system approach, facet system defined as a *concrete* part of the – intended information – system (for instance relevant for evolutionary design methods), the complete information system is split up in a number of parts being developed sequentially. Developing the various parts of the system, the experience gained during the development of previous parts will be applied.

If the *aspect* system approach is used, aspect system defined as an abstract image of the system, then a *model* of the intended information system is built, only containing a number of relevant characteristics. *Relevant* in this context referring to the users and the properties they appreciate.

Compared with the aspect system approach, the facet system approach has two disadvantages:

- in the beginning of the design process, the users only get a vague partial image of the final information system; only after some time during the development process, does this image become more and more clear,
- because the user in the beginning of the design process is confronted with a limited number of system parts, the old information system, to be replaced, is still functioning; so frustrating the opportunity of the new system to demonstrate its value completely.

Therefore, the aspect system approach, instead of the facet system approach, should be preferred.

As we have seen before, prototyping and RAD are both based on prototypes. However, because of synchronous system development, RAD also contains properties of the facet system approach. So, prototyping has an important advantage due to its emphasis on the aspect system approach only.

On the other hand, RAD also has a number of advantages over prototyping, especially in the field of the principles to be taken into account, concerning the composition and functioning of design teams.

Thus, concluding our discussion of general design methods, we prefer to use prototyping facilitating the development of information systems. But it is also recommendable to complement this method with some principles of RAD meant to stimulate speed and quality of the design process.

Finishing this discussion we notice: the objections we made about the application of a facet system approach, referring to RAD, are also relevant to the other two categories of general design methods, discussed in this section, i.e. evolutionary and incremental design methods.

All general design methods, explicitly having room for user involvement during the design process, must handle this phenomenon with care, because otherwise the consequence is 'creeping'. By creeping we mean users formulating again and again new information needs, based on their experiences with parts of the intended information system, often to do with so-called 'nice-to-haves', with a limited meaning for the system's required functionality.

Thus, in regard of the user needs, we distinguish the following four categories:

- must haves; characteristics belonging to the basic functionality of information systems, and therefore absolutely necessary,
- should haves; needs taken into account, unless changed circumstances alter our point of view,

- could haves; normally these needs are not taken into account, unless we come to another point of view based on changing circumstances,
- won't haves; needs absolutely ignored.

The danger of unnecessary fringes is especially present if, for instance applying prototyping, at the start of the design process hardly any action is taken to identify the users' needs more than globally, based on the assumption of sufficiently clarifying the information needs during the design process in every required detail.

A specific method to avoid creeping is the so-called *Process Management Approach*. The fundamental assumption of this method is: creeping is caused by a number of obscurities or shortcomings respectively in the design process, such as inadequate identification of information needs, unclear expectations of users and unknown applications. To solve these problems, the Process Management Approach is based on the following starting points:
- identification of information needs at the start of the design process, as well as possible, by user involvement, already in the phase of the definition study,
- the user must get a clear picture of the solutions offered,
- the user must get what he wants, and what has been agreed upon explicitly.

In summary, using this method we try to get optimal clarity for the user about all kinds of things to be expected in regard of his wishes in every single phase of the design process.

Therefore, application of the Project Management Approach can, next to a number of principles borrowed from RAD, contribute to a further improvement of prototyping as the most preferred general design method, as soon as uncertainty about the needs of the users of information systems has entered the arena.

4. Information management and flexibility

Some species of the general design methods, discussed in section 3 of this chapter, offer the opportunity to take into account changing information needs of future users of information systems until the moment of implementation.

However, because of environmental turbulence, organizations are confronted almost continually with changing information system requirements after implementation. And the proliferation of ICT assets, strongly facilitated by the development of mini computers and personal computers (PC's), makes it even worse.

As a matter of fact, we have two opportunities to solve this problem. On the one hand, it is possible to construct information systems having the necessary flexibility. And on the orther hand, we can use a number of management methods in the exploitation stage enabling us to introduce the required changes adequately.

In this section we pay attention to the subject 'flexibility', and to the so-called 'information technology infrastructure library' method, to manage information systems changes properly.

In designing flexible information systems fundamentally two routes are open;
- information systems consisting of a number of building blocks and
- information systems designed at a higher abstraction level.

The first alternative is about information systems composed by using a number of modules. In daily practice, a specific combination of modules, dependent on the characteristics of the processes to be supported, will be selected and grouped as an information system.

Because of changes in the characteristics and composition of these processes existing modules can be skipped and others added.

Sometimes Workflow management systems are designed this way.

The second alternative relates to the design of information systems based on more general characteristics to be identified in more than one process being supported. For instance, one of the most basic characteristics of any process is the transformation from input into output. In addition, many processes are, as a common property, often characterized by disturbances being distributed bell-shape.

In daily practice, such a general information system has to be specified in more detail, especially by using figures for the relevant parameters like arithmetic mean and standard deviation of the density function of the disturbances just mentioned.

This distinction between more general information systems and information systems for specific applications is, for instance, relevant to decision support systems (see Chapter IX). Traditionally, these systems can be divided into DSS generators (containing general process descriptions), also called 'shells', and specific decision support systems, representing a specific business problem in every relevant detail.

In the situation of more flexible information systems, often an appeal is made to the users' capacity to self design specific applications deduced from more general information systems suited for their own problems in particular. Therefore, such an approach is called 'end user computing' (Rockart and Flannery, 1983).

The management methodology 'information technology infrastructure library' (abbreviated ITIL) chooses as a starting point, speaking about the management of information systems, and the management of ICT respectively, *processes* that have to be supported. The processes involved are the *clients* of the department 'information management'. Between these two parties clear arrangements about the application of ICT have to be made.

All these agreements are, from the point of view of the client, about the necessity of undisturbed and qualitatively good information facilities. As a consequence the client has the obligation to buy the services offered. However, the department 'information management' is not only a seller (in the eyes of the users of information systems), but it is also a client of other supplying departments, such as the department 'maintenance' and of suppliers of software with which it has to come to agreements in a similar way.

Therefore, ITIL is based on the assumeption of quality control of all processes based on mutually agreed and recognized agreements registered in so-called 'Service level Agreements'.

In order to guarantee these quality requirements adequately, coordination is necessary, called 'Service Level Management'. This Service Level Management is responsible for the communication between users and the several units involved in the information system's management; to mention a few units:

Configuration management
- domain:
  all infrastructure now and in the (near) future
- intended result:
  - overview of the expertise inside the organization,
  - source of information to other processes,
  - identification of unwanted substructures.

Helpdesk
- domain:
  operational contacts with users
- intended results:
  - central point for questions and problems,
  - quick solution of disturbances of the service level,
  - active contacts with users,
  - source of relevant management information.

Problem management
- domain:
  identification of causes lying behind disturbances of the service level
- intended results:
  - increased productivity of the users,
  - quicker solutions,
  - to prevent problems instead of offering ad hoc solutions.

Especially because of the necessary connection between all these parts, controlled by Service level Management, ITIL creates more than pure formal results. By applying the ITIL methodology within organizations to manage information systems, we have some guarantee that also after implementation, the future information needs of the users are handled with care.

We wish to finish the subject 'ITIL' with a warning. ITIL is a rather *process* oriented approach. Using such an approach may conflict with the way the organization's internal communication is structured: along the vertical lines of its hierarchy. An organization structure being very suitable in this respect for ITIL is the sociotechnical structure, discussed in Chapter IV, because of its emphasis on organizational processes.

If we intend to apply ITIL in a fruiful way, this method must have its consequences for the organization's communication culture.

5. Specific design methods

In this section we look at a number of specific design methods in more detail. As opposed to general design methods, especially meant to manage information projects adequately, specific methods are about the *focus* of information systems, i.e. the point of view being relevant to shape the data base of information systems, not to be confused with the *technical* or *internal* aspect of information systems, referring to the *internal* structure of the database, such as hierarchical, for instance.

In order to clarify the focus of information systems, we have to identify the processes supported by these systems. For this reason, we need a clear definition of the concept *process*. For our purpose the following definition of a process is adequate:

> *a* process *is a sequence of activities meant to transform input into output, to be interpreted as* objects *undergoing a number of* events, *meanwhile producing* data

In this definition of a process the various concepts written in italics are the possible focal points for shaping the data base, i.e. the orientation of information systems:
- process,
- object,
- event,
- data.

More traditionally, designers of information systems had to choose between two categories of specific design methods: process-oriented and data-oriented approaches. Both have advantages as well as disadvantages. A major advantage of process-orientation is the incorporation of the opportunity to deal with organizational changes due to new information systems and with possible future changes as well, constructing data bases. But this latter is also a weakness because frequent changes of the principles lying behind the data base may lead to regular – and numerous – adaptations of the information system after implementation.

Thus, designers looked for more stable building blocks of information systems and found *data* to meet this need. As a matter of fact, if processes, and also as a consequence events, are changing, then data need not do so because they will, to a certain extent, be produced regardless of the specific processes involved. So, data are less sensitive to changes than processes. Because of this property, in a fast changing world, designers may prefer data-orientation instead of process-orientation. However, using the former, organizational changes caused by new information systems are sometimes paid insufficient attention.

As examples of these two categories specific design methods ISAC (process-oriented) and INFOMOD (data-oriented) can be mentioned (Lundeberg, c.s., 1981; Olle, c.s., 1982; Vangriethuysen and Jardine, 1984;).

One of the major problems of data and process oriented specific design methods relates to the way particular procedures are dependent upon the objects to be manipulated. We will illustrate this problem using the well-known procedure of *counting*. If the sales volume in some period has to be registered, then, for instance, one barrel of raw material added to twenty four barrels of the same kind makes twenty five barrels. So this last figure is generated by using 'normal' counting rules.

However, the counting procedure applied to time, is different. If it is twenty four o'clock, then one hour afterwards it is not twenty five o'clock but one o'clock.

Therefore, procedures, being parts of a process, are sometimes dependent on the objects to be processed. As a consequence, if procedures are specific for some object or the other, it would be sensible to directly relate those procedures to the object in the database, instead of describing it separately elsewhere.

Applying this principle we are dealing with object-oriented data bases (Bakker, 1995).

In addition to the advantage of differentiating between procedures, depending on the specific objects to be processed, object-oriented information systems have still another advantage. If, for instance, in a not object-oriented information system a change in some procedure is made, then this change has to be executed everywhere in the information system where this very procedure is used. If we are dealing with a rather complex and extended information system, this may be very time consuming with a big chance of making mistakes.

However, as opposed to other specific design methods, in using object-oriented design methods, changes are always rather local. If not, it is, applying the principle of so-called 'inheritance', possible to make changes in a number of procedures quickly and safely wherever it is necessary.

In respect of our definition of process in this section and its relevant components – process, data, objects and events – we may wonder whether also *event*-oriented specific design methods could be distinguished logically. As we have seen, objects are processed, leading to events generating data. Thus, events and data are very closely related to each other. Moreover, we are actually not interested in the event as such but in the effects it brings about, leading to data. Therefore, it suffices to use processes or data or objects (including the applied procedures) alternatively as the focal point for the design of information systems.

VIII POWER AND THE CONTROL OF CONFLICTS DUE TO INFORMATION SYSTEMS AND ICT

1. Introduction

In Chapter I we already observed the close relationship between information and power, especially in our present knowledge-intensive society; the saying 'information is power' is more valid than ever.

Power can be defined in many different ways. We prefer to define power as (Goldhamer and Shils, 1939):

> *someone has power as far as he is able to influence the behaviour of others according to his own preferences*

Power is often associated with ulterior motives because many people believe that power corrupts. However, power is essentially a neutral phenomenon. Depending on the intentions with which power is effectively used we can speak about the use or the abuse of power.

When we analyze the power phenomenon in greater depth we can distinguish two different approaches (French and Raven, 1959):
- the static approach and
- the dynamic approach.

The static approach deals with questions like:
- what is power?
- who has power?
- what sources of power can be identified?

Conversely, the dynamic approach focuses on the process of dealing with power (Clegg, 1989).

In view of our problem field we are especially interested in the question in what way power within organizations is distributed among the various participants (the power structure), and in the changes that arise in this pattern due to the filling of information needs.

In this book we therefore pay attention to the static approach to power in particular, though we also discuss the (dynamic) control of conflicts (see section 3).

Within organizations a number of power *sources* are present, such as (French and Raven, 1959; Pfeffer, 1981):

- resources,
- money,
- reduction of uncertainty,
- status,
- information/professional knowledge.

Because of the central position of information and information systems from our point of view, we are only interested in the relationship between information, or professional knowledge respectively, and power.

As the reader will remember, in Chapter II we defined the relationship between information and professional knowledge – not to be confused with knowledge as the human capacity to use information effectively – in such a way that information is the *increase* of this professional knowledge. Because of this relation, we only speak of information in the passage below, while we assume that professional knowledge is included as well.

In order to illustrate the relationship between information and power we discuss two possible applications here.

For instance, if someone has an advantage in the field of information/professional knowledge this lends him authority in relation to other organizational participants in case of differences in view. So this advantage can be used to convince those participants, because they were not able to prepare themselves beforehand.

A second use of information as an instrument of power relates to the influence of particular employees on the organization's flows of information and to their opportunity to manipulate these flows. For example, this is relevant for the information transmitted to top management, and to the chief executive officer respectively.

As Aguilar stipulates, based on his research in the sixties, it is usual for top management to be rather dependent on subordinates for information they obtain (Aguilar, 1967). These subordinates may be members of staff who function as some sort of internal consultants. They are more involved in the information processing of management than other organizational participants, and they are therefore able to influence the decisions which are based on that information.

The same is true for employees who have a lot of contact with others outside the organization, such as the marketing department. Because of their position they are able to influence the crucial external information (in)flows of the organization.

This influence, illustrated above, is realized in a number of ways. For instance, the people involved have the opportunity to – consciously or unconsciously – pass on information selectively or to present information in such a way that some sort of development is suggested in order to manipulate the decisions that are based on the information in a certain direction. It is not a coincidence that a book was once published with the title *How to lie with figures* (Moroney, 1965).

The *(added) value* of people for organizations is the basis of their power. Increasingly this added value is no longer based on their formal position within the organization, but on their knowledge, or even their knowledge lead. Knowledge is particularly relevant for organizations with a delayered structure, such as organizations designed according to principles of the sociotechnical approach. In other words, because of the relationship between professional knowledge (information), added value and power, the information structure and power structure of organizations are closely related.

Generally, it is the possession of some quality or other which creates a solid basis for the power of organizational participants. If this is also valid for professional knowledge and information, the following conditions will have to be fulfilled (Hickson, c.s., 1971):

- scarcity and
- importance.

Scarcity means that the resources concerned, in this case information and professional knowledge, cannot easily be acquired by other means. *Importance* means the value of these resources to people who want to use them while they are dependent on others who are in control of these resources.

Both qualities are relevant here, depending on the kind of information involved and the way people use it.

The filling of organizational information needs will often result in a reshuffling of the flows of information. Whether the filling of these needs is realized by organizational measures or by new information systems based on ICT, reshuffling will take place.

Therefore, solving information problems often implies adaptation of the information structure, and as a result the power structure will change also. As long as the organizational participants involved will only benefit from these changes, they will probably have a cooperative attitude; unlike another category of participants who feel badly done by. This contrast is a potential source of conflicts.

So, when there are information problems to be solved, it is very important to have a clear picture in advance of the changes to the information structure as well as to the power structure. This topic – the impact of information systems and/or ICT on the power structure of organizations – will be discussed in section 2.

It is not sufficient to have a proper understanding of changes in the power structure due to new information systems, but it is also necessary to have a number of instruments for handling these changes adequately; thus reducing the potential damage of the selected solution, and reducing possible conflicts to an acceptable level.

In section 3 we will pay attention to this subject from the point of view of handling conflicts effectively. We will especially focus on information problems that are solved by using new information systems in combination with ICT.

If the reader of the book understands the approach we advocate for handling power conflicts that are due to new information systems, he will also be able to get a clear picture of the effects on the power structure, if organizational solutions to information problems are used instead of ICT ones, and how possible conflicts can be solved effectively.

2. Changes in the power structure of organizations due to new information systems based on ICT

The introduction of new information systems based on ICT into organizations, may, in addition to a number of positive effects, have negative consequences for organizational participants as well. For instance, Argyris lists the following (Argyris, 1971):
1. reduction of room to manoeuvre,
2. reduced feelings of importance,
3. increased visibility of job performance.

ad 1.
Some information systems automatically produce reports which lead to recommendations to take specific measures, without any human interference. Sometimes these recommendations affect the personal interests of the people involved, without offering them the opportunity to express their opinions beforehand. The resulting reduction of their room to manoeuvre has negative consequences for their power.

ad 2.
Data processing by information systems which leads to a number of recommendations may, and this is closely related to the former point, devaluate the role of the decision maker. By this we mean that the information system no longer supports the user; on the contrary, the user has become no more than an 'extension piece' of the system; at least he feels this way.

ad 3.
Generally speaking, the use of information systems within organizations implies an increase in the transparency of the behaviour of the organizational participants. By applying these systems, management is able to get information about the functioning of subordinates more quickly and more completely. This may severely upset their feelings of 'freedom' and privacy. A feeling of being under permanent supervision is the consequence ('Big Brother is watching you').

In addition, when ICT is applied, personal supervision is replaced by invisible electronic supervision. This may cause feelings of powerlessness, increased stress and – finally – deterioration of mental and physical health (Markus, 1984).

An important aspect of the application of ICT which is closely connected with the problem field described in the preceding passages, concerns the relationship between this technology and the control structure of organizations and its resultant impact on the power of the organizational participants.

In our discussion of this subject we assume that the source of power relevant here is not the possession of information/professional knowledge, as before, but the organization's formal authority structure.

Generally speaking, we can postulate that the motivation of organizational participants heavily depends on the degree to which they are authorized to take decisions independently in carrying out their jobs; in other words their degree of autonomy or control capacity (Ashby, 1969; Jenkins, 1974). According to Ashby's Law of Requisite Variety (see Chapter IV) this control capacity has to be in the right proportion to the uncertainty the participants have to deal with. In other words, the more uncertainty, the more control capacity they need.

A lack of control capacity creates feelings of powerlessness, whereas too much of this capacity burdens participants with control and responsibilities that are unnecessary for their functioning. This creates stress too.

Leaving aside the question what is the optimal configuration of responsibilities and control, two opposing views can be identified in respect of the degree to which management is prepared to delegate authority under the influence of ICT. Some students in this field predicted that ICT would cause more centralization (Leavitt and Whisler, 1958). This tendency can be explained as follows. This technology enables management to supervise its subordinates more closely than before.

Other students, however, claim just the opposite: the use of ICT causes increasing decentralization (Pfeffer, 1978). This view is based on the idea that the management of the organization is able to supervise its subordinates from a larger distance, geographically as well as functionally, without losing control, by applying ICT. Therefore, it is willing to delegate more authority than before.

Both views are more or less plausible and based on empirical research activities, which reveal that neither of these two tendencies prevails; though perhaps a slight preference for centralization can be observed (Robey, 1977). It seems we are confronted here with two irreconcilable points of view.

However, a rather obvious explanation of these opposite results with respect to the willingness of management to delegate authority and responsibilities due to ICT can be found in the management's more fundamental attitude towards a more autocratic or a more democratic leadership.

If managers are rather democratic, they will try to use ICT as a means to delegate more authority to subordinates without losing their grip on the organization. The other participants get more power in this way while the power of managers is left untouched.

On the other hand, autocratic managers will use any development, technological or otherwise, to establish a tighter control over their organization. Power will increasingly be concentrated at the management level; even if it harms the participants at lower levels.

Summarizing the relationship between power and information, we can conclude that information systems, and ICT respectively, can be used to:

- create more power for the organization as a whole and
- change the existing balance of power, either by centralization or by decentralization.

As to potential shifts of power within organizations due to the introduction of new information systems, and of ICT respectively, we can distinguish *supposed* shifts and *real* shifts.

By supposed shifts of power we mean that some organizational participants *expect* a decrease of their power, due to new information systems, whereas this is not at all the case. Examples of real shifts of power frequently occurred in the starting period of the application of ICT when organizations in particular pursued efficiency advantages. This led to the replacement of people by machines, and various organizational processes became automated.

Because of these experiences, some employees fear that the introduction of new information systems, and/or ICT will make them redundant. It is evident that dismissal, seen from the perspective of power, is a very extreme form of power shift; in this case the power of the people involved is reduced to zero.

If organizational participants wrongly assess the – negative – effects of information systems and ICT, we are confronted with *supposed* shifts of power.

This problem can be solved effectively by informing people quite well about the impact of the new technology, in order to create a more realistic attitude.

Things are different with *real* shifts of power. They may happen when new information systems are introduced. Such a change will eventually cause a conflict. We define a conflict as:

> *a situation, consisting of two persons, a person and a group or two groups, in which at least one of both parties is of the opinion that the other party is thwarting him/them*

The formulation used above ('will eventually cause a conflict') means that, in spite of the threat of power shifts, a conflict does not always become manifest. Whether conflicts will stay latent or become manifest depends among other things on the differences in power between the parties involved. Sometimes these differences are so great that the weakest party, when it sees its power diminished, is not able to offer resistance and reconciles itself to its changed position beforehand.

Therefore, the chances of actual conflicts are the greatest if the differences in power between the parties involved are only moderate, and both may gain from a struggle.

In such a situation, the organization has to use instruments to control the conflict. This topic will be discussed in the next section.

3. The control of conflicts

One rather obvious form of conflict control is preventing conflicts from becoming manifest; in other words, conflicts stay latent or they are solved.

As a rule, this goal can be achieved by using the following measures; measures which are also relevant for power conflicts in the field of information systems and of ICT (Cyert and March, 1963):

- local rationality,
- decision rules specified by acceptable goal levels,
- sequential goal attention and
- slack.

Local rationality means splitting up problems which may lead to conflicts into a number of smaller problems that can be solved locally in a number of subdepartments which are involved in the problem situation. In this way, these subdepartments have to deal with a smaller number of problems in relation to goals which are limited as well.

When we design information systems, and use information/communication technology, this approach can be practised by splitting up the intended system into a number of parts if this is possible: one for each subdepartment. The potential power conflicts are more easy to solve per part, compared with conflicts that are generated by a larger, more integrated and more complex information system.

If the specification of the decision rules is based on *acceptable* goal levels, we have to consider defining the intended results in terms of satisfactory criteria instead of optimal or maximal ones. Usually, the set of satisfactory criteria is called 'aspiration level'. The application of this level means a decrease in the ambition level of the parties involved, and often prevents conflicts from becoming manifest.

If sequential goal attention is used, the parties involved in a conflict get what they want, not synchronously but one after another (*sequentially*), and, if necessary, in different fields. Therefore, this approach means that today one party has to give up some of its wishes and tomorrow the other.

For instance, this conflict strategy is used if the party whose position is harmed in a power conflict is promised that it will get extra resources in the next round.

Most of the time, organizations have more resources than the total amount – in terms of money, status, power, etc. – they minimally have to pay to participants in order to keep the organization viable as a coalition of its members. The difference between available resources and required payments is called *slack*.

Firstly, the presence of slack means that if some (groups of) organizational participants see their power diminish due to new information systems, this development is not unacceptable as long as the total amount of payments they receive at least equals the minimum amount required. If this is not the case, then perhaps part of the slack of other groups could be used to offer the necessary compensation to keep them on board.

Secondly, it is possible to pursue a more balanced distribution of slack, regardless of the possibility that real shifts in power might occur which would result in an unacceptable reduction of the slack of some (groups of) organizational participants. In order to diffuse organizational pain, it may happen that one party gets less power while another has to be content with more limited resources.

If the measures to keep conflicts latent which were discussed above are exhausted, the conflicts will become manifest. In this situation we also have a number of instruments to control conflicts effectively.

Before discussing these instruments in more detail it is important to pay attention to the types of manifest conflicts that can be distinguished:

- conflicts of interest,
- disagreements about goals and procedures,
- role conflicts about individual behaviours and
- socio-emotional conflicts.

The power conflicts due to new information systems can be classified as 'conflicts of interest' about the allocation of scarce resources, such as money or budgets for capital outlays and materials. Power conflicts caused by information systems may also occur in the sphere of attention, prestige and status.

In the case of conflicts in general, and conflicts of interest in particular, the following methods for controlling conflicts can be used (Koopman and Pool, 1992):

- forcing proposals through,
- persuading,
- postponement,
- compromise.

Forcing proposals through means that one group tries to get what it wants without taking into account the interests of other groups. Formally this is only possible if there is a clear power difference between both parties. Actually, such an approach is always counterproductive. This is because the stronger group only succeeds in the short run, while in the long(er) run the weaker group will always look for opportunities to get back the power it lost, in order to restore the balance of power.

In the case of new information systems, when conflicts are handled this way the group which was put at a disadvantage may sabotage those systems; and as a matter of fact there is an abundance of opportunities for taking such action, for example by overfeeding the system with data or by literally putting sand into the machine.

Forcing proposals through is an approach which is often dominant if more traditional design methods for information systems are used. Therefore, we can hardly speak of real conflict control in this situation.

Persuasion means that the group which was put at a disadvantage reconciles itself to the final result on the basis of reasonable arguments. They do not engage in subversive actions later on (as opposed to what happens with proposals that are forced though), since they can agree with the result achieved. Of course, an open dialogue is necessary here instead of verbal violence from one or both sides, because otherwise we are in fact dealing with proposals forced through.

Postponement is based on the assumption that, by not taking a decision, the (potential) conflict will fade away after some time. If it does not, this approach at least brings about a decrease in the intensity of the emotions that were stirred up at the beginning of the process; so that people are able to handle the conflict in a more pragmatic and distant way.

Postponement differs from the other three instruments for handling conflicts discussed here in so far that conflicts are not solved or eliminated, but become less important after some time.

Finally, by using the instrument of *compromise*, a solution is looked for which takes into account and weighs against each other the interests of all groups involved. This solution belongs to the same category as the solution used to keep conflicts latent by making use of the slack which is present in the organization. As a matter of fact, most parties have to reduce their claims when attempting to reach a compromise. And they are only prepared to do so if their slack resources have not been fully absorbed.

When we apply these conflict strategies, it is possible to put them into practice in many different ways. As an illustration we mention (Mulder, 1978):
- explaining overall interests or creating them,
- negotiation,
- reducing the public character of conflicts,
- arbitration.

With increasing surprise outsiders may sometimes observe how groups which are involved in a (power) conflict fight each other, while completely losing sight of an interest which both groups share and which is much more important. For instance, a new strategic information system may imply that the activities of the marketing department, which is charged with supplying the intended data, will become more visible. This will therefore create resistance, while for the organization as a whole such a system is of vital importance, since it functions in a turbulent environment. By looking at the *over all interest* of introducing a strategic information system which also benefits the marketing department, it is perhaps possible for this department to give up its resistance.

Negotiation is often a very effective way to handle conflicts. In negotiations, groups which are involved in a conflict are forced to talk to each other. And talks can have a therapeutic effect. Moreover, at least if groups really listen to each other, negotiations normally result in some sort of mutual understanding which favours the willingness of the groups involved in the conflict to come to an agreement.

If conflicts are *fought out in public*, the rigidity of the conflicting groups many times exceeds their rigidity if such things happen behind closed doors. Obviously, it is more difficult for human beings to abandon their points of view if this is witnessed by a large number of people.

Moreover, in the case of a conflict fought out in public, the rank and file of the groups play a dominant role because every step towards the other group will be discussed in public. Such an approach heavily reduces the willingness of the negotiators to come to a compromise.

If the groups which are involved in a conflict are unable to come to an agreement, the instrument of *arbitration* – defined as submitting the conflict to one or more independent experts – can be applied. In order to solve the conflict effectively in this way, it is necessary for the conflicting groups to accept the arbitration verdict unconditionally.

IX INFORMATION SYSTEMS FOR THE CONTROL OF ORGANIZATIONS; CATEGORIZATION AND APPLICATION

1. Introduction

Organizations use information systems for many different purposes. This can be illustrated in the following way: numeric controlled machines, bookkeeping, capital budgeting decision making, brainstorm meetings, strategy conferences, electronic meetings, datamining and many others.

To increase the chance of success of information systems it is absolutely necessary for the user to be well informed about the possibilities and impossibilities those systems offer. On the one hand, a better insight results in more realistic expectations, whereas, on the other hand, information systems will not be used for the 'wrong' purposes.

In order to get, as a reader of this book, better acquainted with the many different categories of information systems we will illustrate these systems by using a real world case history.

This case relates to an organization called Rochester Ltd., a company producing computer controlled cooling equipment for the beef processing sector.

To give Rochester's strategic policy the necessary attention, the company's top management decides to organize a two day strategic meeting. The intention of this happening is to bring the department managers together in some sort of brainstorm setting, under the supervision of a facilitator from outside the company. With such a meeting top management hopes to generate a sufficient number of ideas, leading to new combinations of products, markets and technology to safeguard the company's competitive position for a number of years in the future.

Before discussing the course of events during the strategy meeting in more detail, we first present a rough survey of the various information systems to be used here.

With a view to a fruitful exchange of ideas, the participants at the strategy meeting, for instance, must have the necessary information; about their own company (internal information) as well as about the world around (external information). The internal information can especially be extracted from *data base systems* and *management information systems*, whereas the external information will be generated by using *strategic information systems*. Strategic information systems can be seen as a collection of more specific information systems, such as *document information systems*. The whole of all information systems meant to support the functioning of the organization's top management is called *top information systems*.

During the strategy meeting the participants have to confront the internal with the external information in order to generate creative ideas as a basis for business innovations. With *idea processing systems* we are able to support this idea generating process by registering and structuring new ideas.

Because the participants at the strategy meeting of Rochester Ltd operate as a group, instead of as a collection of individuals without direct interaction, the idea processing systems just mentioned should also facilitate group processes, and therefore, in fact belong to a specific category we call *group information systems.*

When a number of ideas has been generated, at some moment it becomes necessary to judge their feasibility in economic respect. Thus, the meeting's participants must have computing facilities to identify the possible consequences of those ideas. *Decision support systems* can be used here; systems also to be applied afterwards, when preparing the various capital budgeting proposals and decisions that have to be taken to implement the strategic policy on a tactical level (see also Chapter II).

The course of the strategy meeting

After some time the strategy meeting takes place and is characterized by a fruitful exchange of thoughts and ideas. The tendency of a number of ideas especially concerns the question how ICT can be used to strengthen the organization's competitive position and pretty soon an idea has been generated that is acceptable for almost every participant.

This idea is about the possibility of the automatic reporting of cooling equipment problems to the service department of Rochester Ltd. in case of emergency. As a matter of fact, the company's service is the weak spot, for a number of reasons.

Firstly, the present emergency procedure is rather slow, leading to a waste of time (and money) and dissatisfied customers.

Secondly, the client is not always capable of describing the emergency problem adequately. As a consequence, the service mechanics are more or less obliged to have an extensive assortment of spare parts.

A third problem is caused by the degree of specialization within the service department. In fact, the company has two categories of mechanics: one category is specialized in the mechanical part of the cooling machines and the other category is specialized in the electronic part. And unfortunately sometimes the wrong expert is mobilized.

With its strategic decision just mentioned, the company hopes to realize a number of advantages leading to quicker (more effective) and cheaper (more efficient) service.

The next step to implement this idea of electronic emergency reporting is the planning of additional capital expenditures. This is because of the new equipment required for the production process of Rochester Ltd.; equipment to be used to provide its products (cooling machines) with an electronical device.

An other important investment category relates to the installation of a new information system to register and to process the emergency reports received. In this context *processing* means the mobilization of a service mechanic.

This new information system must be shaped in such a way that, on the one hand, it is able to exchange emergency data between customer and supplier automatically (called *electronic data interchange*) and, on the other hand, it can take the decision to call a service mechanic (*structured decision system).*

In addition to this, among other things the time a service mechanic needs to repair a cooling machine has to be processed administratively in order to send clients a bill. For this purpose Rochester Ltd. can use a *transaction processing system.*

In the remainder of this chapter, using the Rochester case, after this first identification of a number of categories of information systems, we pay attention to these systems and the roles they play within organizations in more detail; not only in the context of the strategy meeting, but also as instruments to implement its desisions, and to support the good functioning of organizations.

Before doing so we will discuss a more thorough categorization of information systems.

This chapter is about information systems in a *concrete* form. Using the terminology from Chapter II subsystems are discussed signifying *facet* systems.

Information systems can be classified in many different ways. We make a categorization of information systems based on human activities from the point of view of the *structure* criterium of problems: structured/semi-structured/unstructured.

Furthermore, we notice that when discussing information systems, we use the concepts *process*, *problem*, *activity* and *decision* interchangeably. This is because to solve a *problem* we can identify a particular sort of transformation *process*, composed of a number of *activities* resulting in a *decision.*

The classification 'structured/semi-structured/unstructured' we already met in Chapter II. In that chapter we defined *structured* processes as a number of activities to be described in such a way that the order of these activities can be determined unambiguously. *Semi-structured* processes are characterized by a number of activities whose order can only partially be determined beforehand, meaning that during the execution of these processes human intervention is absolutely necessary. Finally, *unstructured* processes concern processes whose order of activities cannot be determined in advance unambiguously.

Structured activities can be left completely to computers. In doing so, the human factor is *replaced.*

As opposed to structured activities, semi-structured and unstructured activities relate to activities where human beings are not replaced but *supported.* The decision maker of flesh and blood, in this situation, always takes the final decision. In this respect, the difference between semi-structured and unstructured activities is only gradual.

As a matter of fact, the less structured a problem is, the more modest the role of computers will be.

If we focus on the phenomenon of computer *support* in more detail, we can make the following observations.

Actually supporting human beings by using computers also means their replacement, though now not totally but partially. Before describing this replacement phenomenon more precisely, we have to distinguish between:

- the structuring of processes and
- the execution of processes.

For both categories of activities computers may be helpful. The assistance to the *structuring* of processes takes place by using information systems, for instance, by asking critical questions and offering stereotypes for structuring, like idea processing systems. This category information systems contains *qualitative* data (see below).

In addition, information systems to support the *execution* of processes are available; and these systems are also taking over parts of human tasks. For instance, this can be illustrated by looking at decision support systems used to make huge calculations for investment proposals that can also be executed 'by hand' but are hardly time-consuming if executed by computers. So the computer is used to replace the user here.

Moreover, in this context another phenomenon appears. Evidently, such systems are also able to execute calculations that, because of the limited time we have to take a decision, would not have been made without these machines. In this situation we are not replacing human beings but are supplementing them with extra capacity.

Of course, decision support systems are, as opposed to idea processing systems, not based on qualitative data but are only able to manipulate *quantitative* data.

Looking at our distinction of the structure of activities – structured, semi-structured and unstructured – we can categorize information systems as follows:

- structured activities: structured decision systems, transaction processing systems, electronic data interchange,
- semi-structured activities: decision support systems, management information systems, idea processing systems,
- unstructured activities: executive information systems, strategic information systems, idea processing systems.

In addition to this categorization we distinguish four other kinds of information systems: data base systems, document information systems, knowledge-based systems and group information systems.

The name 'knowledge-based systems' concerns the *way* these systems are shaped and structured inside. As far as knowledge-based systems are *applied*, they belong to one of the categories just mentioned, such as structured decision systems or decision support systems.

Most information systems are designed to be used by individual human beings. In many cases within organizations, however, we are dealing with a collection of individuals, called *groups*, doing a job. In order to offer these groups the necessary support, out of some kinds of information systems specific group variants have been developed. A well-known example is the category called 'group decision support systems'.

Different kinds of information systems: a summary

In the next section we discuss different kinds of information systems in the order identical to the successive information systems examined during the strategic meeting of Rochester Ltd. and the consequences of the decision having been taken, leading to a specific system of electronic emergency signalling and its administrative follow up.

Therefore, in section 2 we start with a discussion about executive information systems and strategic information systems.

In section 3 we focus on data base systems and document information systems.

Idea processing systems meant to be used individually and to manipulate qualitative data are the subject of section 4.

If those systems are used by groups, instead of individuals, we speak about group information systems, discussed in section 5.

These (group) information systems can be divided into two categories: group idea processing systems and group decision support systems.

Decision support systems, meant to manipulate quantitative data, are the individual variant of this latter category (section 6).

Closely related to decision support systems, and structured decision systems as far as its application in daily practice is concerned, we meet knowledge-based systems in section 7. In discussing this category information systems we also pay attention to artificial intelligence.

Speaking about structured activities we note that, structured decision systems are available; the subject of section 8. Next to this category, in section 8 we discuss electronic data interchange, too.

Transaction processing systems, also in respect of structured activities, are the subject of of section 9.

Section 10 is devoted to business process redesign, a line of thought rather dominated by innovative applications of ICT. Though a little bit outdated already, business process redesign is still a relevant topic for us because of its emphasis on innovation.

Section 11 focuses on the phenomenon of telework as an example of innovative applications of ICT and telematic, a phenomenon that would be quite impossible without the availability of these technologies.

This chapter will be finished in section 12 with a discussion of the relationship between information systems and the decision making process in so far as the various stages applicable to the Rochester Ltd. case have not yet been explored.

2. Executive information systems and strategic information systems

The availability of a number of supporting information systems is a precondition for the adequate functioning of the (chief) management of organizations. By executive information systems (also called executive support systems) we mean information systems at the highest level of the organization's hierarchy (Rockart and Treacy, 1981).

Here we meet a category information systems formed by a number of other information systems, such as data base systems, strategic information systems, document information systems and management information systems. In this section we pay attention to some aspects of executive information systems as a whole and to strategic information systems. As we already know, the other categories will be discussed in the following sections.

Specifying executive information systems we meet a number of problems, closely related to the nature of the activities of executive managers. In regard of the identification of the properties of these activities by Mintzberg, and discussed in a previous chapter (Chapter VII), the following image emerges:
- a quickly changing need of information during relatively short periods of time,
- a preference for verbal communication and
- information needs particularly concerning external developments.

Due to these properties we may have some doubt about the usefulness of ICT as a part of information systems at the highest management level of the organization. In spite of this position many students of the topic 'executive information systems' assume that such systems may contain an ICT component, a topic that we will adress ourselves to in the remainder of this section (Rockart and DeLong, 1988).

Because of executive managers' preference for verbal information flows and communication, we may wonder what the added value could be of executive information systems based on ICT. Recent research reveals that executive information systems should have the following functions (Cullen, 1995):
- drill down (the possibility to look at data at different levels of aggregation, for instance per division, per department, per product or per district),
- exception reporting (developments are reported if tolerance limits, specified for the variables involved, are exceeded),
- trend analysis (to get a clear view of relevant development patterns),
- status reports (electronically generating standard reports; reports in many organizations part of their management information system).

Next to these functionalities of executive information systems, we can think about a number of additional possibilities, such as:
- sensitivity analysis (computing the impact of alternative development patterns of a number of key variables),
- issue management (combining data originating from various sources),
- business intelligence (possibilities to disclose external data bases, relevant for the organization's long term viability; when discussing strategic information systems we return to this subject),
- communication (in daily practice electronic communication, especially electronic mail (abbreviated e-mail) is able to save a lot of time, compared with more traditional media),
- office functions (these functions relate to the personal and to the day-to-day support of various activities, such as electronic calendering of meetings; by the way an activity that is usually done by a secretary and not by top management itself).

Above we already mentioned some problems, based on the properties identified by Mintzberg about managerial work, designing executive information systems. These problems point out that the role of such systems is, in addition to other information sources used by managers, rather modest. These latter sources are particularly based on their personal network, containing many different contacts, regular as well as ad hoc, inside and outside the organization.

Therefore, we should not be surprised that, as far as organizations report successful applications of executive information systems, the real users must not be sought among executive managers, but outside this circle such as middle management and other staff.

By the way, the number of applications of executive information systems seeming to be successful is not very promising. Research on this matter reveals that 18 to 70% of the executive information systems involved has failed actually (Klaver, 1995).

Now we proceed, returning to the strategic meeting of our case company, Rochester Ltd. with a more detailed identification of the kinds of information systems which are part of an executive information system; first of all information systems meant to generate strategic information; called strategic information systems.

The concept 'strategic information system' can be interpreted in two different ways:
- information systems supporting the strategic policy of organizations and
- information systems processing (especially external) strategic flows of information.

In Chapter IV we already paid attention to the meaning of information systems in respect of the – strategic – policy of organizations. Now we focus on information systems helpful in generating strategic information. This is also the particular meaning we attach to strategic information systems.

Looking at strategic information systems their main task is tracing external developments. Therefore, these information systems have an important role in the 'signalling' phase of the decision making process. Thus, in Anglo-American literature this sort of activities is called environmental scanning or intelligence surveillance (Aguilar, 1967; Campbell, 1977).

Usually the input data of strategic information systems will not be gathered by the system itself, because strategic relevant developments cannot always be identified in advance and programmed, but by parts of the organization which have contacts with the world outside; particularly the organization's management and the selling department. Therefore, the information system containing these strategic data actually is our strategic information system. In fact, a strategic information system is no more than a data base, consisting of a specific kind of data, supplemented with some grouping and computing facilities and filled by humans.

Because of the strategic meaning of these information systems it is important for the organization's executive management to be directly responsible here.

In order to have an effective policy, organizations not only need information about their environment and external developments but also information about the organization's position as well. Not until information from these two resources is mutually confronted, are organizations able to diagnose their position and have a platform to shape their strategic policy properly.

3. Data base systems and document information systems

As we already know, the strategic meeting of Rochester Ltd. resulted in the decision of electronically detecting break downs of cooling equipment. However, before reaching such a decision the company must be aware of its position in relation to its environment. In this section we discuss information systems helpful in identifying the position of Rochester Ltd.: data base systems and document information systems.

These systems play, in connection with strategic information systems shown in the preceding section, a role especially in the signalling phase of the organization's strategic decision-making process.

Furthermore, we notice that our point of view from which to look at data base systems and document information systems is, compared with the other information systems discussed in this chapter, not their field of application. On the contrary our point of view is the technological opportunities to store and retrieve collections of data.

Office automation has increased enormously since a number of decades. Initially, ICT was especially used because of its opportunities of data storage (data bases). In fact, computers were functioning then as electronic card files. And these facilities were used, not because of their enormous storing capacity but more because of the opportunities of data access, meaning that the data needed are almost available on line and all kinds of cut outs can be made, applying various retrieval keys.

Hence, at the strategy meeting of Rochester Ltd. data base systems are well suited to picture the organization in a number of different ways. For instance, it is very easy to compare the organization's departments from various points of view.

And also it is possible to show specific developments such as in the field of sales. Using data base systems we are able to get a clear and detailed view of the company's position and its changes in the preceding years.

The character of the data being stored in data base systems is about alpha numeric quantities; in respect of storing quantitative data (numbers) as well as qualitative data (text). The management of these data collections is called data base management.

After some time users became aware of the capability of computers not only to store and retrieve data, but also to process and to manipulate these data.

If it is about the manipulation of quantitative data, i.c. the execution of calculations, then we are confronted with decision support systems.

A text processor is a well-known example of the manipulation of qualitative data. And an idea processing system is another one.

An important disadvantage of qualitative collections of data, being part of information systems, is the very laborious way of registering these data. In the beginning documents could only be stored by putting in every single symbol, characters most of the time, one after another; an activity which is very time-consuming.

This procedure was feasible as an alternative for typewriters, only for the *production* of documents, but not if already existing documents had to be copied. In the latter case paper, that could simply be multiplied by using a copy machine, was a lot more efficient.

In addition to this, because of practical reasons, it may be necessary to use documents on paper; for instance, in the case of contracts having to be signed by the parties involved.

So, it should not surprise us that until the eighties paper was pre-eminently used as the registering and transmitting device for documents.

And based on research, already mentioned in Chapter IV, at the end of that decade the storage of data over several media was as follows (CanningMcNurlin, 1989):
- 95% on paper,
- 4% on microfilm, magnetic disc, etc.
- 1% on line in computers.

What especially strikes us is the modest role of microfilm, because it has a number of advantages over paper, viz.
- less store room,
- simplified access,
- better protection,
- longer life span.

Finishing this discussion about data base systems we notice that data base systems can exist as independent information systems but can also be part of other information systems such as those already discussed in the previous section and those to be discussed in the following sections. By looking at these latter applications the – derived – functionality of data base subsystems may also be clarified.

In reaction to the things we said about document information systems and about the management of documents some changes could be identified at the beginning of the eighties, these being due to specific developments in the field of peripheral computer equipment and miniaturization of ICT.

As to this peripheral equipment, the availability of optical discs and scanners, for instance, to be used to read documents as a whole, instead of symbol after symbol, was of the utmost importance.

Moreover, the miniaturization of ICT caused the birth of mini computers and micro computers (PC's), facilitating the access of users to all sorts of data bases, including documents.

Based on these technical opportunities, the concept 'document', originally closely related to paper as a medium, assumed a broader significance. Nowadays, speaking about documents, we are pointing at all data collections having a specific significance as a whole for the user, and that can be recorded by image and/or tone media. Because it is especially about the registering of *images* – texts, diagrams, figures, etc. – here, we call this image processing. The systems involved, therefore, are called document image systems or document information systems.

These information systems, actually to be called document *data* systems, can be defined as follows:

> *systems used to manage – to be split up into inputting, storing, processing, retrieving, reproducing and circulating – data laid down in documents*

Based on this definition we conclude that document information systems play a supporting role within organizations. And the role of these systems to support the strategic meeting of Rochester Ltd. can be specified in more detail by showing specific internal or external developments, for instance, by screening documents, using different keys.

Compared with the storing of data (documents) on microfilm, document information systems offer the following advantages:

- the costs of recording and of storing documents are considerably lower,
- the accessibility of documents is many times larger and
- it is possible to make connections between documents from a number of angles.

Moreover, the technology lying behind document information systems also has advantages in the field of telegraphic transmission. For example, by using fax, complete documents can be transmitted via the telephone cable.

Both information systems discussed in this section – data base systems and document information systems – play, in mutual dependence, a role vis-a-vis the storage and the creation of accessibility of internal as well as external data.

Finally, the applicability of these systems is not only limited to the strategic policy of organizations but they can also be helpful on both the tactical and operational policy levels.

4. Idea processing systems

As was pointed out in section 2, discussing executive and strategic information systems, for a fruitful course of the strategy meeting of Rochester Ltd. idea processing systems play a rather dominant role. This role particularly relates to – supporting – idea generation. In the framework of the decision making process this is crucial for the phases 'recognition', 'interpretation' and 'formulation' as a part of the intelligence stage, and for the 'generation of alternatives' within the design stage.

Before defining idea processing systems, we pay attention to the components known as: 'idea' and 'idea processing'.

Ideas we define as (Young, 1989):

elementary mental representations of objects or concepts

Therefore, ideas are the building blocks of bigger wholes such as plans or problems (meaning 'something' asking for a decision). As a consequence, idea processing concerns the process resulting in these plans or in the identification of these problems and helping to find solutions. Now idea processing can be described as (Young, 1989):

the transformation process with ideas as input and resulting in output laid down in plans or the identification of problems

If we add the concept 'system' to idea processing, perhaps the impression is made that we are speaking about a category of information systems able to transform ideas into plans or into the solutions of problems independently; and so are able to replace mankind in this respect. In order to clarify this topic we pay attention to a number of levels to be identified in applying idea processing systems. Therefore, let us return to the strategy meeting of Rochester Ltd.

Secretary level

One opportunity to apply idea processing systems, provisionally individually, with coupling the idea processing systems of the meeting's participants, relates to the registering, and as a consequence keeping available for the user, thoughts, ideas, etc., emerging during the (strategy) meeting.

Applied this way the computer functions as a data base, containing data, consisting of text elements. As a matter of fact, the system is used as an electronic secretary, registering what is seen as important by the user.

Because of progress in the field of speech recognition, it is imaginable for the system to be able to record spoken text immediately and reproducing it afterwards in written or spoken form. Compared, for instance, with a dictaphone, the added value of such an idea processing system is its capability to select specific text elements at the request of the user.

Because of the way just mentioned the meeting's participants are able to use their idea processing system, it is called the secretary level (Young, 1989).

Framework level

At the framework level, the idea processing system supports the meeting's participants by structuring their thoughts and ideas. Such a structuring, for example, takes place by combining and grouping the input text elements from various points of view, having been programmed in advance.

Moreover, at this level we meet the capacity of the information system to watch over the procedures to stimulate the users' creativity by posing critical questions. In this latter case the system functions as a mirror. This is especially important if the idea processing system is used on a stand alone basis without communicating with other people who otherwise would pose such questions.

Within the setting of the strategy meeting of Rochester Ltd., where group interaction is very important, this isolated application is therefore less relevant.

Of course, it is out of the question that we would be very pleased if idea processing systems themselves were able to generate ideas opening new ways for the strategic policy of Rochester Ltd. In that situation we are dealing with the generative level, to be discussed now.

Generative level

As opposed to the two preceding levels – secretary level and framework level – where the user is *supported*, on the generative level the role of the user will be (partially) taken over. On this level, after the user has taken care of the necessary input consisting of a number of text elements, the information system itself generates new ideas.

The individual applications of idea processing systems developed so far have reached the second level. As to the chances of the emergence of such systems, capable of functioning on the third level, within a reasonable period of time, we can only speculate. Notwithstanding this, some idea processing systems are claimed to be equiped with generative characteristics. For instance the software program EURISKO seems to be able to defeat human experts in the field of particular military strategic issues (Lenat and Seely Brown, 1984).

For the rest in this context we refer to the subject of 'artificial intelligence, to be discussed in section 7 of this chapter.

As an example of the opportunities for applying idea processing systems we discuss the so-called 'scenario analysis'. Such a technique can be defined as taking into consideration a number of potential alternative development patterns in the future; a technique also used during the strategy meeting of our case company, Rochester Ltd.

At the secretary level several scenarios, that have been distinguished by the strategy meeting's participants are registered by using the idea processing system. The system contributes to this procedure by offering a registration format and by preventing the participants from neglecting important elements.

At the framework level, using our scenario analysis example again, the idea processing system offers the user a menu containing a number of examples of scenarios concerning specific combinations of variables to be selected by the meeting's participants. Within these scenarios a further differentiation is feasible; among other things by distinguishing between an optimistic, a pessimistic and a most probable future development pattern.

Of course, at this level the specific problem situation has to be modelled by the meeting's participants in more detail.

Furthermore, at this level the idea processing system is able to execute a number of analyses, for instance, by determining the – statistical – significance of the differences between the outcomes of alternative scenarios.

If finally, we should have an idea processing system at the generative level, then several scenarios could be generated automatically. In such a situation, the contribution of the meeting's participants consists, as mentioned above, only of the starting up of the system by putting in a number of text elements. In addition to this task, a substantial contribution of the participants is required in discussing the scenarios generated by the system.

As we have seen previously, a fundamental aspect of the strategic policy of organizations is the adaptation of their self image in order to make them attentive to possible developments that would otherwise not have been perceived, using the existing mental model. The opportunities we have discussed there to practice this second order learning relate to the creation of genetic diversity and the mobilization of external consultants. Now the question rises to what extent information systems, more precisely idea processing systems, are able to play an important role here.

To answer this question we return to the distinction we made in discussing the 'level' topic. If we are speaking about the strategic policy of organizations, then the application of idea processing systems at the generative level is not possible, as we know already. Such systems, in our opinion, only have the potential to *support* users;

support in the field of the structuring of problems (secretary level), posing critical questions (framework level), etc.

Essentially, this application has much similarity with the contribution of new organizational participants, or external consultants respectively. As a matter of fact, idea processing systems function more or less as external electronic consultants, having the task to evaluate our behaviour carefully and holding up a mirror to us. So idea processing systems are very relevant devices for supporting techniques like brain storming; a technique also used during the strategic meeting of Rochester Ltd. Applying an idea processing system, the meeting's participants are able to have their ideas checked by the system, before revealing these ideas to the other members.

Moreover, it is also possible to have ideas checked afterwards by the system, in the same way.

'ThinkTank' is a software program being able to support us adapting our mental models in view of the strategic policy of organizations (Young, 1989).

A closely related issue to idea processing is 'cognitive mapping' (Eden, 1989). This technique means the generation of several conceptual models, describing a specific problem situation to be compared and analysed. A software program very helpful here is 'Graphics COPE'.

5. Group information systems

Looking at the strategic meeting of Rochester Ltd. a *group*, consisting of a number of members closely related to each other during the meeting, can be identified. The success of the meeting also depends on the tools to be applied to stimulate the group's idea processing capacity. In this section such tools in the field of information systems will be discussed, meaning that attention is paid to group information systems, also called 'groupware'.

Group information systems can be defined as information systems supporting the activities *of* and *within* groups. By *group activities* we mean (Bostrom, Anson and Clawson, 1993):

> *mutual dependent activities executed by a number of people meant to transform the actual problem situation of the group into a desired future situation using a number of actions or steps*

The concept 'group' therefore, is used here in its task-oriented significance, no matter whether mental or physical tasks have to be executed. All other interpretations of this concept, such as a collection of human beings carrying the same – for instance, ethnic – characteristics, are eliminated this way.

In order to accomplish its task, the group must have the necessary information and the instruments to handle this information adequately.

If people are working together in groups, this may happen simultaneously (same time) as well as diachronously (different times) and located (same location) as well as dislocated (different locations), at least if the intended group process is not hampered.

Group information systems must be carefully distinguished from other information systems, ICT applications respectively, such as e-mail. As opposed to such systems, group information systems offer the opportunity of communication of many people *to* many people.

In the Anglo-American language area, group information systems are often called 'Computer Supported Cooperative Work, (abbreviated: CSCW), a name introduced in 1984 by Paul Cashman and Irene Greif (Grudin, 1991).

Because of the domination of groups, looking at group information systems, and the positive contribution of such systems to the group process, in this section we pay attention to the functioning of groups in more detail.

Compared with a collection of rather isolated working individuals, executing the same tasks, a group has a number of advantages as well as disadvantages.

The advantages of people working in groups, instead of in an isolated manner, can be summarized as follows (Forsyth, 1990; Nunamaker, c.s., 1993), viz.

- synergy (because of the differences between the group members added value is created),
- more objective judgement (group judgements are more balanced due to richer inputs of ideas and discussions),
- encouraging behaviour (belonging to a group is stimulating for the group members),
- learning (group members learn from each other).

In addition, groups also have some disadvantages, compared with a collection of rather autonomously operating individuals (Forsyth, 1990; Nunamaker, c.s., 1993):

- loss of time (if a group is discussing a problem, no more than one member is speaking at a given moment, one after another),
- blocking of results (because the other members have to listen, if one of them is speaking, they have to stop thinking about other opportunities than those revealed by the speaking member),
- adaptive behaviour (if the group has a majority point of view, the members with a deviant opinion are exposed to pressure from the others to adapt),
- groupthink (this phenomenon is closely related to the previous issue and means that group members will try to agree, and therefore run some risk of making mistakes or of neglecting relevant ideas; in fact, for the group, a common opinion is more important than other considerations),
- fear of the group's judgement (some members are afraid that the group will evaluate them negatively or will laugh at them; this issue is especially important if the group consists of people from different hierarchical organizational levels),
- free riding (people hide themselves within the group, meaning that they participate in the group process insufficiently),
- inertia (the group only pays attention to ideas as far as they correspond with the group's current problem, meanwhile neglecting other ideas perhaps also relevant to other – future – problems),
- socialization (part of the communication between the group members has nothing to do with the tasks to be accomplished, but can be qualified as 'social talk'),

- dominance (some group members try to dominate the group by using a number of manipulation devices: speaking very loudly, interrupting others, using rather inaccessible technical terms, etc.),
- information overload (the number of ideas generated by the group exceeds the group's idea processing capacity),
- coordination problems (the group does not have an effective strategy to cope with the ideas generated, and consequently confusion and premature discussions will follow),
- incomplete use of available information (the group does not make good use of all the information the individual group members have access to),
- lacking objective judgement of ideas (because an idea is introduced by a specific member of the group there may be a tendency to evaluate it as positive or negative, depending on the – organizational – position of the member involved).

In designing information systems, it is our intention to equip these systems with a functionality reducing the disadvantages of groups, meanwhile strengthening their advantages.

First of all we draw our attention to the role and significance of group information systems and their ability to *avoid* the *dis*advantages of the functioning of groups carrying out structured tasks. In order to make things clear here we use the strategy meeting of Rochester Ltd. as our starting point.

As we know, the participants in the strategic meeting, in normal – organizational – circumstances have different hierarchical positions. Thus, for some of them it could be very helpful to set out their ideas anonymously. Anonymous communication also is an effective instrument against dominant and adaptive behavior and encourages more objective evaluations.

So we have identified an important first feature of group information systems: facilities to communicate anonymously. However, anonymous communication also has a disadvantage; the disadvantage of 'free riding', meaning that some members use this facility to withdraw from effective participation. In order to prevent this sort of behavior we can imagine certain technical solutions such as the registering, by the process leader (usually called facilitator) or by the system itself, of the number of times members participated in the discussion.

A second category of disadvantages of the functioning of groups relates to the practice of ignoring some ideas. By storing these ideas in a common database, accessible to the members at any moment, the impact of this disadvantage will be diminished considerably. Therefore, it is an important requirement for group information systems to have sufficient *storage* capacity combined with adequate retrieval facilities.

In order to eliminate the disadvantage of time loss, group information systems should not only have communication capacities as such, there must also be facilities for *parallel* communication.

Using this functionality, however, it is possible to strengthen another disadvantage, the disadvantage of information overload, this way and eventually outweighing the positive impact of parallel communication. Therefore, the application of this kind of communication is contingent, meaning it should only be used in the specific situation where the disadvantage of information overload is outweighed by the advantage of preventing lost time.

A number of other disadvantages of group processes, such as inertia, can be avoided, for instance, by adding idea processing like elements to group information systems.

About the strengthening of the *advantages* of group processes by using group information systems we can be rather brief. Summarizing, the advantages of group work mainly relate to the availability of a pool of ideas and information. Combined with the features of group information systems just mentioned, these systems imply that:

- the ideas and other contributions of all the group members will be handled in a more balanced way,
- the contributions of the group members are stored and permanently available, in spite of hardly paying any attention to some of them.

If people are working together in groups, then for the group members it is normally necessary to be present in the same place at the same time. In other words, group work requires unity of *location* and *time*. Now, group information systems create the opportunity, and so the potential advantage, of abandoning these two conditions, whereas a group, in our definition, is still present.

In what way one or both of these features is absent depends on the character of the task to be executed by the group. To clarify this, we distinguish three alternatives:

- tasks requiring unity of location and time,
- tasks only requiring unity of time,
- tasks only requiring unity of location.

Tasks characterized by unity of time and location can be illustrated by meetings requiring immediate feedback between the group members (unity of time), whereas non verbal communication plays an important role, leading to the requirement of unity of location. In such a situation also, group information systems may have added value as a supporting device, next to the more traditional modes of communication, instead of replacing this sort of communication between the group members.

The sociotechnical task group, explained in Chapter IV, normally also requires unity of time and location, at least if it produces physical goods, and during the production process these goods are being transmitted from one member to another, or if the team members are same-time processing the same good, such as an automobile.

Tasks characterized by the unity of time have to be executed simultaneously. For example, this is relevant for board meetings in most organizations. However, if technical means facilitating telecommunication are available, it is often not strictly necessary to be at the same location also. Therefore, telecommunication makes it possible to drop the requirement of unity of location.

Compared with traditional means in the field of telecommunication, group information systems have, as mentioned above, the advantage of facilitating the synchronous communication of many people with many people and of using integrated multi media applications; especially combining image and sound.

With the help of group information systems, such as teleconferencing, the requirement of unity of location is no longer present.

Group tasks, not characterized by the requirement of unity of time and of location, can be illustrated by the ongoing discussion about some topic, such as the organization's strategic policy, which is not finished during a short period of time and where creative ideas of many people are paramount. Because of a lack of specific tools the organization could be forced to execute this task during a limited number of meetings, requiring unity of time and location, with a limited number of participants (remember the strategic meeting of Rochester Ltd.). Such an approach has a major disadvantage because the participants are obliged to spend a lot of their precious time meeting each other and being creative during that very short period the meeting lasts.

However, because creative ideas come to our minds at the most unexpected moments, such meetings are often not very effective (Lamb, 1991). So, it would be very helpful if the people participating in this group process, stay away from it unless they have something to communicate or if they want to react to the ideas of others. Only group information systems offer this opportunity.

Moreover, using these systems the number of participants can be increased tremendously, leading to much more added value than a traditional strategy meeting.

Just like information systems for individual applications, such as idea processing systems, group information systems can be used for the same purposes; for instance *group* idea processing systems. These information systems we call *specific* group information systems. As a matter of fact, all individual information systems can be expanded with a group variant; except information systems not *directly* used to support the decision making process, such as transaction processing systems and structured decision systems. All other information systems have individual variants as well as group variants.

To illustrate this, we pay attention to the group variant of idea processing systems. Compared with individual idea processing systems, the group variant has to offer the same possibilities of being used *simultaneously* now by the group members, for instance scenario analyses. The results of these analyses have to be immediately available for the group members to function effectively.

Furthermore, it must be clear for the other members what sort of interaction takes place between some member and the information system, and the results of this interaction. Only in this way will the group process be supported adequately and loss of the group's synergy can be prevented, because otherwise the danger exists for several group members that they are trying to get the same questions answered without being aware of each other.

Lotus Notes and *Microsoft Exchange* are examples of group information systems, combining the functions of a number of individual systems, namely idea processing systems and decision support systems (see also the next section).

At the end of this section we discuss the following concepts: *group decision room* and *virtual group*.

A group decision room can be described as:

a room equiped with a group information system

Usually, the group using the group information system is also present in this very room. So the system supports a group discussion, same time, same place.

If people are working together in a task-oriented group not requiring unity of time and/or location, then we are not dealing with a group in its original – physical – meaning. Nevertheless, using group information systems it is, as was demonstrated above, quite possible to function as a group, without face-to-face contact. Such groups are called *virtual* groups.

Research about the functioning of group information systems reveals the presence of a number of idiosyncracies for the successful application of these systems, especially:
- facilities for the synchronous execution of activities,
- anonymity,
- group size,
- structure of group processes.

Research concerning the simultaneous execution of activities points out the increase of group effectiveness in applying group information systems.

Among other things, anonymity can be guaranteed using group information systems. This requirement is particularly important if groups are composed of members with different ranks and hierarchical positions within the organization. Moreover, some research points to anonymous groups being more critical (Valacich, c.s., 1992).

As to group size, this variable positively influences the group's effectiveness as well as the satisfaction of the members of groups being supported by group information systems, because the larger the group the greater the advantages of group information systems on the dimensions 'effectiveness' and 'satisfaction' (Dennis and Gallupe, 1993).

Applying group information systems, groups executing structured tasks seem to be more effective than groups with unstructured tasks (Dennis and Gallupe, 1993).

6. Decision support systems

During the strategic meeting of Rochester Ltd. a lot of ideas have been generated. Before exploring some of these ideas in more detail it is desirable to investigate their economic feasibility.

After rejecting several ideas, as a result of this evaluation, the members of the strategic meeting finally embrace the idea of electronically signalling break downs of cooling machines.

The next step is to elaborate this idea in more detail. This elaboration, for instance, boils down to the identification of the size of the capital budgeting outlays to be made in order to realize the proposed system. This is the tactical level of the organization's policy, relating to a planning horizon of three to five years.

To take an adequate capital budgeting decision, the organization has to predict relevant developments during this period. However, due to turbulence in the world around us this is almost impossible. Still, investment calculations are based on data about the – future – course of many different variables, such as expected sales, expected price developments of raw materials, salaries, changes in competitive position, etc.

Because these assumptions are rather uncertain it is necessary for Rochester Ltd. to wonder what the result of the investment calculations would be if the assumptions were different; for instance, lower sales or higher expenditures on raw materials.

Repeating the calculations in order to identify the influence of alternative combinations – or even permutations – of assumptions is a hell of a job, almost impossible to execute without computer assistance.

Meanwhile, by executing these calculations based on different assumptions, we reach the phase 'evaluation of alternatives' of the process of decision making; a stage which is part of the design phase.

To make global economic evaluations during the strategic meeting, as well as calculating the consequences of different assumptions embedded in capital budgeting analyses, decision support systems are very helpful.

Moreover, these systems can also be used if it is necessary to convince higher level managers to get their approval about that very decision.

Decision support systems can be interpreted broadly as well as narrowly. Broadly interpreted, decision support systems are information systems at any organizational level supporting any decision taken by man whatsoever. Decision support systems interpreted this way concern, for instance, bookkeeping or transaction processing systems respectively, just like information systems meant to support the policy of organizations.

However, in doing so we create a container concept with only limited discriminating value. In other words almost any information system belongs to the category 'decision support systems'. Therefore, we prefer to interpret decision support systems in a more narrow sense.

Before discussing this interpretation we make some comments about information systems in a supporting role. Using these systems to support complicated (control) processes, we intend to stimulate process quality, leading to better results. In other words, our line of attack is not efficiency like information systems used to replace people (to automate human activities), but the effectiveness of the processes being supported where man takes the – final – decision.

Now decision support systems (in the narrow sense) can be defined as follows (Keen and Scott Morton, 1978; Freyenfeld, 1984; Mallach, 1994):

> interactive *information systems, based on* quantitative *data, used to* support *middle management, executing* complex *(ill structured) decision making processes, in respect of the* tactical *policy of organizations to improve the* quality *(effectiveness) of those processes*

One aspect of this definition needing some clarification is the *interactive* character of decision support systems. By this character we mean the possibility to communicate with the information system using some sort of dialogue. In other words, the user should have the opportunity to ask the system all kinds of questions, as far as they do not reach beyond the scope of the problem being modeled in the decision support system.

Because of this requirement decision support systems have to be very user-friendly, especially in regard of the lay out of the interface (the medium that is directly used to communicate with the computer – such as (touch)screen, mouse and keyboard) – and response time (the time it takes for the system to answer a question).

Spread sheet programs, such as 'Visicalc' and 'Supercalc', are a rather 'primitive' example of decision support systems. In addition to these more advanced and sophisticated decision support systems, to simulate business processes, such as MDSS, have been developed (Turban, 1990).

We want to illustrate the practical application of decision support systems by returning to our case company Rochester Ltd. Some weeks after the strategic decision about a system of electronic break down signalling of cooling machines, the organization arrives at the tactical policy level; it has to make a choice between a number of systems to be used to implement break down signalling automatically.

As to these systems, our organization has four possible alternatives of which one has to be selected. The most important differences between these alternatives can be identified as follows:

- technical options,
- price,
- user-friendliness,
- integration with existing systems,
- expected exploitation costs,
- cost of additional functionality.

The next step is to make capital budgeting calculations for the four alternatives, based on these six criteria, using a specific decision support system.

As was mentioned above, these calculations, in the case of Rochester Ltd. too, are based on a number of assumptions concerning uncertain future developments. Thus, it is of the utmost importance to repeat these calculations several times, using different values for the key variables.

In making these calculations, the focal point is the impact of changed assumptions on the project's return on investment. Because of this reason we are speaking here about a *sensitivity* analysis, using a decision support system.

Finally, applying the decision support system, Rochester Ltd. gets the following picture. Equiping cooling machines with electronic break down signalling devices, and additional facilities to receive these signals, seems to be feasible economically. However, the option also implying a diagnosis of the *character* of machine break downs is less attractive than the more simple option of electronic break down signalling only, without additional information.

So Rochester Ltd. decides to select an information system facilitating timely machine break down signalling, without informing the service riggers about the specific character of the break down.

The number of possible combinations of assumptions to be investigated, relating to the strategic decision of Rochester Ltd, seems, in respect of the factors listed above, to be rather small. However, if we are dealing with a larger number of uncertain factors, then the number of possible combinations increases quickly. If the company is, for instance, confronted with fifteen variables and for each variable three different assumptions about their future development pattern have to be incorporated, then the maximum number of combinations equals 3**10, i.e. 59,049. It is out of the question that Rochester Ltd. is able to make the necessary calculations for such a number of combinations within an acceptable period of time without using ICT applications.

Here the added value of decision support systems can be demonstrated clearly. As opposed to human beings, such systems have the capacity to make gigantic computations during a short period of time. Because of this property the application of ICT in the framework of decision support systems is absolutely necessary.

The added value of decision support systems can be increased additionally by not using these systems for large numbers of calculations only but also by applying these systems to *simulate* the business processes generating the returns and expenditures as input for these calculations. In doing so, organizations get a better insight into the causes of changing financial results, without experimenting with the real world situation; an approach that could be very dangerous.

As a matter of fact, in this latter situation decision support systems are used similar to the laboratory experiments in the technical sciences, such as experiments with scale models of seaships to investigate their water resistance. Using decision support systems this way, we are confronted with a very effective and powerful application.

Especially at the structure level all kinds of business processes reveal a number of similarities. For instance, any process can be characterized by the sequence: input-transformation-output. And this scheme also holds for the process parts to be distiguished within the main process.

A second common property of processes concerns the phenomenon of the events, triggering the transformation process to happen at irregular moments in such a way that the time lags between the events can be adequately described, using a so-called 'negative exponential' density function.

An other common property of transformation processes can be found in the random disturbances of those processes. As a rule these disturbances are distributed according to the Gauss density function.

Because of these common characteristics it is possible to develop a decision support model to be used for the modelling of quite different situations. This general model is called 'DSS generator' or 'DSS shell'. A specific application for a specific situation can be derived from this general model by specifying the parameters of the general model based on data originating from that very situation. Thus, this specific model is not surprisingly called 'specific DSS' (Sprague and Carlson, 1982).

7. Knowledge-based systems and artificial intelligence

The concept 'knowledge-based systems' originally denotes systems processing knowledge in a similar way as human beings handle knowledge. In this context we define knowledge as a collection of views in respect of a specific (scientific) domain.

A number of concepts is narrowly related with knowledge-based systems, such as 'artificial intelligence' and 'expert systems'. We will discuss these concepts first, before returning to knowledge-based systems.

If computer systems, defined as combinations of hardware and software, are intended to simulate the way human beings handle knowledge we meet the concept 'artificial intelligence'. According to Minsky we define artificial intelligence as (Minsky, 1967):

> *the science concerning the design of machines able to take actions that require intelligence if executed by man*

After a period of euphoria about the result of 'intelligent' information systems the development in this field of research stagnated considerably. And this stagnation has everything to do with the meaning of the concept 'intelligence' (Dreyfus, 1992).

According to Douglas Hofstadter we can sum up the following requirements about the abilities of intelligent beings (Hofstadter, 1979):
- they react flexibly to circumstances,
- they take advantage of circumstances as much as possible,
- they give a clear interpretation of ambiguity and inconsistencies,
- they are able to balance the relative importance of various factors,
- they determine similarities and differences between various phenomena,
- they form new concepts based on old ones,
- they formulate new ideas.

Obviously, looking at this list of requirements, we have a long way to go before computer systems are able to equal people in this respect.

Nevertheless, in some fields, such as chess playing, computer systems are available, able to compete with players at world level. For instance, the match between the FIDE-world champion Kasparov and the chess playing program 'Deep Blue' resulted in the Spring of 1997 for the first time in a defeat (2 1/2-3 1/2) for the human of flesh and blood. However, this performance of Deep Blue has nothing to do with human intelligence but is especially achieved by using the principle of 'brute force' combined with efficient search based on the technique of 'pattern recognition'.

Deep Blue's chess capability relates to its gigantic storing and computing capacity effectuated by two hundred and fifty six parallel coupled micro processors. Based on this capacity a tremendous number of different chess game configurations is stored. Using these configurations the computer 'recognizes' specific patterns and is able to investigate the consequences of all possible moves of both parties during a limited number of seconds. So it almost always chooses the best move.

Indeed, such an approach has nothing to do with the intelligence requirements formulated by Hofstadter. Only the final result is comparable and fits Minsky's definition of artificial intelligence.

The development of artificial intelligence is more or less similar to the way human beings have learned to move forward in the air. After originally trying to imitate the flying behaviour of birds (think about Icarus from Greek mythology) man finally succeeded in moving forward in the air using a completely different technique from birds, i.e. a technique based on the principle of *decoupling* the vertical and horizontal forces needed for lifting and propelling.

Man still does not 'fly' like birds, using aeroplanes, but the final *result* is comparable.

Expert systems are a subset of knowledge-based systems containing the professional knowledge of (top) experts.

The oldest expert system ever developed is Geoffrey Clarkson's system in the field of management, relating to the management of stock portfolios (Clarkson, 1963).

One of the earliest and most well-known examples of expert systems in other fields can be find in the domain of medicine and is called MYCIN, used for diagnosing blood and meningitis infections (Shortliffe, 1976).

In the meantime by now expert systems have been developed in many different fields (Turban, 1990; Sprague and Watson, 1996; Luger and Stubblefield, 1998).

In order to identify the specifice characteristics of knowledge-based systems, as opposed to other information systems such as decision support systems, we pay in some detail attention to the architecture of knowledge-based systems; i.e. the specific parts constituting such systems:
- inference engine,
- knowledge base,
- database,
- explanation facility.

Inference engine
The inference engine forms the heart of the knowledge-based system because this part contains procedural knowledge concerning the way man handles knowledge and solves problems, irrespective of the professional domain where the knowledge is applied. In other words, the inference engine contains a number of rules. Actually, this inference engine is the most general part of the system and is for any knowledge-based system almost the same. Therefore, the knowledge stored in the inference engine is *knowledge* specific.

Without explaining in detail how man handles knowledge we notice the following process. If, for instance, human beings have to solve a problem, they do not use the logical approach well-known from the field of mathematics: going from lemma to proof, taking a number of steps in a strictly following order. On the contrary, in their memory problem solvers look for analogies: similar problems and their solutions. Next they determine how these problems differ from the present problem and finally come to a solution. In fact, such behaviour could more accurately be labeled as: jumping to conclusions. In other words problem solvers, reaching solutions for problems, do *infer*.

Here we meet an important aspect of handling knowledge: new knowledge is always connected with existing knowledge by comparing the present situation with former ones. If, for instance, a medical doctor observes a number of symptoms he will – partly unconsciously – compare these with well-known diseases and accompanying diagnoses, whether based on literature or based on his own experience.

Knowledge base

The knowledge base contains knowledge relating to the specific professional domain of the knowledge-based system in question. This knowledge, being *domain* specific, can be divided into two parts: *procedural* knowledge and *declarative* knowledge. Procedural knowledge is about rules; rules relevant to the specific domain now. Declarative knowledge contains facts, also relevant to the specific domain.

Database

In order to solve a problem using knowledge-based systems, we need information, stored in the underlying data, about that very problem. Thus, a third base can be distiguished: the database.

The data in this base are *problem* specific.

Explanation facility

Finally knowledge-based systems are equiped with an explanation facility. Using this facility the system 'explains' how it came to its conclusion/decision. This part is important because we are, using knowledge-based systems and more especially expert systems, often confronted with ill structured problems. This lack of structure often results in more than one possible solution. So the user has to make a final choice. Therefore, to come to a well-considered decision, it is important to offer the decision maker information about the way the system has reached its conclusion. This is the task of the explanation facility.

We will clarify the use of knowledge-based systems with an illustration in the field of diagnostic applications; applications being rather familiar to organizations. In doing so we return to our case company, Rochester Ltd.

As we know already, the capital budgeting calculations, using a decision support system, resulted in the decision to equip cooling machines in the future with a device for electronic break down signalling, without giving information about the specific character of the break down. So service mechanics have to diagnose the problem in more detail at location.

In order to find the cause of machine break downs quickly, they use a knowledge-based system; actually an expert system. This diagnosis, in the present situation also relevant, proceeds as follows.

A service mechanic is mobilized by the client to repair a cooling machine. After activating the expert system it 'asks' the mechanic a number of questions about the symptoms accompanying the break down. The system stops asking questions as soon it 'knows' enough, or if the mechanic is, together with the client, not able to answer further questions. Finally, the expert system suggests a solution, i.e. it diagnoses the problem.

However, it is quite imaginable that the system cannot give unambiguous advice. If this happens, the expert systems suggests a number of conditioned alternatives, meaning that *if* the problem could be characterized by some additional symptoms *then* the solution is as follows. Therefore, we call this the if/then approach.

Looking at the illustration of the use of knowledge-based systems and expert systems respectively, the functionality of these systems is similar to the functionality of structured decision systems (see the next section) replacing human beings or to the functionality of decision support systems supporting them.

If the system is completely informed it can take an unambiguous decision comparable with the decisions of structured decision systems. Here, the user of the system does not need to add his own judgment.

If sufficient information is lacking, then the system is only able to suggest some direction for solving the problem, eventually combined with probability scores. In such a situation the system is only supportive and the user has to make the final decision.

The use of knowledge-based systems has a number of advantages:

- scarce knowledge is used better; these systems make it possible to multiply the knowledge restricted to a small number of experts,
- by registering knowledge in knowledge-based systems this knowledge stays within the organization if the experts involved leave,
- applying expert systems makes it possible to reveal knowledge to others in a learning situation,
- part of the routine work of organizational participants can be executed by knowledge-based systems; for instance, this concerns the construction of complex computer programs using so-called I-CASE tools,
- the activities of experts are improved quantitatively as well as qualitatively; quantitatively because knowledge-based systems are active twenty four hours a day; and qualitatively because knowledge-based systems can be fed by the knowledge of more than one expert.

8. Structured decision systems and electronic data interchange

As we know, structured decisions relate to activities composed of a sequence of steps to be taken many times in the past. So this sequence can be described completely. Structured decision systems can be defined as follows:

> *applications of ICT used to replace people taking (structured) decisions*

A decision making process can be described, using system theoretical concepts, as a transformation process with a problem as input and a decision as output.

Studying organizations we can meet many examples of structured decision systems. Illustrating the use of structured decision systems we discuss two real world examples in more detail; we start with the decision process about determining a personal loan.

Based on the gathered data the structured decision system makes some calculations, leading to a certain outcome, relating to the bank's conditions to make a loan. Confronted with the amount the client asks for, and the period of paying the money back, the system can take a decision. If the request of the client is rejected, the system can indicate on what terms – for instance, a lesser amount – it can still be honoured. Strictly speaking the structured decision system's task ends here.

Communicating the decision to the client and executing it (transmitting the money to the client's account), we meet two possibilities: whether the system itself takes these actions or whether it is the task of a clerk of the bank. Of course, the point of view can be defended that communicating a decision is inextricably bound up with the decision itself. However, if the system is used by a bank clerk, it functions more or less as a calculating device and the clerk communicates the outcomes to the client.

On the other hand, hardly any phantasy is required to imagine a situation characterized by an information system executing all these activities; especially if clients use some sort of system of distant banking at home.

Our second example of structured decision systems concerns electronic inventory control systems.

To understand this application properly we have to think about an organization, for instance, using a minimum ordering level for a specific raw material; for insiders such an ordering system is well-known as the 'two bin' system. This system means that, if the inventory reaches the minimum ordering level, a new quantity of raw material will be ordered. Because this inventory control process can be described by using a finite number of unambiguous steps, it can be automated; and this is what many organizations do. The structured decision system registers every decrease of the inventory and compares the rest with the minimum ordering level. As soon as this level is reached a new order will be generated.

Naturally, this order can also be communicated to the supplier automatically. However, in doing so, the structured decision system has to be complemented with a second system, for instance, based on electronic data interchange, to be discussed below.

The system of automatic break down signalling selected by Rochester Ltd. is also an example of a combination of a structured decision system and electronic data interchange.

The use of structured decision systems as such is restricted to the field of efficiency applications because the purchase of these systems is based on considerations about cost reduction due to the replacement of people by ICT.

With this point in mind it is relevant to return for a moment to our bank providing personal loans discussed above. In this situation it is quite possible for the bank to see also its effectiveness increasing, due to the fact that the procedure in respect of personal loans becomes much simpler for its clients. However, this advantage is not generated by the structured decision system as such, but particularly by automating the follow up procedure of communicating the decision to the client and by automating especially the transmission of money.

A topic already mentioned above, with a strong relationship with structured decision systems, relates to electronic data interchange (abbreviated: EDI). Electronic data interchange we define as:

the electronic data traffic between two or more organizations

In other words, we are confronted here with communication between the information systems of various organizations.

We will clarify this application of ICT by using the case of Rochester Ltd. As we know, the strategic meeting resulted in a decision to equip cooling machines in the future with an electronic break down signalling device.

As a consequence of this decision Rochester Ltd. needs an (information) system, not only to receive break down signals from clients, but also to process these signals in such a way that a service mechanic can be mobilized.

So the information systems in this respect used by both organizations can be described as follows. The cooling machines bought from Rochester Ltd. and operating in the meat processing industry contain a device for electronic break down signalling. This is an electronic diagnosing system perhaps belonging to the category of knowledge-based systems; even more precisely: expert systems. But probably it is not necessary here to use such a system because for break down signalling alone the architecture of knowledge-based systems is not required. In fact these diagnostic problems are too simple for that.

As soon as a break down occurs the system detects it and 'takes the decision' to inform Rochester Ltd. So here we are dealing with a structured decision system.

Informing Rochester Ltd. electronically means automated communication between the information systems of two organizations: electronic data interchange. Here the task of the various information systems functioning in a specific order stops and human follow up is needed, because if the message is received by Rochester Ltd. then man has to read it and a service mechanic is mobilized 'by hand' to repair the machine.

In addition to this electronic data interchange system a transaction processing system can be used in view of the administrative follow up, such as the registration of the time mechanics are in action and sending a bill afterwards.

A recent development not to be neglected here, concerns 'extranet'. Extranet we define as:

a communication network between an organization and a number of its clients, based on internet technology

Without discussing this topic in much detail, because we are only interested in ICT applications as far as the control of organizations can be improved, we note that extranet also can be used to exchange messages between organizations automatically.

In addition to this functionality extranet has a major advantage: the opportunity to do business electronically; like advertising, ordering products, sending bills and paying bills. As a matter of fact, extranet facilitates the development of electronic commerce (abbreviated: e-commerce) considerably.

Returning to the concepts 'information content' and 'information intensity', discussed in Chapter II, the application of electronic data interchange by Rochester Ltd. is an illustration of both. On the one hand, the information system needed to implement the strategic decision implies an increase in the information intensity of its process, because more ICT will be used in the future.

On the other hand, the information systems, as a part of the cooling machines (electronic break down signalling devices) do increase the information content of Rochester Ltd.'s products. In this situation the concept 'product' has to be interpreted rather broadly as is usual in the marketing field. In that context we must not only think about the physical product (cooling machines), but also about the obtainability of products, product information, service level, etc. In particular the service level increases due to the extra device cooling machines will be equiped with.

9. Transaction processing systems

As the name already suggests, transaction processing systems, also called 'data processing systems' or 'transaction information systems', concern transactions of organizations. In this context a *transaction* can be defined as (O'Leary and Williams, 1985):

> *any businesslike event occurring within an organization and leading to mutations*

Transactions may happen in many different fields. As an example we can think about operational activities to execute the organization's primary process, such as buying raw materials, paying salaries, receiving payments from clients, etc.

In all these cases, mutations take place having to be registered. And this registration (administrative processing) is the main activity of transaction processing systems.

One of the most well-known examples of these systems is the organization's bookkeeping system.

If we speak in the remainder of this section about transaction processing systems we mean:

> *the whole of all (sub) systems used for administrative processing transactions within organizations*

Such a system is composed of a number of subsystems concerning specific activities within the organization. At the end of this section we return to this topic of transaction processing subsystems using a concrete example.

The processing of transactions can be divided into four different activities (O'Leary and Williams, 1985):
- input of data,
- processing of data,
- storing of data and
- output of data.

Input of data
Any event within the organization, causing a mutation, has to be registered. This means that the data, relating to these mutations, form the input for the system handled in an efficient and an effective way.

The document, serving as the basis for the input of data is called the 'basic document'. Many sorts of basic documents can be distinguished, such as a bill, a letter of resignation, etc. Usually, at least until today, we are speaking here about paper documents. But data can also be made available in electronic form.

Processing of data
After the input of data they have to be processed, meaning the storage of the mutation due to a specific event in the transaction processing system.

It is possible to process data, combined with input, in three different ways:
- on line input and batch processing,
- on line input and on line processing,
- batch input and batch processing.

In the situation of on line (real time) input and batch processing the data input takes place at the moment of the transaction and the processing happens later on. As a matter of fact, the data are collected one at a time and processed if they reach a certain number or if a certain period of time has expired.

This approach is, for instance, followed in retail companies where electronic stand alone check-outs permanently register sales whereas at the end of the day total sales form the input for the transaction processing system.

As opposed to the former situation on line input combined with on line processing means that data are not collected one at a time and processed collectively but every single data is processed separately.

For instance, this procedure is necessary for specific raw materials having to be ordered if the minimum inventory ordering level, being part of the so-called 'two bin' inventory control system, is reached. An out of stock position may temporarily be the consequence of delaying a new order, and so the production will stagnate. Therefore, any decrease must immediately be registered by the system, to prevent stock problems.

Using the combination of batch input and batch processing of data, the basic documents containing data are collected first. Because we are confronted here with a clustering due to the selection process, the data are also processed as clusters.

This method of input and processing will, for instance, be applied to determine the number of hours each labour force member has worked and will be registered on a card. At the end of the day the cards are handed in to the clerical department, so they can be processed immediately.

Data output

Of course, data are not stored because of their own sake but because of a specific objective: support of the functioning of the organization. Therefore, on the one hand, the transaction processing system will be used at the initiative of one or more organizational participants, whereas, on the other hand, the system makes certain output available automatically. As to this latter activity we have to think about the production of data, including possible documents, concerning information needs to be specified in advance. For instance, we are confronted here with generating invoices if products are sold, periodical summaries (once a week) of the sales per product and the production of salary data (once a month).

Above, transaction processing systems were discussed in general. Additionally, a second point of view, in respect of the several *parts* (subsystems) of the transaction processing system, can be identified.

Because this subject can only fruitfully be discussed with a real world case in mind we will illustrate these subsystems using the example of a company producing several types of automobiles. Within this organization two categories of transaction processing subsystems can be identified:

- transaction processing systems concerning the primary process (*primary* transaction processing subsystems) and
- transaction processing systems in regard of facilitating and supporting processes, such as sales, maintenance and personnel (*facilitating* transaction processing subsystems).

Primary transaction processing systems

It goes without saying that the structure of the primary process is a dominant factor for the shape of the organization's structure and thus also for the resulting transaction processing subsystems. For instance, such a transaction processing subsystem in a situation characterized by the assembly line approach will be quite different from a production process structure based on sociotechnical principles. In our automobile example we assume that these latter principles are being used.

This situation means that, as far as some sort of registration of the products in process is used – i.e. registration of the ever changing status of products in process – the teams involved have to do this themselves. This is certainly relevant to the situation where the teams have all the necessary equipment to make a complete product, without sharing equipment with other teams. Only at the end of the planning period will management be informed about the team's output, administratively characterized as a combination of batch input and batch output.

Depending on the properties of the production process, in other situations, different combination of input and output, both divided in batch and on line, will be relevant.

Facilitating transaction processing systems
Assuming that the team principle of our automobile company is only used for the *production* function on the shopfloor, it is possible to formulate the properties of facilitating transaction processing systems in a more general way.

In any – market oriented – organization we will be confronted with a number of stocks (apart from the products in process, discussed in the context of primary transaction processing systems), often meant literally, changing again and again, that have to be registered.

In this context we have to think about the following stocks:
- raw materials,
- finished goods,
- machinery,
- furniture,
- money,
- personnel,
- etc.

For instance, controlling raw materials we need the following transaction processing subsystems:
- creditor administration (including a suppliers database),
- stock administration for the several sorts of raw materials,
- sales administration.

In the same way we can think about the following personnel transaction processing subsystems:
- personnel administration,
- sick leave administration,
- salary administration.

Just like any other information system, transaction processing systems concern, as said before, the control of organizations. For instance, the registration of stock changes is necessary because otherwise the risk of running out of stock may become unacceptable, as was mentionend before.

However, transaction processing can also be used to reconstruct the processes involved if there is disagreement. For example, a supplier could blame us for not having ordered our bank to pay a bill in time. With a well-functioning clerical department it is easy to investigate this problem.

Of course, this opportunity to reconstruct processes can also be used for the control of organizations. Especially, reconstruction could be relevant here to prevent mistakes in the future, for instance due to specific procedures falling short.

So, transaction processing systems are an important instrument for checking all sorts of operations as part of the control cycle of organizations.

10. Business process redesign

From time to time new management and control concepts are launched. As illustrations originating in the past we mention (Block, 1987; Juran, 1984):
- just in time,
- empowerment and
- total quality management.

A rather recent development in the field of management techniques, and almost outdated today already, is business process redesign, closely associated with the names of Michael Hammer and James Champy (Hammer and Champy, 1993). In addition to the concept 'business process redesign', 'business process reengineering' and 'business process improvement' are also used (Harrington, 1991: Davenport, 1993).

For the redesign of organizations, as advocated by business process redesign, the use of ICT, or information systems respectively, is rather dominant. This is why we discuss this topic here.

In this section we firstly pay attention to the principles of business process redesign. Secondly the role of ICT especially applied innovatively, as well as the role of information systems, will be discussed.

The following case story may be used to illustrate the technique of business process redesign.

Because of high salaries and unacceptable losses during a number of years, the owner of a pub had no other choice but to fire some of his staff. After some time, however, this measure caused complaints about the pub's service level, in particular due to increased waiting time for the clients.

Moreover, the waiters did not feel very happy with the way they were functioning. On the one hand, they were constantly in a hurry to register orders and to deliver drinks, etc. to the customers, whereas, on the other, hand they had to wait at the bar until the bar personnel had prepared these drinks and other foods. For the waiters, waiting time was not only boring but also caused them more fatigue.

By the way, honestly speaking, this latter waiting and idle time problem already existed before some of the waiters were fired. But now it became more pressing because of the customers' complaints just mentioned.

In the past the owner had looked for solutions to solve this problem, for instance, by enlarging the tasks of the waiters with task elements of the bar personnel. However, this seemed not to solve the problem adequately because of the limited room behind the bar.

Finally our pub owner found the following solution, solving both problems: customer complaints and idle time. The waiters were given a device, particularly developed at the request of our pub owner, the size of a pocket calculator, to be applied to transmit the customers' orders by remote control to a new information system at the bar, used by the bar personnel. While the waiters were registering a number of other orders and came to the bar, several orders had meanwhile already been carried out by the bar personnel and could immediately be taken to the customers.

Obviously, the redesign of the (pub) process, by using an information system, or ICT respectively, contibutes to the solution of both problems effectively.

In almost any organization, especially manufacturing organizations, the organization's structure is based on *specialization* at all levels and within almost every part. Because we are speaking here about specialization within functions in respect of organizational participants, we use the concept of *functional* or *horizontal* specialization.

The activities, to be executed by these participants are parts of a larger whole, contributing to the products resulting from the primary process. So these activities have to be coordinated.

And because the product, during the production process, matures from raw material to consumer good, i.e. a good to be sold on the external market, by passing several departments *horizontally*, the coordination should also be horizontal. However, usually control and coordination within organizations, and especially the coordination of the primary process, takes place vertically starting from the organization's hierarchy.

And also within this hierarchy functional specialization is dominant. Therefore, this sort of coordination strengthens the functional specialization at the workfloor level instead of mitigating it. As a consequence all departments only have a limited scope, determined by their own self interest, without caring about the interest of the larger organization. And often this attitude not only means ignoring the interests of other departments but even harming these interests explicitly.

The utmost consequence of a production and organization structure based on the principle of functional specialization is the assembly line system. Not only is the necessary variety in task elements missing here but also variety in product characteristics for the customer is completely absent. Because of this mass production the customer only has two options: to buy or not to buy.

This dilemma is well-illustrated by the point of view of Henry Ford in regard of his famous T-Ford:

you can get any colour if it is black

In addition to a number of efficiency advantages, the assembly line system is especially accompanied by large amounts of more or less hidden costs. For instance, we can mention:

- the design costs of the production process, because the total process has to be split up in a large number of parts, every one taking the same amount of time,
- the consequence of stagnation of one part of the process for all the other parts,
- attuning the speed of the assembly line to the mean employee, meaning that for fifty percent the speed is too low and for the other fifty percent the speed is too high, both leading to negative side effects,
- the relatively large number of hierarchical levels within the organization's structure, due to the limited authority of the organizational participants,
- the time lost because of internal transport and waiting time, at least if not all activities are coupled in a completely fixed way,

- lack of involvement of people in their activities because they are not motivated at all, but feel bored and alienated from their work and from the products they contribute to.

Because of lack of motivation, among other things, there is a lot of sick leave and there are wasted products. Therefore, this shortcoming (lack of motivation) is a major cause of hidden costs.

According to Hackman and Oldham, people's motivation is closely related to the following function characteristics (Hackman and Oldham, 1976):
- variation in skills,
- opportunities to identify oneself with the task,
- importance of the task,
- sufficient authority,
- feedback.

In view of what is said about the coordination problems previously, the point of impact of business process redesign concerns functional specialization combined with the position of the client of each organizational process.

Functional specialization results, as far as business process redesign is concerned, in many connection points between functions within the primary process, where things can go wrong. And, due to Murphy's Law ('if anything can go wrong then it will'), this will happen indeed. Therefore, it is absolutely necessary to stop the development of further functional specialization and to strive for functional integration.

Not only functional specialized organizations are a collection of rather isolated departments, but they also loose sight of the *client*. As a consequence, goods will be produced which no one is actually asking for, but are still bought in some quantities because the customer does not have feasible alternatives. So it is important for each process within the organization to give the client a central position in order to realize results really wanted; no matter where the client may be located, inside or outside the organization.

To realize functional integration the organization has to be redesigned fundamentally. In view of this redesign process two principles are very important:
- the cornerstone of the new organization structure and
- the levers facilitating the process of redesign.

Cornerstone and levers

As opposed to functional specialized organization structures, based on *tasks*, business process redesign uses as its cornerstone *processes*, meaning:

> *a combination of activities leading to a final result for a specific client with clearly and unambiguously defined product requirements*

By emphasizing processes, tasks will be integrated, activities coordinated and attuned to the requirements formulated by the next phase in the (production) process.

Levers, also called *enablers*, can be defined as instruments facilitating functional integration. As to levers we make a distinction between two different categories (Davenport, 1993):
- organizational levers and
- ICT levers.

Organizational levers can be further distinguished in 'structural' and 'cultural' kinds. *Structural* levers relate to the design of the organization structure, facilitating the process of functional integration. For instance, we can think about team based work here according to sociotechnical principles (see also Chapter IV).

With *cultural* levers we mean the system of norms, values, etc. characterizing an organization. For instance, instead of dominating hierarchical relationships one could strive for a more participative culture and management style.

Of course, in this book the ICT levers are the most important to us. Therefore we discuss these levers separately.

ICT applications make it possible to integrate process parts previously located in separate tasks. This is not only relevant to processes inside the organization but to processes outside the organization as well.

For instance, a company in the pharmaceutical line of business got the idea to give the buyers of its products, i.e. pharmacists, access to its computer system to order medicines. Because of this integration, the number of personnel in the sales department could be decreased from seven hundred to fifteen (!) meanwhile considerably accelerating the deliveries of products ordered.

As a matter of fact, ICT is, as this example demonstrates, a very powerful lever for business process redesign.

The organizational changes just mentioned are actually not a byproduct of the use of information systems, or of ICT respectively, but the intended target whose realization is facilitated by using these resources.

In order to take full advantage of the opportunities of ICT it is of the utmost importance to look for *new* and *innovative* applications instead of imitating existing ones. For instance, this is relevant for mini and micro computers, because a tendency to see this equipment as a cheap alternative for mainframes can be identified. If this is so, then its impact is almost exclusively restricted to efficiency advantages and we cannot expect results leading to a radical redesign of existing structures, based on innovative applications.

However, due to using ICT as a lever for business process redesign, innovative applications of this technology are emerging slowly, because of the emphasis on existing applications. To really reap the fruits of ICT, to fight the productivity paradox (see Chapter I) a radical turn around within organizations is required (Beatty and Gordon, 1988). The turn around we have to think about here could be illustrated with the invention of the cinema movie.

The medium 'movie' was already known in the nineteenth century, and was originally used to register and to reproduce theatre plays in a linear manner. At first, people did like to look at plays registered on film tape in a dark cinema. But after some time they changed their mind and preferred to visit the theatre to watch plays executed by real actors of flesh and blood, as a result of which cinemas were left with more and more idle capacity. Only when the technique of *montage* was discovered (movie fragments can be edited in any following order, completely different from the registering process) did the medium movie really get added value and the cinema was back again.

The same sort of consideration is relevant to ICT. If we try to do the same things as before with this technology, its contribution is only marginal. A breakthrough in the field of ICT can only happen if we are dealing with applications which are impossible without this technology, applications which open up new horizons by looking at the fundamental needs of the organization and its customers.

Moreover, in doing so it is very important to develop applications in respect of the organization's core business, because their impact here is far-reaching, more than in any other field (Keen, 1991).

The theory mentioned above will be illustrated here with three cases of innovative applications of ICT. The first case we borrow from Hammer and Champy, the champions of business process redesign (Hammer and Champy, 1993).

In a certain company the department 'product design' was geographically dispersed over more than one location. This dispersion required regular meetings of the designers. To facilitate the design process the idea was born to make use of the opportunities of teleconferencing, belonging to the category 'group information systems' (see section 5), originally meant by the company to replace the time and money consuming group meetings of this company's designers.

But, after some time it became evident that electronic meetings were not a good alternative to face-to-face meetings because of the limited opportunities of non verbal communication, and informal contacts outside the meeting room. Therefore, it was decided to restore the original meetings, and to use the system of teleconferencing – because it was still available – not to replace but to supplement the regular meetings for contacts on an ad hoc basis. After a number of months the organization discovered that, due to this combination of instruments, by using teleconferencing in a more innovative way, the required design time has been reduced considerably.

A second example of innovative applications of ICT relates to an organization which is a wholesaler of bathroom devices. This wholesaler buys all kinds of devices from many different suppliers that, in a lot of combinations, are sold to its customers, such as retail companies and installers. Originally, the added value of wholesalers is created by bridging time and location gaps between factories and their customers. However, a major problem our wholesale company felt was its very limited influence on the needs of the final consumers (the occupants of the houses where the bathroom devices are installed), which they did not have direct contact with. Of course, advertising could be an instrument to bypass the installers. ICT could help to solve this problem. And indeed the company came to the conclusion that this technology creates opportunities to inform the consumer more directly, particularly by giving them a disk to be used at home to compose many different bathroom designs combining a number of building blocks. Hence, the concept 'virtual' bathroom was born. This approach has been facilitated due to advanced techniques and the widespread availability of ICT applications.

In addition to the sources of added value just mentioned (bridging time and location gaps), our wholesaler got an extra one: providing information to, and directly influencing the customer thanks to modern ICT.

A third and more general example of the innovative application of ICT concerns a mass production system, able to cope with the individual wishes of clients to a certain extent by applying this technology: CAD/CAM (Computer Aided Design/Computer Aided Manufacturing) systems. For instance, these systems are used in the automobile sector, where the client can make a choice between a number of properties in addition to a standard model, to compose the car he likes most.

It is completely impossible to produce all these potential combinations in advance, because of its gigantic number. If, for instance, we are confronted with fifteen different additional properties, then the total number of combinations is almost thirty three thousand (2**15). And any additional property increases this number exponentially. So stocks containing all these combinations are very expensive, or even almost impossible. But, if we do not want to restrict the clients' choice opportunities beforehand, the car with a specific combination of properties can only be produced afterwards if the company is well-informed about the combination desired by the client. Without the help of ICT (embedded in a CAD/CAM system) such an individualization of production orders would be absolutely impossible.

In this situation the application of ICT takes place as follows. At the design department the required combination of properties will be determined, using Computer Aided Design. Next, the execution order is automatically transmitted to numerically controlled machines in the production department. So we are dealing here with Computer Aided Manufacturing. Hence a CAD/CAM production system means that, after the specific car is designed in the designing room using a computer, it will leave the assembly line automatically after some time.

As a consequence CAD/CAM systems increase the production process' information intensity.

In order to identify possible opportunities offered by the application of ICT we start with an enumeration borrowed from Davenport (1993):

- Automational: eliminating human labour from a process,
- Informational: capturing process information for purposes of understanding,
- Sequential: changing process sequence, or enabling parallelism,
- Tracking: closely monitoring process status and objects,
- Analytical: improving analysis of information and decision making,
- Geographical: coordinating processes across distances,
- Integrative: coordination between tasks and processes,
- Intellectual: capturing and distributing intellectual assets,
- Disintermediating: eliminating intermediaries from a process.

In addition to this enumeration we pay attention to the levels of innovative applications of ICT as distinguished by Venkatraman (1991).

Level 1: localized exploitation
This is the most basic level of exploiting ICT capabilities within organizations, limited to local applications without mutual relations. The advantages of such an approach concern efficiency and sometimes effectiveness.

Level 2: internal integration
In this situation organizations recognize the centrality of an ICT platform, or infrastructure. We may expect such a platform to permit the exploitation of efficiency-related benefits of compression of time and distance as well as effectiveness-related benefits of information distributing and sharing across business processes.

Level 3: business process redesign
As opposed to the two former evolutionary levels, requiring rather modest changes in business processes to exploit ICT, this third level is revolutionary, meaning that radical changes in organization practices are necessary. The central premise at this level is that ICT is a lever for designing business processes; an approach that would not have been possible without this technology. Organizations initiating radical business process redesigns do not only become more efficient but are also more competitive (effective).

Level 4: business network redesign
So far, we have seen ICT inducing a reconfiguration within a single organization. In contrast, the fourth level represents the use of this technology for redesigning the nature of exchange relations among multiple participants in a business network. Therefore, this strategy is called *electronic integration*; not to be confused with electronic data interchange, for instance. In contrast to this latter application, relating to the technical features of networks, strategies for electronic integration address business issues involving the relative authority and responsibilities of the different participants. As a matter of fact, electronic integration can be used to shape relations between organizations that previously only could be realized by complete horizontal and/or vertical integration.

For instance, organization A is a supplier of organization B. Instead of taking over A by B (vertical integration) it now suffices to couple the processes of both organizations using ICT. It is no longer necessary to merge the two organizations; a network of organizations alone can do the job (Rockart and Short, 1991).

The advantages at this level can be identified in a wide range: from operational efficiency to strategic capabilities.

Extranet, already defined above, is a kind of network very valuable for putting business network redesign into practice.

Level 5: business scope redefinition
This final level assesses the potential role of ICT in the redefinition of business scope. In fact two specific issues are considered here: (1) business scope enlargement and (2)

business scope shift. Business scope enlargement can, for instance, be realized by offering value-added services related to the original business by applying ICT. Shifting the business scope concerns changes in the organization's strategic combination: the combination of products, markets and technologies. The impact of ICT from a strategic management perspective lies, on the one hand, in its potential to render many of the traditional tasks and skills obsolete, whereas, on the other hand, new opportunities are emerging being far beyond our phantasy as long as this technology is only used to gain efficiency benefits. This is only possible if we look behind the products we manufacture, in order to identify their real functionality, the relevant core competencies and the contribution ICT can make; not only in the production process but also in the product or service and in the exchange process as well.

Therefore, at this level the advantages of ICT are especially strategic

The identification of – innovative – applications of ICT discussed above raises the question how organizations are able to recognize themselves here as far as really creative breakthroughs are concerned (Fransman, 1999). To shed light on this matter we return to our discussion of mental models. However, before doing so, we pay attention to two categories of characteristics of ICT: more general characteristics and more specific characteristics. This discussion may be helpful in generating innovative applications of ICT.

Speaking about more general characteristics we mean the dimensions in which ICT differs more or less from other technologies, i.e. rate of change, impact, contagion and character; four viewpoints to be discussed in more detail now.

Rate of change

As to the *rate of change* we can make the observation that ICT differs considerably. For instance, according to Moore's Law, every year the storage capacity of integrated circuits, or chips, doubles (Chattell, 1998). Hence, this technology offers a lot of opportunities, especially to early adapters.

Impact

Metaphorically, the functioning of organizational and societal information systems can be compared with the human nervous system. If this system breaks down, the human body will be paralyzed. In quite the same way, organizations and society suffer from paralysis if they do not have adequate information systems, often based on ICT. And moreover, because of environmental turbulence, information becomes more and more important. Therefore, the *impact* of ICT is rather high and still increasing.

Contagion

One striking property of ICT, especially due to miniaturization and cost reduction, relates to its *contagion* within organizations and within households as well. In almost any part of our present society we are confronted with applications of this technology. And this process of penetration will go on, leading to an increasing number of self controlling products and processes. Here we meet the concept 'embedded software'; the software being embedded in products and processes to improve their functioning.

Character
Looking at the *character* of ICT, an important difference between older technologies and this one can be distinguished. This first category of technologies, dating back to ancient human history, aimed to extend the physical capabilities of mankind, ranging from simple tools, like spades, to rather complex modern automobiles. ICT, however, concerns the human mind in respect of storing, processing and retrieving information. With this technology it is possible to increase our mental capabilities to a large extent, such as in numerically controlled machines and all kinds of information systems (Chattell, 1998).

Apart from the more general characteristics of ICT we also distinguish a number of specific properties. To identify these properties we have to make a distinction between the two basic elements of this technology, i.e. information and communication.

Information
In the field of information computers have three powerful properties: storage capacity, processing speed and retrieval capabilities.

Though human beings have an enormous *storage capacity* (about one gigabyte each) nowadays several computers are already superior in this respect. And combined with their *retrieval capabilities*, many times superior to human beings, they are very helpful as our background memory. Moreover, the *processing speed* of computers also exceeds the capacity of human beings also many times. Taken together these three properties are responsible for computers that outperform people in many fields. So their added value may be enormous.

Communication
As to the communication aspect of ICT two powerful properties can be identified: unity of time and place are no longer required. Of course, some of our older communication means, such as the telephone, make it also possible to bridge geographically dispersed locations in real time, but the *combination* of the properties just mentioned is new, enabling a lot of novel products such as – more or less – interactive distance learning (also called telelearning) and telework. The subject 'telework' will be discussed in more detail in the next section.

About 'telelearning' we notice that this phenomenon is rather different from traditional distance learning, as has been practised by the Open University 'for ages'. The most important medium for facilitating distance learning is printed paper combined with hardly any – on line – interaction between teachers and students. Compared with distance learning, telelearning is heavily based on the application of modern ICT tools, facilitating interactive learning and virtual class room experiences.

Once more, we stipulate that, using ICT, two main streams can be identified: replacement and support. If this technology is used to *replace* people, then we are in fact doing the same things more cheaply and more efficiently. In spite of the cost reduction caused by such applications we cannot expect to realize large positive effects. Only if we are able to generate completely new applications, often *supporting* people and making them more effective, will the potential benefits of ICT rise quickly.

With this discussion about a number of properties of ICT in mind we return to the subject 'mental model', already paid attention to in the context of the strategic policy of organizations. And just like the necessity to adapt our mental models to generate new strategic options, this adaptation is relevant to innovative breakthroughs in the field of ICT as well.

However, many organizations, using this technology, also seem to prefer not to cross the limits of existing applications very much, innovative applications are not numerous. In this way, new opportunities are often discovered ad hoc and haphazardly.

In order to generate innovative applications of ICT in a more systematic way it is necessary not to see the technology as a starting point (technology push) but the organizational processes and the function of their products to be supported (demand pull). By this point of view we mean that organizations should wonder what technological capabilities they need for their products and processes without being guided or limited by the possibilities they perceive at a given moment. As was said before, organizations have to look not at their specific products they accidentally happen to produce, but at the functions of their products. In doing so, perhaps new ideas will be generated to shape these functions in a quite different way.

By freeing our creative energy and creativity, if necessary supported by idea processing systems, we are perhaps able to formulate the required ICT applications to make our phantasy come true.

Analogous to the well-known saying in the domain of strategic policy 'structure follows strategy', here the leading principle is: 'technology follows phantasy'.

To illustrate this we return to the example at the start of this section; the case of the process redesign of a pub, using ICT.

As a matter of fact this company did not ask for external advice to identify the – existing – technical opportunities. On the contrary, it invented a solution itself by mobilizing its phantasy. Not until then did a computer company get the order to realize this solution.

This case makes clear that our starting point just mentioned makes sense. A company has a problem, whether offensive or defensive, and imagines a solution (the wireless transmission of orders at a limited distance) without posing questions about its technical feasibility. It is not the technique which should be dominant but the need of the organization to get new applications.

In other words, the technology push in the field of ICT has to be turned around into a demand pull in order to generate major breakthroughs.

We wish to finish our discussion of business process redesign with an enumeration of a number of benefits of process integration:

- shorter waiting time or through put time,
- fewer overhead costs,
- the customer's wishes become more dominant, leading to increased effectiveness,
- increased control by organizational participants of their own work,
- task variety,
- better motivation.

11. Telework

A phenomenon, developing rather quickly due to ICT, and to innovative applications in this domain, relates to teleworking or telework.

Telework we define as:

a situation characterized by a geographic separation between the employee's workplace and the employer's residence, using ICT

Looking at this definition, we notice that – similar to the difference between distant learning and telelearning – well-known forms of working at home like packaging products, already existing for many years, are not classified as telework. For telework the application of ICT is absolutely necessary.

As will be clear, telework causes flexibilisation of activities as regards the dimensions of time and location. When using modern communication means, it is no longer necessary to execute a number of activities at specific times and at specific locations. Even, by using ICT, it is possible for the members of teams to do their jobs at different locations; thus giving birth to virtual teams (Townsend, DeMarie and Hendrickson, 1998).

As to telework we can distinguish between a number of appearances:

- work at home,
- satellite work,
- neighbourhood work.

The most well-known form of telework is *work at home* meaning that employees pursue some activities at home instead of being occupied in the organization's residence where they are normally employed. However, the application of ICT is sometimes not absolutely necessary here (for example, a school teacher marking test papers of his pupils at home usually does not need this technology to do his work properly). But still the use of ICT has to be required to clasify these activities as 'telework'.

Satellite work concerns activities concentrated at a place which is not the organization's main residence. This is a form of telework to be met in many organizations, for example because of the necessity of geographically dispersed selling departments to be near to the local markets of their products. In this situation the focus is not upon single employees but upon complete departments being dislocated.

A third possibility of telework we want to distinguish is *neighbourhood work.* Using this form of telework a number of employees of more than one organization work in the same building in their own neighbourhood.

Telework is characterized by advantages and disadvantages for employers and for employees as well, to be identified below.

Advantages for the employer

The most important advantages of telework for the employer are a higher labour productivity combined with lower costs. As to these lower costs we have especially to think about housing costs and travelling costs from home to work and back.

The increased labour productivity of telework originates in a number of factors, such as:

- efficient design of individual working hours attuned to the individual day and night cycle,
- less risk of getting diverted if concentration is necessary,
- decrease of sick leave because teleworkers tend to be less ill and the period of their recovery process is shorter.

Disadvantages for the employer

Unfortunately, telework does not only have advantages for the employer, but displays a number of disadvantages as well. Firstly, the involvement of teleworkers is not always optimal. So their personal interest may dominate the organization's interest.

Closely related with this disadvantage there is a second one, the danger of social isolation and loneliness, which is sometimes rather detrimental to the employees' output.

A third disadvantage concerns the possibilities to check the activities of employees. Because these activities cannot be monitored by the management, only control based on output norms is feasible. Activities needing control based on input are therefore not well-suited for telework.

Fourthly, for teleworkers it is important to have the required equipment to do their job elsewhere without losing contact with the organization. Hence, considerable amounts of money have to be invested to buy and maintain ICT applications; though in many households several applications of ICT are available.

It is even possible that in some situations ICT falls short because adequate communication between the people involved requires face-to-face contacts. For instance, this requirement is met if non verbal communication plays an important role whereas modern ICT is not yet able to incorporate this aspect sufficiently. In this situation the – lack of – feasible opportunities is prohibitive for the practice of telework.

Advantages for employees

The following advantages of telework for employees can be identified. Firstly, employees can save travelling time and travelling money. A second advantage relates to the opportunity of more flexibele working hours attuned to their individual wishes. This characteristic of telework is especially important for employees whose labour market entrance is blocked without the opportunities of telework, such as people who want to combine caring tasks with parttime participation in paid labour or people with a mobility problem because of a physical handicap.

Disadvantages for employees

There is only one, but a very important, disadvantage of telework for employees: social isolation. If people work at home, it is clear that their contacts, particularly informal contacts, with colleagues will decrease considerably. Hence, to mitigate this disavantage, frequently telework is combined with a limited number of working hours at the organization's (main) residence. Also, this isolation problem can be solved by satellite labour, or even neighbourhood labour, though in this latter situation employees only have the opportunity to make direct – face-to-face – contact with other people not being employed in their own organization.

Because the impact of telework on feelings of isolation is not the same for every employee, this topic will be discussed separately.

Feelings of social isolation are closely related to the motivation of people to join organizations and the needs, in respect of Maslov's 'need hierarchy', which they try to satisfy this way.

Without discussing this need hierarchy thoroughly we want to distinguish here three groups of employees as far as their needs in connection with paid labour are concerned:

- employees motivated by primary needs,
- employees motivated by social needs and
- employees motivated by the need of self actualisation.

If employees are only motivated by the satisfaction of their *primary* needs – food, clothes, lodging – as was relevant to many participants in the early years of this century, then contact with fellow human beings (satisfaction of social needs) does not play a role. In such circumstances, from this point of view, the execution of tasks can happen in a rather isolated manner and telework could be a real option.

On the other hand, however, the technical lay out of the production process may obstruct telework as we will see below.

What has been said before about the opportunities of telework for employees motivated by primary needs is also relevant to people motivated by the need of *self actualisation*; self actualisation meaning that their personal ambition level is very high. So they are more oriented to themselves and to their work than to others. In fact, we are speaking here about highly skilled professionals. Often they communicate more frequently with the same professionals within other organizations, especially in writing contributions in scientific periodicals or attending conferences, than with their direct colleagues. Such employees do not so much participate in satisfying social needs as in reaching top-notch performance. As far as it is technically feasible they can be considered for telework.

Finally, we distinguished a category of employees participating in organizations motivated by opportunities to satisfy *social* needs. Not surprisingly, telework undoubtedly conflicts with this state of mind.

In addition to the social consequences, and the opportunities to apply telework, we have to distinguish between three categories of employees, or activities, from the angle of the physical limitations of telework:

- employees having jobs requiring physical proximity,
- employees having jobs not requiring physical proximity,
- employees not being able to participate in paid labour without opportunities for telework, i.e. using ICT.

For this first category of employees, we do not take telework into consideration, whereas in the third situation telework is an absolute prerequisite. The first category especially concerns blue collar workers cooperating in highly interdependent jobs; for instance, this is relevant to the production of automobiles. For such jobs, among other things, telework leads to huge transportation costs and a waste of (production) time.

As mentioned before, employees belonging to our third category, for example people with a physical handicap, are considerably benefited by using ICT applications to facilitate their participation in paid labour.

The second category of employees has a position in between: telework is possible but is not required. So this category has some degrees of freedom, especially relating to:
- what job elements are well-suited for telework,
- on what days employees prefer to work at home and
- what additional facilities are necessary.

Answering these questions a well-considered balance has to be struck between work at the organization's residence and work at home, based on the advantages and disadvantages of both, as discussed above.

Concerning the organizational consequences of telework we return to our discussion about output registration. Because telework does not include the opportunities of direct supervision – unless the activities of the employees involved are monitored by a videocamera: Big brother is watching you – the yardsticks for control can be solely based on *output*, with clear agreements for each period. For the employees output control implies a higher degree of independence with accompanying authorities and responsibilities.

As a consequence, from the information point of view, in applying telework, fewer contacts between employees and their supervisors will result, i.e. the vertical flows of information decrease; quantitatively (the number of the contacts in each period) as well as qualitatively (the content of the contacts). Therefore, it is possible to manage a larger number of employees effectively. In other words, the span of control increases. This development means a decrease of the organization's hierarchical levels, combined with fewer staff management positions. Hence, organizations will be delayered and become more flat.

The delayering of organizations has a positive effect on the overhead costs and it takes a message less transmission time to pass the vertical communication channels. Moreover, the risk that a message, because of wrong interpretations, is changed during the transmission process diminishes considerably.

Thus, telework is not a purely technological phenomenon, in the same way as a newly purchased machine. In addition it is of the utmost importance to determine carefully in advance whether the employees are able to cope with their larger responsibilities and whether the managers involved are able to play a – literally – more distant role.

As a consequence, to make well-considered choices here, the technology, i.e. the opportunities of telework, should not be the leading factor but the organization's needs to redesign its workprocesses: the technology push, as far as it is present, has to be turned into a demand pull.

12. The relationship between information systems and the decision making *process*

A number of pages ago we already paid attention to the relationship between information systems and several (sub)stages of the decision making process in the field of strategic problems. In summary, we identified the following substages combined with possible applications of information systems:

- *intelligence*
  - signalling: strategic information systems,
  - identifying: idea processing systems,
  - interpreting: idea processing systems,
  - formulating: idea processing systems,
  - recognizing: decision support systems,
- *design*
  - generating: idea processing systems,
  - evaluating: decision support systems.

The stages not discussed so far are *choice* and *implementation*. Before focusing on the information systems within these two stages we pay attention to the question about the influence of the degree of *structure* of problems on the relationship between the (sub)stages and information systems.

If problems are completely structured, then the intelligence stage can be passed quickly, leading to the application of a structured decision system, responsible for the rest of the decision making process, until the implementation stage is reached.

And also in this latter stage, dealing with structured problems, special attention points do not have to be expected.

However, for semi-structured and unstructured problems the course of events is quite different.

The less problems are structured the more we have to make an appeal to our creativity. This is clearly demonstrated by the application of idea processing systems within our case company in regard of a strategic problem, Rochester Ltd.

Now we continue our discussion of the relationship between (sub)stages of the decision making process and information systems with the stages of choice and implementation.

Choice

As its name already suggests, at this stage it is time to take a decision. And if the available alternatives are evaluated unambiguously, meaning that the several evaluation criteria are translated into a common standard (for example, money), the final decision is no more than a formality: the alternative with the highest overall score will be chosen, and the choice stage is completed.

However, sometimes we are confronted with criteria that cannot be translated into a common standard, without solving measuring problems arbitrarily. Of course, this is not a problem if we have one alternative which is the best in every respect. But usually this is an exception. In most cases the available alternatives' priority order changes, looking at different decision criteria.

In this situation, in order to arrive at a decision, it is necessary to process the outcomes based on the different criteria in such a way that a clear evaluation and priority order results. This process is the main activity in the choice stage. Several methods have been developed to solve this evaluation problem; for instance, scorecard methods, equivalence procedures and multi criteria analysis. Some of these will be discussed in Chapter X more thouroughly.

It is rather obvious that these techniques are part of a number of decision support systems to help the user in making the necessary calculations.

Implementation

If in the choice stage a decision is taken it is time for the final step in our decision making procedure: implementation. By this stage we actually mean that organizational participants, not involved in the preparation of the decision, who become confronted with its consequences afterwards in doing their jobs, have to be convinced about its positive effect. Hence, at this stage we look for consensus.

Trying to get consensus we are in a similar situation as in the substage, where we tried to get recognition, with only the difference that in the implementation stage recognition does not come from higher management but from others; peers and/or subordinates. Therefore, we can also use here the same decision support system.

However, apart from the difference just mentioned, another difference between recognition and implementation, as a part of the intelligence stage, exists. In fact, recognition relates to the willingness of the organization as a *whole* to raise funds in order to solve the problem, whereas achieving consensus concerns *individual* organizational participants. Perhaps the decision to be taken will result in opposed interests. If, for instance, a decision has to be taken about a new information system, the department involved will benefit as a whole. But this does not hold for any individual departmental participant. It is quite normal for some of them to be, or to feel, harmed by the new system.

Therefore, in addition to using the decision support system to demonstrate the information system's benefits for the larger organizational subsystem, it is also necessary to deal with the – sometimes unfounded – fear of subordinates about their future position in a responsible way. Especially because we are dealing with a rather sensitive topic here, a group information system, guaranteeing the subordinates' anonimity, may be very helpful in giving adequate support.

Summarizing the application of information systems, in addition to the list at the beginning of this section, we can complete it and conclude as follows:

- *choice*: decision support systems,
- *implementation*: decision support systems, group information systems.

X THE (ECONOMIC) EVALUATION OF INVESTMENTS IN INFORMATION SYSTEMS AND IN ICT

1. Introduction

Investments in the field of ICT are usually major capital budgeting projects, involving a lot of money. Hence, they have to compete with other projects also claiming a part of the organization's scarce resources. In this context, the concept 'scarce' has to be interpreted as follows: the organization's budget is insufficient to realize all the profitable capital budgeting projects, identified at a given moment.

For organizations in this comfortable position it is necessary to make careful comparisons between the alternative ways the funds can be used. And this is only possible with methods meeting the following two requirements:

- the methods give the organization a clear view of the advantages and disadvantages of capital budgeting projects and
- the several advantages and disadvantages can be compared with each other, i.e. they have to be expressed in a common standard to arrive at an unambiguous priority order.

Often information systems, based on ICT, do not meet these requirements.

In addition to the expenditures in buying and designing information systems, changing information needs after implementation often cause costly adjustments (see Chapter I) which are rather difficult to predict. Therefore they cannot be taken into account during the design stage.

However, if we do not want to abandon information projects in a preliminary stage we have no other choice than to realize the required adaptations. Moreover, the degree of change of information systems afterwards differs from project to project and from time to time. Obviously, information systems belong to a class of projects with large risks.

In designing information systems, a specific cost category is the amount of *time* the future users have to invest if participatory design methods are applied. This factor is also very difficult to predict.

Compared with estimating the costs of information systems the identification of the benefits of these systems is even more difficult. As long as the impact of information systems is restricted to efficiency targets, such as in the initial phase of the application of ICT, then quantifying the expected benefits is relatively easy. In fact, in this situation the benefits only concern reduced labour costs, by automating organizational tasks. As mentioned before, the concept *automation*, for laymen equivalent to the use of ICT, stems from this period.

However, as happens more and more, the targets of information projects are less well-defined – for example improvement of the organization's competitive position – so that the identification of the benefits of these projects in advance is far from easy; apart from *quantifying* the effects properly.

Another problem, closely related to the problems just mentioned, relates to the *timing* of the expected benefits. Usually, if benefits can be less well-defined, it takes more time before the positive effects of the investment emerge. Also, this property contributes to the project's uncertainty.

A further complication in quantifying the benefits of information projects is present if these projects have positive or negative side effects, not only for the department involved, but also for other departments. For instance, a new system of numerically controlled machines (Computer Aided Manufacturing) may not only solve stagnation in a specific subprocess, but can also create benefits for the client-department; the next link in the production chain.

In section 3 of this Chapter we will discuss the identification of the benefits of information systems in more detail.

It is not only difficult to identify the costs and benefits of information projects adequately, but an unambiguous assessment of these projects is also far from easy.

In solving capital budgeting problems of organizations (apart from situations with considerable risks, where a – short – pay-back period is preferred, or situations where, because of strategic reasons, an extended investment analysis is not opportune) the criterium 'rate of return' is generally used, in order to express costs and benefits in terms of money. Hence, as far as return on investment or pay-back period is applied, both criteria not only require a complete quantification of all costs and benefits of the projects to be evaluated, but it is also necessary to quantify them in terms of money. This requirement raises an important problem in evaluating investments in ICT.

The impact of information systems is usually not restricted to one specific area only, for instance either efficiency or effectiveness, but includes both. If for example, an organization considers buying a decision support system the aim is to *improve* the decision making process, by executing complex calculations or by simulating business processes, omitted until now. However, some of the calculations, taking place before, will also be executed by the system. Therefore, the new information system not only has advantages in the effectiveness domain but also in the efficiency domain.

The effectiveness advantages are more difficult to quantify than efficiency advantages. In many cases, these former advantages cannot even be quantified at all, so we can only describe them in qualitative terms.

Above we tried to make clear that capital budgeting decisions about information projects, i.e. ICT projects, raise a number of specific problems. Thus, we need an adapted procedure for the evaluation of these projects; a procedure to be discussed in this chapter. In addition to the more traditional capital budgeting methods, attention will be paid to:

- a thorough analysis of the costs and benefits of information projects, in quantitative as well as qualitative terms,
- methods to deal with risks explicitly,
- methods making it easier to deal with both categories (qualitative and quantitative variables), in order to arrive at an unambiguous evaluation of these projects and a clear priority order.

In the remainder of this chapter these topics will be paid attention to. Firstly, in section 2 we will briefly discuss a number of traditional capital budgeting methods. Secondly, in section 3 we will pay attention to the distinction between quantitative and qualitative variables. Thirdly, handling the risks of information projects is the subject of section 4. Fourthly, in section 5 methods to generate data about the costs and benefits of information projects will be discussed. Finally, section 6 is dedicated to the comparison of investment projects in different fields.

2. Traditional capital budgeting techniques

The majority of the traditional capital budgeting techniques, developed so far, belong to the category of 'discounted cash flow methods'. These methods are based on the principle of discounting the future costs and benefits caused by a capital budgeting project.

Of the discounted cash flow methods we discuss two variants: the net present value method and the internal rate of return method.

Net present value method

The net present value method implies discounting future cash flows (inflows and outflows) using a discounting rate based on the – risk adjusted – costs of capital; the latter interpreted as the costs of borrowing the capital involved (borrowing rate), or the income that can be generated alternatively (lending rate). This method can be described in the following formula:

$$NPV = -I + (O\text{-}U)_i / (1+c) + ... + (O\text{-}U)_n / (1+c)^n$$

In this equation the symbols used are defined as follows:

NPV = net present value,
I = the investment amount before the project is operational, i.e. generates positive net cash flows
O = the periodical cash inflows
U = the periodical cash outflows
c = cost of capital
n = total lifetime of the project

Projects having a positive net present value are in principle acceptable. Whether a project will be selected indeed, also depends, apart from other reasons such as urgency, on the net present value of other projects, i.e. its position in the priority order.

Internal rate of return method
The internal rate of return method only slightly differs from the net present value method. As we have seen, using this latter method the net present value will be calculated. So this value is the dependent variable. Now, the only difference between both methods concerns the discounting rate being used. For the internal rate of return method this rate is not an independent variable determined outside the model, but is its outcome, meaning that a discounting rate is calculated leading to a net present value of zero.

Both methods have some advantages and disadvantages. However, in view of the evaluation of *information* projects, we prefer the net present value method, because this method facilitates weighting quantitative and qualitative factors when we are evaluating these projects (see also our discussion of 'value analysis' in section 5 of this chapter).

The pay back-period
A method that should not be neglected here is the method of the pay-back period. Originally, in the field of capital budgeting this method had a rather negative image. As a matter of fact this method actually does not measure the profitability of capital budgeting projects because profits are not realized until the pay-back period has come to an end.

Notwithstanding this, in an adapted form of the pay-back period can be an adequate yardstick for the selection of capital budgeting projects.

The pay-back period can be defined as the number of periods required to recover the initial investment by generating positive net cash flows. This period (T) can be calculated by using the following formula:

$$T = I / (O\text{-}U)$$

Looking at this formula we observe that the timing (discounting) of future cash flows is completely neglected. And here we meet the most important shortcoming of this method. However, it is very simple to take timing into account here, by discounting the cash flows involved.

In doing so, the pay-back period can be defined as the period that expires at the moment that the aggregated discounted cash flows at least equal the intitial investment.

$$\text{If } \sum_{i=1}^{n} (O\text{-}U) / (1+c)^i = I \text{ then } T = n$$

A second shortcoming of the method of the pay-back period, already mentioned above, relates to the criterium 'pay-back period' as such. In fact this period does not measure the profitability of capital budgeting projects, because the profits of the projects are not generated until this period has come to an end. This problem can be solved by taking into consideration all positive net cash flows during the total lifetime of investment projects.

The method of the pay-back period should not be used to replace, but to supplement the methods discussed above, and is especially useful for projects with high risks. Due to the size of the discounting rate, in such a situation, the cash flows in the first few years are relatively much more important and less uncertain too. And precisely, by applying the pay-back criterion, this aspect will be emphasized.

Notwithstanding this, a warning has to be given if the pay-back period is used. If we are confronted with projects needing much time to generate positive net cash flows, this criterion is far from adequate because of its emphasis on cash flows in the first few years. So, taking capital budgeting decisions, the pay back-period can only make a positive contribution if projects, that have to be compared, show a similar timing of their cash flows.

A general problem of the capital budgeting techniques, mentioned above, concerns the – limited – reliability of the data used to make the necessary calculations. As a matter of fact, speaking about capital budgeting decision making we are dealing with a rather long time horizon; three to five years is not unusual. And because of environmental turbulence, organizations are confronted with, it is almost impossible to make reliable predictions.

Under the heading 'tacit knowledge' in section 5 we return to this problem which is also important for information projects.

3. Quantitative and qualitative factors and the evaluation of information projects

Quantitative factors

Quantitative factors are defined as factors to be measured on a ratio scale. A ratio scale is a scale characterized by a so-called natural zero point, which means that if a certain variable is zero it does not exist at all. If for instance a check list is used to identify – future – expenditures for an information project it may happen that some expenditure categories do not occur in a specific situation. Then they are valued as zero. So, the ratio scale is the only scale characterized by *absolute* values. All other scales (see below) have more or less *relative* values, which means that the evaluation of capital budgeting alternatives is only meaningful if mutual comparisons are made, either comparisons between several possible outcomes of one specific project or between possible outcomes of more than one project or both.

The requirement of ratio scale measurements has to be met if we want to make calculations concerning the traditional capital budgeting methods discussed in the previous section. As soon as other scales – particularly nominal scale and ordinal scale – have to be used, then such calculations are no longer allowed.

Therefore, we will try to measure the variables, relevant for capital budgeting decisions, on a ratio scale when even possible.

As most costs of information projects can be expressed in terms of money, which is a quantitative factor, the requirement for the application of a ratio scale has been fulfilled.

However, the problems that can be identified when measuring benefits are rather complex. In general, only the benefits of information systems caused by efficiency aspects are ratio-scaled from the beginning. Unfortunately, this is not true for all other positive effects, especially those of effectiveness.

Before discussing the identification of qualitative advantages of information projects in more detail we must first of all pay attention to a description of qualitative variables and how they are related to the choice of an appropriate scale. This will be done below.

Qualitative variables

We start our discussion here by giving a definition of qualitative variables: as variables *not* to be measured using a ratio scale. Above we already mentioned three other scales:
- the nominal scale,
- the ordinal scale,
- the interval scale.

The nominal scale presupposes that the phenomena involved only have – different – *names*. If for instance we have to choose between two information systems whose benefits can only be designated as efficiency benefits for one system and effectiveness benefits for the other, without further specification, then only the nominal scale will be appropriate. However, this is rather exceptional. In most situations we have more specific information.

Imagine the following case. An organization has to choose between two information systems, both having a positive impact on the organization's competitive position. Moreover the organization is convinced that the project with score 2 is better on this dimension than the project having score 1, without knowing the difference between their scores exactly. In fact, the organization is able to specify a ranking order here, so that an ordinal scale is at least appropriate.

Ranking orders do not have an *absolute* meaning. Therefore, it is not allowed to perform arithmetic operations on these numbers. For instance, it is meaningless to conclude that the distance between project score 1 and project score 2 is half the distance between project score 1 and project score 3.

This example exactly illustrates the difference between an ordinal scale and an interval scale. If the interval scale is used it is legitimate to express the distances between the scores of the projects in terms of their arithmetic differences. The only difference between an interval scale and a ratio scale is that the latter lacks a natural zero point.

Of course, confronted with qualitative variables, organizations will try to employ the most informative scale. They are in fact looking for opportunities to use the interval scale if a ratio scale is not allowed. And, as will be demonstrated below in the next section and in section 5 of this chapter, usually the interval scale is a justifiable, due to the way organizations generate scores for qualitative variables.

Information systems can, in addition to cost reduction (efficiency advantages), have other positive effects on organizations, in the sense that other organizational targets (effectiveness advantages) are reached. These latter advantages originate from causes that can be enumerated as follows (Parker, Benson and Trainor, 1989):

- value linking,
- value acceleration,
- value restructuring,
- innovation valuation.

Though these four phenomena are primarily mentioned by Parker c.s. because of the identification of side benefits due to investments in ICT, they are also helpful in determining qualitative effects. The dominance of these effects increases as we move from value linking via value acceleration and value restructuring to innovation valuation.

We will explain these phenomena by some illustrative examples.

We speak of value linking if investments in ICT have positive side-effects in other fields, inside or outside the department involved. For instance value linking is present if the 'invoice' department decides to generate invoices electronically in the future. By using a new computer system, the 'bookkeeping' department will be provided with invoice data on disc, so that both departments profit by saving time and money for the latter department.

Value acceleration occurs if some organizational benefits, due to a new investment, are realized faster. In our former example of value linking, perhaps the invoicing process is not only cheaper, but also quicker, leading to a shorter payment period by debtors and thus to a decrease in the loss of interest.

Value restructuring means the elimination of tasks with limited added value under the influence of the new ICT application, resulting in tasks with higher added value, as far as the employees involved are not fired. As an example of this phenomenon we can think of decision support systems taking over calculations originally made 'by hand'.

Innovation valuation relates to the innovative potential of investments in ICT. Here the organization's competitive position is central, because new applications of this technology in processes and in products particularly strengthen its position among competitors. For instance innovation valuation can be illustrated with our case of Rochester Ltd. (see Chapter IX) a company that during a strategic meeting decided to acquire an information system for automatic signalling and processing of break downs of cooling equipment. Because of raising its service to a higher level Rochester Ltd. will strengthen its competitive position.

Looking at qualitative variables it is often – implicitly – assumed that their effects materialize almost immediately, without delay. But usually this is not the case.

If for example one of the criteria of an investment in ICT concerns the effect of 'increased customer satisfaction' due to a higher service level, this satisfaction will usually not immediately rise to the intended level, by simply 'pushing a button', i.e. by implementing the new system. As has been mentioned before, a new information system and the organization have to be well-attuned to one another. The conditions for this have to be created during the design process, but getting used to the changed situation is a matter of learning by doing. So, it takes the organization – a lot of – time, during a growth process, to reach the intended service level.

In addition to this delay, caused by internal organizational processes, it also takes the customers, apart from the level to be reached, (some) time to perceive any improvement. And finally, the positive effects of increased customer satisfaction grow little by little, and will be reaped in the *future*.

As soon as the outcomes of variables, relevant for capital budgeting decisions, do not materialize immediately, the time factor has to be taken into account explicitly. The procedure to be applied here for variables that can be quantified by using a ratio scale, is well-known from the traditional capital budgeting literature, and was briefly discussed above.

However, the question is: how should time preference be handled when dealing with qualitative variables?

At first sight we could try to find methods to solve our timing problem in the well-known domain of (expected) utility theory. For instance, this theory enables us to draw a number of indifference curves representing different combinations of delay time and service level with the same utility level, resulting in an 'indifference map'.

However, this approach does not make very much sense here, because of a number of reasons. Firstly, what does the expression 'utility' mean? Probably, this is not the utility judgement of one person in particular but the utility judgment of all the people involved in the decision making process, because many decisions within organizations, including capital budgeting decisions about investment in ICT, are often group decisions. Unfortunately, one important assumption of utility theory relates to the impossibility of interpersonal utility comparison. So, it is not allowed to add up the utility scores given by several individuals. Secondly, increases of the realization level of qualitative variables need not to be equally distributed over time. This handicap makes it very difficult to specify our variable 'time' adequately in utility theory models.

But, is it appropriate to apply an (adapted) version of a procedure which was used to express our time preference, when we were dealing with quantitative variables? Answering this question means that we have to investigate the feasibility of *discounting* qualitative variables.

As to our three scales vis-a-vis qualitative variables and the possibilities of performing arithmetical operations – such as calculating the mean or using discounting techniques – we must distinguish between two categories: on the one hand the interval scale and on the other hand the ordinal scale and the nominal scale. Arithmetical calculations are only allowed in the first category. For instance, it makes no sense to calculate a mean if we are using an ordinal scale, because the numbers involved are, as opposed to interval-scaled numbers, no more than ranking numbers. In fact, arithmetical operations of ranking numbers are a useless activity.

Thus, the possibilities to apply the discounting technique are closely connected with the scale used to measure the variables involved. We will discuss the scale problem first and then answer the question whether the discounting procedure is appopriate.

Returning to our service level example, it is our intention to increase this level in a number of steps, during the project's lifetime. For instance, based on the estimations of experts, the following time profile could be identified (in this figure the abbreviation sl means the evaluation of the service level reached at any – discrete – moment in the future):

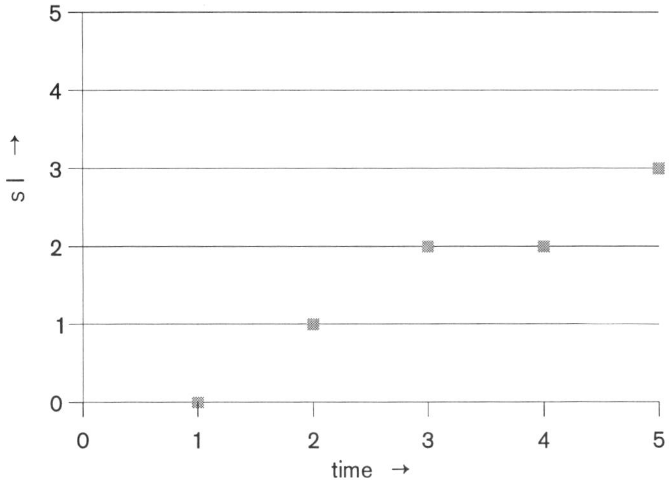

By the way, perhaps there is some doubt about the reliability of the expectations represented here and in similar cases. However, the same doubt is relevant to data concerning quantitative variables, because they are also estimates of uncertain future developments. In fact, the only difference is the scale used to measure them.

Moreover, asking the experts to specify their estimations using time profiles, they are forced to be more explicit, which may increase their reliability. This topic of generating expert estimations will be discussed in more detail in section 5 of this chapter.

The next step in our procedure is to determine the yearly improvements of the service level, that can easily be derived from the figure above. Finally, the improvements have to be discounted and added up, resulting in a so-called 'discounted qualitative benefit'. This procedure does not differ from the one followed in similar cases with quantitaive data. As to the discounting rate there is no reason to use one that is different from the one used to determine the discounted value of quantitative variables.

Of course it is not always possible to measure qualitative variables applying an interval scale. Sometimes we have to rest content with ordinal-scaled ariables. In this situation it is not allowed to discount the project scores. However, there is an alternative here. By taking the timing of the projects' qualitative costs and benefits into account an independent variable, representing the time dimension, can be introduced and handled in a similar way as the other qualitative variables.

4. A procedure to handle the risks of information projects

In Chapter V we presented an extended enumeration of factors liable to get out of control. Because of this list and of what has been said about this subject in Chapter I the conclusion is clear: information projects are very risky, implying that big differences – positive as well as negative – may occur between the expected value of the return on investment and its realization at a later stage.

In order to clarify this problem we use the net present value, explained in section 2 of this chapter. If this value can be predicted with complete accuracy the project's risks are zero. In our experience this situation seldom presents itself. Although we are able to calculate a net present value using a simple formula resulting in an exact outcome, its realization is still far from certain. The risks involved can be made clear by specifying an interval combined with the relevant probabilities of the outcomes of this variable.

In order to get an insight into the density function of the net present value, the following procedure can be applied. First of all, the density functions of all the variables taken together in a composite variable, i.e. the net present value, has to be specified. We have to consider here density functions of variables such as the expected sales, the prices of raw materials, etc. The next step is to calculate the net present value a number of times using different values for the several independent values selected randomly. In this way we also get a number of outcomes for the net present value, which together represent a sample to be used to estimate the parameters of the net present value's density function.

For this analysis, decision support systems, especially designed to make complex capital budgeting calculations, are very helpful. Not only is such a decision support system able to make the necessary calculations very quickly, but it is also, as a standard procedure, equiped with a so-called 'random generator', a piece of software to be used to generate the different values of the independent variables, in order to randomly calculate a number of net present value outcomes.

Assuming a normal – bell shaped – distribution to describe net present values, i.e. a distribution of net present values described by a Gauss curve – we are able to deal with risks, evaluating capital budgeting projects, as follows: use as an evaluation criterion the expected net present value (the mean of the density function) minus two times the standard deviation. The chance of the net present value to be lower after finishing the project, is, as can be easily determined in the table for the normal distribution, no more than 2.28%.

The preceding approach is based on two assumptions. Firstly, it is not allowed here, as is common practice, to raise the cost of capital, used to calculate the net present value, due to business risks. Secondly, this approach requires sufficient knowledge of the density function of the net present value. However, usually we only have subjective estimations, creating additional risks.

Because of the latter problem it would be wise to decompose the net present value by identifying the factors responsible for possible deviations; negative as well as positive. When we have described these factors in terms of the mean and the standard deviation, a sensitivity analysis can be applied. With this analysis, frequently belonging to the tool kit of decision support systems, we are able to determine the possible consequences for the net present value, especially the negative ones.

After processing these results statistically the available projects can be ranked unambiguously and a decision is made.

5. The evaluation of information projects

In evaluating information projects, not only are quantitative factors important, but also qualitative factors have to be dealt with. In order to be able to do that we have to measure these factors beforehand.

To shed light on the question of how to measure them we have to analyse the origins of these factors. In general, factors are of a qualitative nature because of a lack of knowledge of the phenomena involved. So, we can only describe them in rather global terms.

To illustrate this problem we return to our example of innovation valuation discussed in the previous section. As we have seen, it is Rochester Ltd.'s intention to strengthen its competitive position by introducing a system of automatic signalling and processing of break downs of cooling equipment. Probably participants in the strategic meeting have no doubt about some sort of product improvement when such a system is acquired. But is this improvement large enough to justify its costs? In other words, are the expected benefits sufficient?

Daily practice reveals that organizations usually make such decisions based on some sort of vague belief or trust in their strategic importance, without a profound analysis. Though we do not reject this approach outright we strongly prefer first to try out some methods that may be helpful in identifying the potential advantages of information projects more explicitly.

Three of these methods will be discussed below:

- the Delphi method,
- goal seeking, and value analysis respectively,
- ratio analysis.

Before doing so we pay some attention to the topic of 'tacit knowledge'.

Using the methods just mentioned we assume the presence of a lot of hidden knowledge within organizations; knowledge which can be made explicit in order to use it in a profitable way during the decision making process. Therefore, we have no objections against decisions based on human intuition. As a matter of fact this intuition is based on a lot of experience and implicit knowledge. And there is nothing wrong with using this knowledge, provided the necessary precautions are taken.

In discussing this subject, the only objection we have relates to the attitude of some organizations that they don't use methods to make implicit knowledge more explicit. This is because some facts will, as opposed to others, be emphasized disproportionately, without being able to judge the underlying reasons. Hence, it is only allowed to use implicit knowledge directly if methods to make it more explicit do not succeed.

Compared with the other methods, just mentioned, the Delphi method is the most profound one. Therefore, we recommend to apply this method first. If the Delphi method fails, then we should switch to goal seeking, or value analysis respectively, and finally to ratio analysis.

The Delphi method, deriving its name from the residence of the famous oracle well-known from ancient Greek history because of its ability to predict future developments, is in some way a reaction to brainstorming; a method very popular some decades ago. Brainstorming was especially meant to facilitate people in stimulating each other within groups, to generate creative ideas.

However, after some time of experiments with brainstorming, group processes appeared to influence the outcomes negatively; a subject already discussed in Chapter IX. One of the main problems of this method is connected with the direct contact between the participants in brainstorming and social interaction, sometimes leading to negative influences on the group process. Especially, the habit in the United States to (ab)use brainstorm sessions to give vent to one's negative personal feelings about other group members was detrimental.

Thus, a new method has been developed, avoiding the disadvantages of direct contact between the participants: the Delphi method (Linstone and Turoff, 1975).

The Delphi method has to be applied as follows. First of all a panel is composed by inviting some experts, in the field of the subject of interest, to join it (the required number of participants and their expertise will be discussed later in section 5). The experts report their opinion to the coordinator. This latter person summarizes the opinions and gives the participants feedback in order to offer them the opportunity to adapt their original opinion. As experiences with this method show, these adapted opinions will usually converge. As a matter of fact convergence appears not because of social interaction but because of increasing insight.

After a limited number of such convergence rounds a group opinion acceptable for the members will frequently result (a communis opinio).

As mentioned before the Delphi method can be helpful in generating data about different phenomena. To illustrate this we return to the Rochester Ltd. case where, among other things, the decision was made to use a system of electronic data interchange. It should not surprise us that within several departments – such as the selling deparment and the maintenance department – employees could be found who had an opinion about the impact of the intended system on the company's sales. Therefore, a number of them was invited to participate in a Delphi panel.

During the panel sessions several questions had to be answered, for example the question: how much will our sales increase, due to the new system, over the next five years?

Suppose, answering this question, in the first round we got a number of percentages showing rather big differences. However, after four convergence rounds a common opinion had emerged: sales increase 19.8%.

This is an interesting number. However, what is its significance? In our discussion of risks in the preceding section it was made clear that this prediction of a sales increase can in fact turn out to be higher or lower. Of course we will be pleased if it is higher, but beforehand we are particularly interested in the consequences of *lower* increases for the profitability of the investment and the decision to be made. Therefore, insight into the distribution of the possible outcomes of the sales is required. In other words, how do we get information about the density function of the sales' increases?

To solve this problem we return to the first round of the Delphi experiment, revealing differences between the estimations of the participants. Looking at these differences the question is: why do the participants differ? For these differences we have a rather obvious explanation: the participants do not fully agree beforehand, because of uncertainty. And the more uncertainty, the larger the differences are between their estimations. These differences can now be used to quantify the risks of the phenomenon involved. However, this latter approach is only allowed if an important requirement, concerning the panel's composition, has been fulfilled: the participants should have quite *different* kinds of expertise. If not, then in the first round there could be near consensus, whereas the estimations are still very uncertain. Hence, if not adequately composed (see also below), the Delphi panel prevents us from getting reliable information about the risks involved.

The way we try to measure risks, using the Delphi method, may raise another question: is it still necessary to have convergence rounds, because these rounds cause decreasing differences between the estimations? In other words, does it suffice to use the first round's estimations to calculate a mean and a standard deviation? Put another way: does the convergence process generate additional information? In fact it does. Based on the results of a lot of Delphi experiments the common opinion from the last round, or its mean, seems a more reliable guess of the density function's mean which we are looking for, than the mean from the first round (Scott Armstrong, 1985).

Therefore, we recommend the following procedure. Using the opinions from the *first* round a standard deviation has to be calculated, being the best guess of the uncertainty, i.e. the standard deviation of the density function, whereas the mean of the *last* round is the expected value, i.e. the best guess of the mean of this density function.

Further, we have to shed light on the question of the role of the Delphi method vis-a-vis the distinction between quantitative and qualitative variables. As can be easily demonstrated the answer depends on the scale that will be used. In the Rochester Ltd. case the participants were asked to make estimations of sales increases using *absolute* numbers. With such a question a ratio scale is implicitly assumed and the variables involved are quantitative.

But we can also imagine the following question to be answered by the Rochester Ltd. panel: what is the improvement of the organization's service level, due to the new system of automatic signalling and processing equipment break downs, using a five point scale. Often the present level is indicated as 0. By the way, this does not mean there is no service. On the contrary, but we only want to improve it. Therefore, 0 is a rather arbitrarily determined 'value', not relating to a natural zero point but indicating the present level. As a consequence we are dealing here with an *interval* scale, at least if the differences between the scores can be expressed in each other, meaning that the variable involved is, according to our definition, *qualitative*. Because on interval-scaled numbers some arithmetic operations are allowed, we will try, as much as possible, to measure qualitative variables using an interval scale.

In the same way as described above the Delphi procedure will be applied here.

To enrich the Delphi procedure we can supplement it with a so-called 'policy Delphi'. Policy Delphi concerns a group discussion after finishing the original Delphi procedure described above. The policy Delphi could have added value if the consensus reached in the last round is insufficient. Though the shortcomings of brainstorming, in connection with direct confrontation of the participants, may occur here too, we do not expect many problems, because the discussion is strictly limited to the subject the panel is composed for and to the discussion of the outcomes during the first session.

Moreover, the Delphi method is not only useful in determining the significance of the properties of alternative (information) projects but can also be used to determine the relative importance – weights – of the quantitative and qualitative characteristics of information systems in order to express them in a common standard.

Discussing the Delphi method we will finally pay attention to the degree of expertise of the panel members and the seize of the panel. Based on experiences with the Delphi method the panel does not have to be composed of top experts but of people with only moderate expertise. In contrast to participants with moderate expertise, the estimates of top experts of future developments tend to be more conservatively (pessimistic) than more realistic. And it is the latter quality that we need. By the way, top experts outperform moderate experts if the *present* situation in a certain domain has to be diagnosed (Scott Armstrong, 1985).

As far as its size is concerned the number of particpants is optimal between eight and twelve. If the size is less than eight, its multiform character is at stake. On the other hand, if the size exceeds twelve the added value of additional participants diminishes quickly.

The results of the Delphi experiments have to be dealt with by following the same procedure as in section 4, identifyting the density function of the net present. So, whether the independent variables involved are determined by observation or by appliying the Delphi method, in both situations the net present value has to be calculated a number of times, using different values of these variables, generated by chance.

As has been demonstrated before, the Delphi method is based on estimates of one or more quantifiable aspects of a certain phenomenon made by experts. However, sometimes we are confronted with almost unpredictable phenomena. In such a situation the Delphi method can not be applied adequately and we have to look for other instruments to shed some light on those phenomena. Here the method of goal seeking may be useful.

In fact, goal seeking is rather similar to sensitivity analysis. The main difference between the two methods relates to the way in which they have to be carried out. Instead of using predetermined values, for instance generated by the Delphi method, goal seeking means the application of sensitivity analysis to determine the values of – combinations of – factors causing a zero net present value. After finishing these calculations the values are presented to experts to judge the probability of these values. We will illustrate this procedure with an example.

Rochester Ltd. tries to gather information about the influence of the system of automatic signalling and processing break downs of equipment on the company's sales volume, in order to make a well-considered decision. However, after some time it appears to be very difficult to get this information about expected future sales growth with some degree of probability. Therefore, a sensitivity analysis is carried out with other factors the company is able to quantify adequately, combined with a sales growth together causing a *zero* net present value. Resulting from a number of trial and error calculations, the minimum rate of required growth of sales is to be 3.7%.

The next step in the procedure is to present this growth percentage to a group of experts, composed in the same way as a Delphi panel, asking them to estimate the chance of a *lower* sales growth percentage, resulting from the intended new information system. If the complete panel has the opinion that this chance is almost zero, then the sales growth is at least 3.7%.

In addition, we can ask the same question for a higher rate of growth, for instance 4%, 4.3%, etc. The response will show more experts perceive the rate of growth as improbable.

What we in fact really are looking for in applying this approach concerns the following three values:

- the lowest value of the variable involved perceived by all the experts as almost improbable (l),
- the value perceived by 50% as improbable and the other half as probable (m),
- the highest value perceived by all the experts as almost improbable (h).

With these three values we are usually able to determine a density function whose parameters – mean and standard deviation – can be used in a sensitivity analysis.

If the following equation holds:

$$m - l = h - m,$$

then we assume the property of the phenomenon involved is a normal – bell shaped – distribution with parameters m (mean) and (h – l)/6 (standard deviation) (Prakken, 1989).

In addition to goal seeking, value analysis can also play a role if sufficient information about the future development of some factors is lacking. As opposed to goal seeking, value analysis concerns the evaluation of complete projects instead of single factors, if too many of the relevant factors are of a qualitative nature (by the way, here we meet a link to the next section where we focus on the evaluation of information *projects*).

Value analysis is based on the following question for the decision maker to answer: what amount of money are you prepared to spend for an information system having a specific combination of properties (Keen, 1986)?

As is well-known a major problem of qualitative factors relates to determining the positive future effects of information systems. And these effects are highly dependent on the properties of the system. Hence, applying value analysis, it is necessary to begin taking into consideration only the properties with sufficient transparency. And for this part of the properties the user has to answer the question just mentioned. If the amount he is willing to spend does not exceed the price of the information system, it is acceptable as such.

If this amount is lower, then it will be necessary to identify other positive properties of the system being neglected so far.

In the same way value analysis is useful for projects characterized by a combination of quantitative and qualitative factors; so-called *miscellaneous* projects. In this situation the following procedure is available. Firstly, based on quantitative factors the net present value has to be calculated. If this value is at least zero then the procedure is ended.

In the opposite situation, however, or if a choice has to be made between more than one project, the maximum amount, the user is prepared to pay at most for the remaining functionality based on qualitative factors, has to be determined too. As soon as this amount, added to the amount based on the judgement of quantitative factors, at least equals the net present value then the project is acceptable.

Because of the opportunity to compare the contribution of qualitative factors, expressed in terms of money, directly with the net present value resulting from quantitative factors, as has just been demonstrated, we prefer the net present value method for evaluating the profitability of information projects (also see section 2).

The difference between the price of information projects and the maximum amounts the user is prepared to pay, may be helpful in determining the priority order of available projects. This ranking procedure should also be followed for miscellaneous projects to identify the significance of qualitative factors in order to arrive at a well-considered decision.

A third method we pay attention to within the scope of decision making about information systems and ICT is ratio analysis.

Ratio analysis, also called *bench marking*, uses ratios or bench marks, based on the organization's experiences in the past and on experiences of other organizations in comparable circumstances. These ratios have to be within certain predetermined limits to safeguard sound policies and practices. For instance, in some sectors the upper limit for the solvency of the organization (the ratio between equity and debts) is 2 and the lower limit is 1.

Of course, ratios are rather global indicators to be used carefully because of the idiosyncratic position of the organization. Notwithstanding this, ratios can be useful to evaluate the organization's policy.

In the field of ICT ratios can also be applied. In order to keep up with competitors here, organizations may try to spend comparable amounts of money, for instance as a percentage of the organization's total expenditures. It goes without saying that, using this approach successfully, rather decomposed data are necessary.

If only aggregated data on the organizational level should be available, without detailed specification, then these data fall short because they are not able to inform us about the many opportunities ICT offers.

Therefore, ratio analysis, or bench marking respectively, should not be restricted to global financial data but must give insight on a more detailed level. For example, if in some line of business computerized administrative systems are usual, then an organization not having such a system yet, should take its purchase into consideration. And this decision is only triggered if more than unspecified global financial data are available.

Because of this requirement we explicitly distinguish between two different kinds of ratio analysis or bench marking: *global* and *detailed.*

Moreover, using ratio analysis as the paramount method to decide about investments in ICT, many organizations turn into followers instead of leaders or pioneers. Certainly for this technological field such behaviour is very dangerous because of the increasing importance of ICT to realize competitive advantages. Now and in the near future the competitive position of organizations will depend more and more on their ability to use ICT in innovative ways; in products and in processes as well.

Finally, ratio analysis, especially in its global form, is only suitable for evaluating the organization's policy in a certain field as a whole. So, this analysis offers no assistance in judging single ICT projects. As a consequence, ratio analysis has to be used in addition to other methods instead of replacing them. These 'other' methods should have single projects as a starting point. When ratio methods on a global level offer no assistance to the decision maker, a very rare situation, ratio analysis on a detailed level is an alternative if applied carefully.

6. A decision procedure for ICT projects

Before specifying the problems of decision making about information projects in more detail, we will briefly discuss the relation between design and choice phase. In Chapter II we saw a decision making process which is not linear most of the time, but circular. For the evaluation of projects and the phases just mentioned the circular character is of the utmost importance.

As a matter of fact decision makers are normally not sufficiently informed about every available alternative in the field of information systems. Thus, before reaching a decision a search process is started which needs a criterium for putting an end to the process. Here we meet the *aspiration level*; which is composed of a number of minimal requirements that have to be fulfilled by acceptable alternatives. The choice phase will stop with a positive decision, as soon as an alternative, meeting the aspiration level, has been found.

In other words, this procedure means the passing of the (sub) phases 'generating alternatives', 'evaluating alternatives' and 'choice' again and again until a satisficing alternative can be chosen.

Both in theory and in daily practice, this notion of satisfying behaviour is supported broadly and is also adopted by us as a starting point for decision making on information systems, or ICT projects respectively.

However, this pattern of behaviour raises an important question about the *evaluation* of (information) projects, which we have to pay attention to. Before doing so, we will start by giving an example.

An organization considers buying an information system, not only causing quantitative advantages and disadvantages, such as a reduction of labour costs and the price of the information system, but also has qualitative benefits, such as:
- reliability,
- response time and
- maintenance.

For each of the relevant properties the organization specifies a minimum value, as far as possible. The next step in this procedure is to evaluate the first information system to be scrutinized by comparing its properties to the corresponding dimensions of the composite aspiration level. The decision is clear if its scores on every dimension of the aspiration level are positive; then it will be accepted. On the other hand, if its scores are negative on every dimension, then it will be rejected. But what is to be done if this comparison has the following result: some requirements of the aspiration level can be easily met, others cannot? In other words, the scores of the evaluated information system are mixed: some are above and some are below the aspiration level.

And here we have reached the situation where our question of the evaluation of information projects, mentioned above, arises: what is the decision maker's reaction in a situation where we have mixed scores? To answer this question three options can be identified:
- the aspiration level will be adapted because it seems to be less realistic in some respects, so that an alternative that has been rejected becomes acceptable,
- the search process will be continued until an alternative, meeting every requirement, emerges,
- several requirements, may be compensatory; if so, projects as a whole are acceptable if negative scores on certain criteria are compensated by positive scores on others.

The first two options presuppose the existence of clear boderlines between the several requirements in the aspiration level. So, here we don't need a procedure to express these, incomparable, requirements in a common standard because each requirement is prohibitive.

This is opposed to the third option. Using this option the first step is to identify two different categories of requirements: prohibitive and compensatory requirements. Only requirements belonging to this latter category can compensate each other. If compensation is allowed, then we need a procedure to make them comparable. When discussing the evaluation of projects (see below) we will pay attention to this subject too.

In evaluating information projects we prefer to use only methods of judgement capable of producing unambiguous values. For instance, methods belonging to the category of traditional capital budgeting methods, discussed in section 3, meet that requirement. Depending on the criterion used, such as the net present value, these methods make it possible to judge the available projects applying this specific criterion, containing all the factors causing advantages or disadvantages for the organization if the projects involved are realized. This way a unique priority order of projects results, simplifying the choice process drastically.

However, the application of such an approach is only allowed subjected to the following two conditions:

- all relevant factors are quantitative from the start and can be expressed in terms of money or any other standard or
- factors, initially qualitative, can be quantified by using specific techniques (see the Delphi method) and can be expressed in a common standard as mentioned before.

Looking at information projects we usually meet with a number of factors that will remain qualitative, in spite of attempts to use the methods discussed in the preceding section. As a consequence, information projects are miscellaneous: some relevant factors are quantitative and can be processed by applying a common standard, whereas other factors remain qualitative and uncapable of being quantified.

Furthermore, these qualitative factors cause an additional complication because, to the criteria to determine their scores, differ. For instance, the criterion 'reliability of information systems' differs from the criterion 'improving the organization's competitive position'; two criteria which are incomparable without further processing.

When one of the available projects scores better on every criterion, then a decision is not difficult at all. Most of the time, however, we are in a less comfortable position, because, depending on the specific criterion used, the priority order changes. Notwithstanding this problem, only one single project can be selected: the project, supposed to be the best of all.

In order to give such a supposition a solid foundation we have to use methods facilitating the processing of suitable combinations of quantitative and qualitative factors. These methods can be found in the well-known field of information economics.

A wide-spread method belonging to this category relates to so-called business scorecards (Kaplan and Norton, 1992). Though not explicitly developed to evaluate single ICT projects, we are interested in this method because it may be helpful to express quantitative and qualitative variables in a common standard, thus arriving at unambiguous overall scores of the project.

This technique starts with a number of – in principle – incomparable criteria for the evaluation of capital budgeting projects in the field of ICT. For instance, Parker, Benson and Trainor advocate the following criteria (Parker, Benson and Trainor, 1989):

- return on investment,
- strategic match,
- competitive advantage,

- management information,
- competitive response,
- strategic IS architecture,
- project or organisational risk,
- definitional uncertainty,
- technical uncertainty and
- infrastructure risk.

To score single projects on these criteria a 'panel discussion' is often used as an instrument. The next step in the scorecard procedure is to add the scores after multiplying them with coefficients based on their relative importance, resulting in overall scores. In fact this is an application of the so-called 'weighted sum' method. The final step is to classify the projects and to select the project with the highest overall score.

Though this procedure is quite simple, we will, however, meet some problems:
- which scales are used to measure the qualitative variables and what are the consequences?
- how should the time-aspect of qualitative variables be taken into account?
- is the procedure of calculating overall scores using them in order to classify projects feasible?

We will discuss these three questions below.

Scale

Apart from the criterion 'return on investment' the criteria listed above are qualitative. And as we have seen before, the variables involved are measured by using an interval scale or an ordinal scale. We recommend to use the former scale as much as possible. Not only does an interval scale have a higher information content than an ordinal scale but the choice of scale to measure these variables also influences the way in which the time-aspect has to be dealt with (see below). Moreover, the 'weighted sum' method is only allowed if qualitative variables are interval-scaled.

As a consequence of the business scorecard method becomes problematic if ordinal scaled variables are present, because this scale does not permit arithmetic operations.

Timing

Qualitative variables are just like quantitative ones also characterized by a time profile; thus it is necessary to take the time-aspect into consideration. Dependent on the relevant scale two alternative approaches are available: discounting (using an interval scale) or handling this aspect as an independent variable in addition to the other ones (using an ordinal scale).

Overall scores and priority order of projects

One of the attractive features of the business scorecard approach is its rather simple calculation procedure to get overall scores, i.e. their weighted sum. Unfortunately, we also meet one of its weaknesses here. As a matter of fact a major disadvantage of the weighted sum method relates to its lack of reliability because the several criterion scores, constituting the overall score, are not compared mutually. A mutual comparison increases the reliability of the method considerably. This procedure is not incompatible with the business scorecard approach.

Moreover, it is, again in respect of the reliability of the method, necessary to standardize criterion scores and coefficients. Looking at the business scorecard method this requirement can easily be met with.

Finally, as mentioned before, the weighted sum approach is only allowed if we are dealing with ratio-scaled or interval-scaled variables.

Taken together, the answers to our three questions suggest that the business scorecard method is only feasible if:

- all qualitative variables involved can be measured using an interval scale,
- the timing problem is solved adequately,
- the criterion scores are mutually compared and
- the scores and coefficients are standardized.

Actually taking these requirements, and restrictions, into account we can no longer speak of a business scorecard method. Therefore, we turn to other, more adequate, methods to deal with qualitative variables properly. Multi-criteria analysis is a category of methods that are helpful here. One specific method, belonging to this category, the so-called *evamix* method will be discussed below.

As obeserved before, the evamix method is useful to make a final judgement about projects characterized by a combination of quantitative and qualitative factors, regardless of the choice of scale to be used in the latter category. This method starts with the determination of the scores of the alternatives on the several criteria, as well as the weights of these criteria. Both – scores and weights – are (usually) generated during a Delphi experiment.

After this step, the scores have to be processed in a specific way, which is illustrated by the following example.

An organization has to choose between three information systems: A, B, and C. These alternatives are judged, using two quantitative criteria: discounted labour savings during a number of years (criterion 1) and the costs of the system (criterion 2), defined as a – negative – discounted cash flow during the same period.

In addition two qualitative (ordinal) factors are relevant: the creation of competitive advantages (criterion 3) and improved reliability of data (criterion 4).*

The scores of the three alternatives vis-a-vis the four criteria are presented in the form of a so-called score matrix, shown in table X.1 below.

Table X.1 Score matrix

Project	Criterion 1	Criterion 2	Criterion 3	Criterion 4
A	120	170	1	2
B	160	180	2	1
C	110	155	2	3

* If a factor is measured using an interval scale, then, according to the evamix procedure, it has to be treated in de same way as ratio-scaled factors.

In our example, the four criteria have the following weights:
criterion 1: 1
criterion 2: -1
criterion 3: .1
criterion 4: .2

The *sum* of the *absolute* weights is 2 for the quantitative factors and .3 for the qualitative ones.

The next step, completing the score matrix, is the standardization of the *quantitative* scores, using the following formula:

$$SCA = (SA - S_{min})/(S_{max} - S_{min})$$

In this formula, the symbols are defined as follows:
SCA = standardized score of project A
SA = score of project A
S_{min} = minimum score
S_{max} = maximum score

For example, on criterion 1 project A scores as follows:

$$SCA = (120 - 110)/(160 - 110) = .2$$

And on criterion 2:

$$SCA = (170 - 155)/(180 - 155) = .6$$

Applying the SCA-formula to the three projects on the two quantitative criteria, the so-called 'standardized quantitative scorecard' emerges, which is represented in table X.2 below.

Table X.2 Standardized quantitative scorecard

Project	Criterion 1	Criterion 2
A	.2	.6
B	1	1
C	0	0

We proceed with the standardization of scores of the *qualitative* factors. This standardization, as opposed to the standardization of quantitative scores, is reached by determining how projects score in relation to each other by adding weights as follows. If a certain project scores higher, then the *weight* of the other project gets a positive sign in this procedure; if it does not, then the sign will be negative. Finally, if projects have equal scores, then the weight becomes zero.

For instance, on criterion 3 project A scores lower than B and C, then the standardized score of A on criterion 3 equals -.1 + -.1. = -.2.

On criterion 3 project B scores higher than A and so the initial outcome is .1, but its score is equal to that of C, and the final standard score remains .1. The same is true for project C; it also gets a standard score of .1.

If the same procedure for the standardization of the scores on criterion 4 is used then the standardized qualitative scorecard can be composed, represented in table X.3 below.

Table X.3 Standardized qualitative scorecard

Project	Criterion 1	Criterion 2
A	.2	0
B	1	-.4
C	1	.4

As can be easily be demonstrated, for each of the criteria the sum of the standardized scores should equal zero.

The next step in the evamix procedure is to determine the dominance of the projects over each other (for quantitative and qualitative criteria separately), by using the following formula for both:

$$D_{ab} = \sum_{i=1}^{k} (GS_{ai} - GS_{bi}) G_i$$

The symbols in this formula are defined as follows:

D_{ab} = dominance of project A over project B
GS_{ai} = standardized score of project A on criterion i
GS_{bi} = standardized score of project B on criterion i
G_i = weight of criterion i
k = number of criteria

For project A in relation to project B on criterion 1 the dominance outcome is -.8 and on criterion 2 it is .4, resulting in a final dominance of A over B of -.4. In the same way the other dominances are determined, the results of which are presented in table X.4 below.

Table X.4 Quantitative dominance matrix

	A	B	C
A	-	-.4	-.4
B	.4	-	0
C	.4	0	-

The sum of the *absolute* numbers in this dominance matrix is 1.6.

The following step in this procedure is the determination of the dominances of the three information projects in respect of the *qualitative* factors. The 'qualitative dominance matrix' (see table X.5) is the result of these calculations.

Table X.5 Qualitative dominance matrix

	A	B	C
A	-	.05	-.11
B	-.05	-	-.16
C	.11	.16	-

The sum of the absolute numbers in this dominance matrix is .64.

The next – and final – step in the evamix procedure is combining the quantitative and qualitative dominance scores together, in order to calculate a so-called *utility* score. This utility score is an unambiguous yardstick for each project, so that a clear priority order of the available projects is now possible.

Calculating this utility score, we have to take into account:

- the absolute total weights of the quantitative and the qualitative criteria and
- the sum of the absolute dominance scores from both dominance tables.

We are now able to determine the utility score of each project using the following formula:

$$U_i = \sum_{i=1}^{n} \left\{ \frac{D_{kwan(ij)}}{\sum_{i=1}^{n}\sum_{j=1}^{n} D_{kwan(ij)}} \sum_{i=1}^{k} \left| G_{ikwan} \right| + \frac{D_{kwal(ij)}}{\sum_{i=1}^{n}\sum_{j=1}^{n} D_{kwal(ij)}} \sum_{i=1}^{l} \left| G_{ikwal} \right| \right\}$$

In this formula the symbols can be defined as follows:

U_i = utility score of the i-th project

$D_{kwan(ij)}$ = the quantitative dominance of project i over project j

$D_{kwal(ij)}$ = the qualitative dominance of project i over project j

$\sum_{j=1}^{k} G_{ikwan}$ = sum of the absolute weights of the quantitative criteria

$\sum_{i=i}^{l} G_{ikwal}$ = sum of the absolute weights of the qualitative criteria

Applying the formula above, the utility scores of the three projects are calculated as follows:

$U_a = (-.4/1.6)2 + (-.4/1.6)2 + (.05/.64).3 + (-.11/.64).3 = -1.028$

$U_b = (.4/1.6)2 + (0/1.6)2 + (-.05/.64).3 + (-.16/.64).3 = .402$

$U_c = (.4/1.6)2 + (0/1.6)2 + (.11/.64).3 + (.16/.64).3 = .627$

As a consequence, project C will be preferred.

Finally, we should like to make some comments about the evamix method, in particular in regard of its restrictions.

Primarily, during the application of the evamix procedure it is not allowed to add new projects. Secondly, additional criteria should not be introduced. Thus, the evamix procedure should only be started when the design phase in the search process has been completed. Thirdly, in addition to these two caveats a number of more general conditions can be specified for methods based on utility scores, such as the requirement of transitivity. The discussion of a subject like this one, however, is beyond the scope of the book. If the reader is interested in such topics, then publications in the field of decision making have to be consulted.

7. The mutual comparison between projects and the final decision once again

Quantitative projects are, as we know, exclusively evaluated and classified by applying capital budgeting decision methods; for instance by methods discussed in section 2 of this chapter. Because of the unambiguous character of the criteria used here, a unique priority order will emerge and it is sufficient to select the project with the highest score.

However, sometimes we meet a problem here if more than one method is used simultaneously. For example, it is not unusual to use the pay-back period criterion in addition to the net present value. If the priority orders for both criteria are different, then we have to determine the weights of these criteria in advance. These can be obtained in the same way as in the evamix procedure.

It is also possible to use the net present value as the selection criterion, whereas the pay-back period acts as a constraint. In this situation the first step is to divide the available projects, based on their pay-back period, into two categories 'acceptable' and 'unacceptable'. In the second and final step the acceptable projects will be classified using their net present value.

An important aspect of decision making about *miscellaneous* projects, composed of quantitative *and* qualitative factors, concerns the role of the aspiration level; a role especially important for the decision to stop or to continue the search process. If the aspiration level is the 'translation' of the decision maker's frame of reference that is used to evaluate projects, then these projects will not be compared to each other but merely to the aspiration level.

As soon as a project comes up to every criterion score of the aspiration level then a positive decision will be made. However, what procedure do we have to follow if a project does not have positive scores in all respects? If the properties involved are not prohibitive, i.e. they can compensate each other, then we can also use the evamix method, including the aspiration level as well.

As a consequence, the utility score of the aspiration level is the lower limit for projects to be acceptable. As soon as a project score equals at least this limit, then it will be selected and the decsision making process comes to an end. If not, then the well-known procedure – looking for other alternatives and/or adapting the aspiration level – will have to be followed, until a project is found, which comes up to the utility score of the aspiration level.

REFERENCES

Ackoff, R.L. (1978), *The Art of Problem Solving*, New York.

Aguilar, F.J. (1967), *Scanning the Business Environment*, Londen.

Akkerman, T. and H. DeWeerd (1995), *EVOlutionary Systems Development (EVOlutionaire systeemontwikkeling)*, Deventer.

Albrecht, A.J. and J. Jaffney (1983), 'Software Function, Source Lines of Code and Development Effort Prediction', IEEE, *Transactions on Software Engineering*, vol. 9, no. 6.

Alter, S. (1999), *Information Systems: A Management Perspective*, Reading, Mass.

Argyris, C. and D.A. Schon (1978), *Organizational Learning: A Theory of Action Perspective*, Reading Mass.

Argyris, C. (1971), 'Management Information Systems: The Challenge to Rationality and Emotionality', *Management Science*, vol. 17, no. 6, pp. 275-292.

Ashby, W.R. (1969), 'Self-regulation and Requisite Variety' in F.E. Emery (ed.), *Systems Thinking*, Penguin Books.

Bakker,J. (1995), *Object-Oriented Modelling of Information Systems*, Maastricht.

Beatty, C.A. and J.R.M. Gordon (1988), 'Barriers to Implementation of CAD/CAM Systems', *Sloan Management Review*, vol. 29 no. 4, pp. 25-33.

Beauclair, R. (1987), *An Experimental Study of the Effects of Group Decision Support System Process Support Application on Small Group Decision Making*, Bloomington.

Beer, S. (1990), *The Heart of Enterprise*, Chichester.

Bemelmans, T.M.A. (1987), *Management Information Systems and Automation (Bestuurlijke informatiesystemen en automatisering)*, Leiden.

Benbasat, I., A.S. Dexter, D.H. Drury and R.C. Goldsrein (1984), 'A Critique of the "Stage Hypothesis": Theory and Emperical Evidence', *Communications of the ACM*, may, pp. 476-485.

Bertlanffy, L. von (1956), 'General Systems Theory', *General Systems I.*

Bertlanffy, L. von (1968), *General Systems Theory*, New York, 1968.

Beulen, E., P. Ribbers and J. Roos (1994), *Outsourcing of IT* (Outsourcing van IT-dienstverlening), Deventer.

Beynon-Davies, P., D. Tudhope and H. Mackay (1999), 'Information systems prototyping in practice', *JIT; Journal of Information Technology*, vol. 14, no. 1, pp. 107-20.

Bjyrnjolfsson, E. (1993), 'The Productivity Paradox of Information Technology', *Communications of the ACM*, vol. 36, no. 12, dec., pp. 67-77.

Block, P. (1987), *The Empowered Manager*, San Fransisco.

Blumenthal, S.C. (1969), *Management Information Systems: A Framework for Planning and Development*, Englewood Cliffs, N.J.

Bostrom, R.P., R.Anson and V.K. Clawson (1993), 'Group Facilitation and Group Support Systems', in L.M. Jessup and J.S. Valacich (eds.), *Group Support Systems*, New York, pp. 146-169.

Boulding, K.E. (1956), 'General Systems Theory – The Skeleton of Science', *General Systems I.*

Cabelo, C. (1996), 'Returns in IT Investment, the End of the Productivity Paradox?', *The OPTS Report*, april.

Campbell, B.J. (1977), *Understanding Information Systems*, Cambridge, Mass.

Canning McNurlin, B. (1989), 'Electronic Document Management', *I/S Analyzer*, no. 5, may, pp. 1-12.

Chapanis, A., 'Studies in interactive communication: The effects of four communication modes on the behavior of teams during cooperative problem-solving', *Human Factors*, vol. 14, 1972, pp. 487-509.

Chattell, A. (1998), *Creating Value in the Digital Era; Achieving Success through Insight, Imagination and Innovation*, London.

Checkland, P. and J. Scholes (1990), *Soft Systems Methodology in Action*, Chichester.

Clarkson, G.P.E. (1963), 'A Model of the Trust Investment Process', in E.A. Feigenbaum and J. Feldman (eds.), *Computers and Thought*, New York, pp. 347-371.

Clegg, S.R. (1989), *Frameworks of Power*, Londen.

Cullen, R. (1995), *EIS more than data* (*EIS meer dan gegevens*), Technical University Eindhoven.

Cyert, R.M. and J.G. March (1963), *A Behavioral Theory of the Firm*, Englewood Cliffs, N.J.

Czerniawska, F. and G. Potter (1998), *Business in a Virtual World*, London.

Davenport, T.H. (1993), *Process Innovation; Re-engineering Work Through Information Technology*, Boston.

Davis, G.B. and M.H. Olson (1985), *Management Information Systems*, New York.
Dayhoff, J.E. (1990), *Neural Network Architectures*, New York.
DeLooff, L. (1996), *A Model for Information Systems Outsourcing Decision Making*, Delft.
Dennis, A.R. and R.B. Gallupe (1993), 'A History of Group Support Systems Emperical Research', in L.M. Jessup and J.S. Valacich (eds.), *Group Support Systems*, New York, pp. 57-78.
DeVries, M.S. (1992), 'Stepwise Multiple Criteria Evaluation', *Quality and Quantity*, vol. 26, pp. 61-76.
Doll, J.W. (1987), 'Encouraging User Management Participation in Systems Design', *Information & Management*, no. 13, pp. 25-32.
Dreyfus, H.L. (1992), *What Computers Still Can't Do*, Cambridge, Mass.
Drucker, P. (1990), *Managing in Turbulent Times*, London
Eden, C. (1989), 'Using Cognitive Mapping for Strategic Options Development Analysis (SODA)', in J. Rosenhead (ed.), *Rational Analysis for a Problematic World*, Chicester.
Eijnatten, F.M. van (1994), *The Paradigm that changed the work place*, Assen.
Emery, F.E. and E. Thorsrud (1976), *Democracy at Work; Report of the Norwegian industrial democracy program*, Leiden.
Farbey, B., F. Land and D. Targett (1993), *How to Assess Your IT Investment*, Oxford.
Forgionne, G.A., 'A Step Toward Complete Decision Support' (1991), *Information Systems Management*, autumn, pp. 34-44.
Forsyth, D.R. (1990), *Group Dynamics*, Pacific Grove, California.
Fransman, M. (1999), *Visions of innovation: the firm and Japan*, Oxford.
French, J.R.P. and B. Raven (1959), 'The Bases of Social Power', in D. Cartwright (ed.), *Studies in Power*, Ann Arbor, pp. 150-167.
Freyenfeld, W.A. (1984), *Decision Support Systems*, Manchester.
Galbraith, J.R. (1976), *Designing Complex Organizations*, Reading, Mass.
Galbraith, J.R. and E.E. Lawler (1993), *Organizing for the Future: The New Logic for Managing Complex Organizations*, San Francisco.
Gallupe, R.B., W.H. Cooper and L. Bastianutti (1991), 'Unblocking Brainstorms', *Journal of Applied Psychology*, vol. 76, no. 1, pp. 137-142.
Gibson, C.F. and R.L. Nolan (1974), 'Managing the Four Stages of EDP Growth', *Harvard Business Review*, jan./febr. pp. 78-88.
Goldhamer, H. and E.A. Shils (1939), 'Types of Power and Status', *American Journal of Sociology*, vol. 45, pp. 171-182.
Grudin, J. (1991), 'Introduction to CSCW', *Communications of the ACM*, vol. 34, no. 12 dec., pp. 30-34.
Guest, R.H. (1957), 'Job Enlargement – a Revolution in Job Design', *Personnel Administration*, pp. 9-16.
Hackman, J.R. and G.R. Oldham (1976), 'Motivation through the Design of Work: Test of a Theory', *Organizational Behaviour and Human Performance*, vol. 16 no. 2, pp. 250-279.
Hackman, J.R. and G.R. Oldham (1976), 'Motivation Through the Design of Work: Test of a Theory', *Organizational Behavior and Human Performance*, pp. 250-279.
Hamel, G. and C.K. Prahalad (1993), *Competing for the Future*, Harvard Business Review Press.
Hammer, M. and J. Champy (1993), *Reengineering the Corporation*, New York.
Harrington, H.J. (1991), *Business Process Improvement*, New York.
Hendriks, P. (1999), 'Why Share Knowledge? The Influence of ICT on the Motivation for Knowledge Sharing', *Knowledge and Process Management*, vol. 6, no. 2, pp. 91-100.
Herbst, P.G. (1974), *Socio-technical Design: Strategies in Multidisciplinary Research*, London.
Herzberg, F. (1968), 'One More Time: How Do You Motivate Employees', *Harvard Business Review*, pp. 53-62.
Hickson, D.J., C.R. Hinings, A.C. Lee, R.E. Schneck and J.M. Pennings (1971), 'A Strategic Contingency Theory of Intra-Organizational Power', *Administrative Science Quarterly*, vol. 16, pp. 216-229.
Hillier, F.S. (1969), *The Evaluation of Risky Interrelated Projects*, Amsterdam/London.
Hofstadter, D.R. (1979), *Godel, Escher, Bach an Eternal Braid*, New York.
IDC (1998), *Computable*, 27 nov.
Jenkins, A.M., J.D. Naumann and J.C. Wetherbe (1984), 'Empirical Investigation of Systems Development Practices and Results', *Information & Management*, vol. 7.
Jenkins, D. (1974), *Job Power: Blue and White Collar Democracy*, London.
Juran, J.M. (1984), *Managerial Breakthrough*, New York.
Juran, J.M. (1974), *Quality Control Handbook*, McGraw Hill.
Kaplan, R and D. Norton (1992), 'The balanced scorecard – Measures that drive performance', *Harvard Business Review*, jan./febr., pp. 71-79.

Keen, P.G.W., 'Value Analysis: Justifying Decision Support Systems' (1986), in R.H. Sprague and H.J. Watson (eds.), *Decision Support Systems*, Englewood Cliffs, N.J., pp. 48-65.
Keen, P.G.W. (1991), *Shaping the Future*, Harvard Business School Press.
Keen, P.G.W. and M.S. Scott Morton (1978), *Decision Support Systems*, Reading, Mass.
Klaver, L., (1995) 'EIS can hardly support managers' ('EIS kan managers nauwelijks ondersteunen'), *Information Management (Informatiemanagement)*, aug./sept., pp. 12-16.
Koopman, P.L. and J. Pool (1992), *Management and Decision Making in Organizations (Management en besluitvorming in organisaties)*, Assen/Maastricht.
Lamb, D. (1991), *Discovery, Creativity and Problem Solving*, Aldershot (UK).
Leavitt, H.J. and T.L. Whisler (1985), 'Management in the 1980's', *Harvard Business Review*, nov./dec., pp. 41-48.
Ledford, G.E., E.E. Lawler and S.A. Mohrman (1988), 'The Quality Circle and its Variations', in J.P. Campbell and R.J. Campbell (eds.), *Productivity in Organizations: New Perspectives from Industrial Organizational Psychology*, San Francisco.
Lenat, D.B. and J. Seely Brown (1984), 'Why AM and EURISKO Appear to Work', *Artificial Intelligence*, pp. 269-294.
Linstone, H.A. and M. Turoff (1975), *The Delphi Method: Techniques and Applications*, Massachusetts.
Luger, G.F. and W.A. Stubblefield (1998), *Artificial Intelligence*, Harlow.
Lundeberg, M., G. Goldkuhl and A. Nilson (1981), *Information Systems Development; A systematic approach*, Englewood Cliffs, N.J.
Mallach, E. (1994), *Understanding Decision Support Systems and Expert Systems*, Burr Ridge, Ill.
Mansfield, E. (1981), 'Imitation Costs and Patents', *Economic Journal*, dec. pp. 80-97.
March, J.G. and H.A. Simon (1958), *Organizations*, New York.
Markus, M.L. (1984), *Systems in Organizations*, Cambridge, Mass.
Martin, J. (1987), *Information Engineering*, Lancaster.
Martin, J. (1991), *Rapid Application Development*, New York.
Mason, R.D. and I.I. Mitroff (1981), *Challenging Strategic Planning Assumptions*, New York.
Maturana, H.R. and F.J. Varela (1992), *The Tree of Knowledge*, Boston/London.
McMillan, C.J. (1985), *The Japanese Industrial System*, Berlin.
Minsky, M.L. (1968), 'Matter, Mind and Models', in M.L. Minsky (ed.), *Semantic Information Processing*, Cambridge, Mass.
Mintzberg, H. (1976), *The Nature of Managerial Work*, Englewood Cliffs, N.J.
Mirani, R. and A.L. Lederer (1998), 'An instrument for assessing the organizational benefits of IS projects', *Decision Sciences*, vol. 29, no. 4, pp. 803-838.
Mitroff, I.I. and Th. R. Featheringham (1974), 'On Systematic Problem Solving and the Error of the Third Kind', *Behavioral Sciences*, vol. 19, no. 6, pp. 383-93.
Mohrman, S.A., S.G. Cohen and A.M. Mohrman Jr (1995), *Designing Team-Based Organizations*, San francisco.
Morgan, G. (1986), *Images of Organization*, Beverly Hills.
Moroney, M. (1965), *How to Lie with Figures*, Pelican Books.
Mulder, M. (1978), *Dealing with Conflicts (Conflicthantering)*, Leiden.
Mumford, E. (1983), *Designing Human Systems for New Technology: the ETHICS Method*, Manchester.
Naumann, J.D. and A.M. Jenkins (1987), 'Prototyping: The New Paradigm', in H.J. Watson, A.B. Caroll and R.I. Mann (eds), *Information Systems for Management*, Plano Texas, pp. 210-33.
Newell, A. and H.A. Simon (1963), 'GPS: A Program that Simulates Human Thought', in E.A. Feigenbaum and J.A. Feldman (eds.), *Computers and Thought.*, New York.
Nolan, R.L. (1973), 'Managing the Computer Resource: A Stage Hypothesis', *Communications of the ACM*, vol. 16, no. 7, pp. 339-405.
Nolan, R.L. (1991), 'The Strategic Potential of Information Technology', *Financial Executive*, july/aug., pp. 25-27.
Nunamaker, J.F., A.R. Dennis, J.S. Valacich, D.R. Vogel and J.E. George (1993), 'Group Support Systems Research: Experiences from the Lab and Field', in L.M. Jessup and J.S. Valacich (eds.), *Group Support Systems*, New York, pp. 125-146.
O'Leary, T.J. en K. Williams (1985), *Computers & Information Processing, with business applications*, Addison-Wesley.
Olle, T.W., H. Sol and A.A. Verrijn Stuart (1982), *Information Systems Design Methodologies; A comparative review*, Amsterdam.
Parker, M.M., R.J. Benson and H.E. Trainor (1988), *Information Economics*, Englewood Cliffs, N.J.

Pasmore, W.A. (1988), *Designing Complex Organizations: The Sociotechnical Systems Perspective*, New York.

Peters, T.J. and R.H. Waterman (1983), *In Search of Excellence*, New York.

Pfeffer, J.(1978), *Organizational Design*, Arling Heights, Ill.

Pfeffer, J. (1981), *Power in Organizations*, Boston.

Porter, M. and V. Millar, (1985), 'How Information Gives You Competitive Advantage', *Harvard Business Review*, july/august, pp. 149-60.

Prakken, B. (1989), *Strategic and Tactical Information Policy (Strategisch en tactisch informatiebeleid)*, Alphen a/d Rijn.

Prakken, B. (1992), *The tip of the iceberg (Het topje van de ijsberg)*, University of Nijmegen.

Robey, D. (1977), 'Computer and Management Structure: Some Empirical Findings Re-Examined', *Human Relations*, vol. 30, no. 11, pp. 963-976.

Rockart, J.F. (1979), 'Chief Executives Define Their Own Data Needs', *Harvard Business Review*, mrt.-apr., pp. 81-93.

Rockart, J.F. and D.W. De Long (1988), *Executive Support Systems*, Homewood, Ill.

Rockart, J. and L. Flannery (1983), 'The Management of End User Computing', *Communications of the ACM*, vol. 26, no. 10, oct., pp. 779-784.

Rockart, J.F. and J.E. Short (1991), 'The Networked Organization and Management of Interdependence', in M.S. Scott Morton (ed.), *The Corporation of the 1990's*, New York, pp. 189-220.

Rockart, J.F. and M.E. Treacy (1982), 'The CEO Goes On-Line', *Harvard Business Review*, jan./febr.

Scott Armstrong, J. (1985), *Long-Range Forecasting*, New York.

Shortliffe, E.H. (1976), *Computer-based Medical Consultation: MYCIN*, New York.

Simon, H.A. (1959), *Administrative Behaviour*, MacMillan.

Simon, H.A. (1970), 'The New Science of Management Decision', in A. Welsh and R.M. Cyert (eds), *Management Decision Making*, Harmondsworth, pp. 13-30.

Smith, H.J. and J. Hasnas (1999), 'Ethics and information systems: the corporate domain', *Management Information Systems Quarterly*, vol. 23, no. 1, pp. 109-127.

Sprague, R.H. and E.D. Carlson (1982), *Building Effective Decision Support Systems*, Englewood Cliffs, N.J.

Sprague, R.H. and H.J. Watson (1996), *Decision Support for Management*, London.

Teo, T.S.H. and J.K.S. Ang (1999), 'Critical success factors in the alignment of IS plans with business plans', *International Journal of Information Management*, vol. 19, no. 2, pp. 173-85.

Theeuwes, J.A.M. (1986), 'Information policy and information planning; a framework' (Informatiebeleidsvorming en informatieplanning; een raamwerk), *Bedrijfskunde*, vol. 58, no. 3, pp. 248-260.

Thorp, J. (1999), *The information paradox; Realizing the business benefits of information technology*, McGraw Hill.

Townsend, A.M., S. DeMarie and A.R. Hendrickson (1998), 'Virtual teams: technology and the workplace of the future', *Academy of Management Executive*, vol. 12, no. 3, pp. 17-29.

Turban, E. (1990), *Decision Support and Expert Systems*, New York.

Turban, E., E. McLean and J. Wetherbe (1996), *Information technology for management: Improving quality and productivity*, New York.

Turner, W.S., R.P. Langerhorst, H.B. Eilers, R.J.M.M. Castermans, G.F. Hice and L.F. Cahwell (1985), *Systems Development Methodology*, Rijswijk.

Valacich, J.S., A.R. Dennis and J.F. Nunamaker (1992), 'Group Size and Anonimity Effects on Computer-mediated Idea Generation', *Small Group Research*, vol 23, no. 1, pp. 49-73.

VanAmelsvoort, P. and G. Scholtes (1994), *Self steering teams: Design, implementation and management (Zelfsturende teams: Ontwerpen, invoeren en begeleiden)*, Oss.

Vangriethuysen, J.J. and D.A. Jardine (1984), 'The infomod-approach of information modelling (De infomodbenadering van informatiemodellering)', *Informatie*, vol. 26, no. 6, pp. 423-443.

Venkatraman, N. (1991), 'IT-Induced Business Reconfiguration', in M.S. Scott Morton (ed.), *The Corporation of the 1990s*, New York, pp. 122-159.

Ward, A., J.K. Liker, J.J. Cristiano and D.K. Sobek (1995), 'The Second Toyota Paradox: How to Delaying Decisions Can Make Better Cars Faster', *Sloan Management Review*, Spring, pp. 43-61.

Watson, R., G. DeSanctis and M.S. Poole (1988), 'Using a GDSS to Facilitate Group Consensus: Some Intended and Unintended Consequences', *MISQuaterly*, vol. 12, no. 3, pp. 463-478.

Weick, K.E. (1979), *The social psychology of organizing*, Reading, Mass.

Williamson, O. (1985), *The Economic Institutions of Capitalism*, New York.

Willke, R. (1993), *System Theorie*, Campus.

Winograd, T. and F. Flores (1986), *Understanding Computers and Cognition*, Norwood, N.J.

Young, L.F. (1989), *Decision Support and Idea Processing Systems*, Dubuque, Iowa.

INDEX

acceptance 4, 8, 107, 112, 113
Ackoff, R.L. 7, 8, 30, 67
Aguilar, F.J. 28, 140, 155
anchoring 115, 116
Ashby's Law of Requisite Variety 60
aspect approach 52-54
aspect systems 14, 15
aspiration gap 4, 117
autonomous tasks 56
autopoeietic 18

balanced scorecard 9
bench marking 212, 213
Benson, R.J. 203, 215
black box approach 24
Boulding, K.E.17
business process redesign 12, 46, 64, 153, 180, 182-184, 186, 189

Cashman, P. 162
Champy, J. 184
circularity 90, 113, 114, 131
Clarkson, G.P.E. 171
communication gap 4, 8, 96, 117, 125
complexity 17, 44, 48, 56, 63, 65, 105, 121, 122, 127
Computer Aided Manufacturing 185, 198
conceptual structuring 33, 113
concreteness 115
conditioned viewing 28
control cycle 11, 13, 22, 23, 26, 34, 86, 89, 90, 179
creeping 132, 133

data base systems 149, 152, 153, 156-158
data sources 39, 40
datalogical aspect 127
Davis, G.B. 8, 51, 92, 115
decision support systems 25, 32, 42, 134, 150, 152, 153, 156, 165-169, 171, 173, 194, 195, 203, 206, 207
Deep Blue 170
defensive strategy 25

Delphi 9, 41, 207-211, 215, 217
Deming 59
Dinkey toys 19
dissolving 7
document information systems 149, 152, 153, 156-158
double loop learning 20, 75, 76
DSS generators 134
DSS Shell 169

economic evaluation v, 4, 6, 7, 9, 12, 96, 121
electronic data interchange 41, 151-153, 173-176, 186, 208
enactment 18
ETHICS 11
evamix method 217, 221, 222
evolutionary design methods 112, 124-126, 131
executive information systems 120, 152-155
expert systems 171-173, 175
extranet 175, 176, 186

facet systems 14, 54, 151
facilitating processes 15, 16, 103
failure factors 3, 7, 8, 11, 99
Fisherprice 19
Ford, H. 68
formal search 28
formulation of information problems 4, 5, 8, 30

gaps 4, 19, 184, 185
Gauss 169, 206
general design methods 105, 108, 114, 124, 128, 131-133, 136
goal seeking 207, 208, 210, 211
Greif, I. 162
Gresham' Law of Planning 20
group decision room 165, 166
group information systems 150, 152, 153, 161-166, 195

Hackman, J.R. 61, 182
Hamel, G. 9, 21, 25

Hammer, M. 54, 79, 180, 184
Hofstadter, D.R. 170, 171

I-CASE 11, 173
idea processing systems 150, 152, 153, 158-161, 165, 189, 194
incremental design methods 124, 126, 129, 132
infological aspect 127
INFOMOD 136
informal search 28
information content 45, 89, 176, 216
information economics 9, 215
information intensity 45, 89, 176, 185
information policy 7, 9, 14, 25, 34, 44, 63, 85-90, 95, 105, 109, 120
information technology infrastructure library (ITIL) 134, 135
innovation valuation 203, 207
input data 34-37, 155
integrated approach 3, 7, 11
internal rate of return 199, 200
interval scale 202, 204, 205, 210, 216, 217
IPEP analysis 31
ISAC 136

Jenkins, A.M. 2, 3, 126, 143
job enlargement 56, 57, 61, 69, 72, 73
job enrichment 56-58, 61, 69, 72
Juran, J.M. 59, 180

Kasparov 170
knowledge-based systems 152, 153, 170-173, 175

Lashley, K. 18
lateral relations 56-58, 60
Lego 19
local area network 90

maintenance 2, 4, 5, 8, 73, 90, 95, 104, 178, 208, 214
Management Information Science 30
management information systems 7, 12, 51, 52, 96, 149, 152, 153
March, J.G. 20, 41, 144
Maslov's need hierarchy 68, 69, 192
mental filters 28, 29
mental models 12, 18, 19, 21, 116, 161, 187, 189
Minsky, M.L. 170
Mintzberg, H. 31, 119, 154
Moore's Law 12, 187
multi-criteria analysis 9, 217
Murphy's Law 47, 69, 182
MYCIN 171

Naumann, J.D., 2, 3, 126
net present value 43, 199, 200, 206, 207, 210-212, 215, 222
nice-to-haves 8, 122, 125, 126, 130, 132
Nolan, R. 91-95
nominal scale 201, 202, 204

object-oriented design methods 137
offensive strategy 25
Oldham, G.R. 61, 182
Olson, M.H. 8, 51, 92, 115
operational structuring 33, 34
ordinal scale 201, 202, 204, 216
output data 34-38, 127
outsourcing 88, 99-104

PANDATA 111
parallelisation of orders 57, 59
Pareto's Law 8, 130
Parker, M.M. 9, 203, 215
participatory design methods 124, 125, 197
participatory/incremental design methods 124
pay-back period 198, 200, 201, 222
physical filters 28, 29
policy framework 4, 5, 86, 87
policy levels 26, 88, 89, 158
political processes 7, 10
power 4, 6, 7, 10, 12, 22, 30, 94, 96, 116, 117, 139-147
power structure 4, 6, 7, 10, 116, 139, 141, 142
Prahalad, C.K. 9, 21, 25
problem approach 52, 53
Procrustean bed 30
Procrustes-bed 5
productivity paradox 1, 10, 12, 183
project groups 108-110, 117
project management approach 9, 133
project team 10, 105, 108, 110, 123
prototyping 8, 112, 113, 126-133

quality control circles 56, 57, 60

Rapid Application Development 8, 112, 113, 124, 129
rate of responce 44
ratio analysis 207, 208, 212, 213
ratio scale 201, 202, 204, 209
recency 115
recursivity 90
response time 44, 56, 65, 81, 168, 214

sensitivity analysis 9, 32, 42, 154, 168, 207, 211
sequential approach 24
Service Level Management 135
signals 19-21, 27-29, 31, 34, 35, 59, 168, 175
Simon, H.A. 20, 27, 41
single loop learning 19, 76
slack 56-59, 91-93, 144-146
sociotechnical approach v, 12, 60-63, 67, 69, 71, 78, 80, 141
Solow 1
specific decision support systems (specific DSS) 134, 169
specific design methods 105, 120, 136, 137
steering committee 108-110
strategic information systems 149, 152-156, 158, 194
structure of problems 28, 29, 41-43, 194
structured decision system 151, 174, 175, 194
SWAT 130
SWOT (Strengths/Weaknesses/Opportunities/Threats) analysis 30
systelogical aspect 127
Systems Development Methodology 106, 107, 111

tacit knowledge 207
task group 108, 164
Taylor, F.W. 68
Tayloristic organization structure 47, 69
technical aspect 128
teleconferencing 165, 184
telework 153, 188, 190-193
top information systems 149
Trainor, H.E. 215
transaction costs 100, 102
transaction processing systems 152, 153, 165, 167, 176, 178, 179
turn key methods 8

uncertainty 43, 44, 56, 65, 102, 105, 126, 131, 133, 140, 143, 198, 209, 216
undirected viewing 28

value acceleration 203
value analysis 6, 207, 208, 211, 212
value linking 203
value restructuring 203
Venkatraman, N. 186

Weick, K.E. 18
wetherbe 3, 10
wisdom 34, 36, 39

zooming-in procedure 42, 43
zooming-out procedure 30, 55